THE LIMITS OF LIABILITY

THE LIMITS OF LIABILITY

Keeping the Floodgates Shut

J. SPIER (Editor)
C. von Bar
D.B. Dobbs
K.D. Kerameus / K. Roussos
H. Koziol
A. van Oevelen
W.V.H. Rogers
G. Viney
P. Widmer

KLUWER LAW INTERNATIONAL
THE HAGUE / LONDON / BOSTON

A C.I.P. Catalogue record for this book is available from the Library of Congress.

ISBN 90-411-0169-1

Published by Kluwer Law International,
P.O. Box 85889, 2508 CN The Hague, The Netherlands.

Sold and distributed in the U.S.A. and Canada
by Kluwer Law International,
675 Massachusetts Avenue, Cambridge, MA 02139, U.S.A.

In all other countries, sold and distributed
by Kluwer Law International,
P.O. Box 85889, 2508 CN The Hague, The Netherlands.

Printed on acid-free paper

Kluwer Law International incorporates the publishing programmes of
Graham & Trotman Ltd, Kluwer Law and Taxation Publishers,
and Martinus Nijhoff Publishers.

Printed in the Netherlands

Preface

In 1853 Mr Joel Bishop proposed to write a book on the law of torts. He was assured by all the publishers that there was no call for a work on such a subject, and that, "if the book were written by the most eminent and prominent author that ever lived, not a dozen of copies a year could be sold".[1]

Times have changed. Tort law has become a major topic these days. And its importance is still increasing. This is due to various reasons, which are clearly interrelated. First, the developments are caused by changing law, case law and legislation alike.

The above is partly influenced by international developments. Conventions and EC directives play an ever more important role. For example the directive on product liability, the ideas to enact one or more directives on (various) so called defective services, the convention on civil liability for damage resulting from activities dangerous to the environment and the convention on nuclear incidents. They undoubtedly have - as they should - an important effect on the laws of the countries involved. Directives and legislation are becoming more and more mutually influential.

Certain legal concepts which hardly played a role until some decades, if not just a couple of years, ago, emerge, albeit that there still are considerable differences between various countries and legal systems. Only some examples out of many: joint and several liability , proportional liability, loss of a chance, new heads of damages like "ecological damage", the legal implications of slowly progressing personal injury like asbestosis and its consequences as for example limitation (prescription). Strict liability seems to become popular, especially in case of environmental liability and liability for traffic accidents. The question whether pure economic loss should be compensated is highly debated. The same is true for the boundaries of the "duty of care". One cannot escape from the impression that legislators and/or courts are trying to find new ways to compensate victims suffering personal injury. New case law - as well as some legislation - apparently have retro-active effect. This clearly causes difficulties.

1 Bishop, Non-Contract Law, 1889, 2, quoted by Prosser and Keeton on Torts, 5 th ed. page 1.

Scientific research also has an impact on liability law. Diseases (like asbestosis, repetitive strain injury, whiplashes and the like) are "discovered" or at least causation can more readily be established. Victims try to get compensation from those who actually "caused" those diseases, like manufacturers and employers. Even if the law does not change in those respects, this increasing knowledge will in the near future have tremendous effects on liabilities, or more precisely on their quantum. It is open to debate whether the law as it stands, would have been the same, assuming that those who developed it, would have been aware of the possibly draconic consequences. Similar developments occur in relation to environmental liability. To a large extent, the downside and the effects of all kinds of dumping and discharge of waste appeared only quite recently.

People are less inclined to bear their own losses. As von Bar put it: Schicksal und Leiden nimmt man nicht länger widerspruchslos hin".[2] Although reliable figures are hardly available[3], it seems likely that we face an increasing claim-consciousness in many countries, be it not always in the same areas. The amounts awarded are rising too. They sometimes are incredibly high. Even a few "mega award cases" may have a considerable impact on tortfeasors and, even more so, on their insurers.[4]

Insurers sound the alarm. For decades, those who might become the "victim" of liability claims, could cover their potential exposure by taking insurance covers. Of course, insurers have almost without exception always limited the amounts insured, but for practical purposes it is fair to assume that the limits in the insurance contracts were only rarely surpassed. The insurance market is trying to cope with the changes briefly touched upon above. Either by limiting the maximum amounts covered, by specifically excluding certain risks or by introducing claims made policies or similar vehicles.[5]

The reaction of insurers on the developments[6], briefly described above, changes the scene of liability law. Potential tortfeasors may be deprived of insurance cover, while the injured could be left out in the cold, because the tortfeasor is unable to compensate him. This can ruin activities, broadly considered as useful, if not necessary, in our modern society; one could think of liberal professions like

2 C. von Bar, in Gutachten und Vorschläge zur Überarbeitung des Schuldrechts, Vol. 2 page 1691

3 The same observation was made by B.S. Markesinis, Litigation-mania in England, Germany and the USA: are we so very different?, Cambridge Law Journal, 49(2), July 1990, pp 233-276.

4 See e.g. An update on the Liability Crisis, Tort Policy Working Group (1987) page 37. It is true that those figures cannot necessarily be compared with Europe. But also in the "old world", we face claims which are nearing the sky, which is, as we know, "the" limit.

5 See about the claims made phenomenon e.g. Malcolm A. Clarke, The law of insurance contracts, 2nd ed. 17-4D pp 404 ff. For several reasons, it is questionable whether the new clauses will really have the desired effect. National legislators and courts may disapply certain contractual provisions. Sometimes, the precise result of the clauses seem to be insufficiently thought of.

6 I leave aside whether or not they overreact. I am inclined to believe that it might well turn out that they still underestimate rather foreseeable developments.

physicians, accountants and attorneys but also of companies, using or manufacturing dangerous substances or "producing" waste which they have to get rid of in one way or another. On the other hand, the mere fact that liability can no longer be insured is not necessarily sufficient reason to change the law. The choice for what is perceived as the best solution requires taking into account not only the victim and the tortfeasor, but also insurers and the needs of society. After all, unlimited liability could possibly be fair and equitable because the interests of the injured person should prevail. Other solutions, like compensation funds, should also be given thought.

One has to consider the implications of developments in many areas for defendants and plaintiffs, or indeed the whole society. Doing so, one has to reflect on the fundamentals of this part of the law. This is certainly a challenge for legal doctrine. In an ideal world, it should equally be for legislators and courts. In reality this challenge is hardly ever taken up, which is partly due to lack of information. But as far as legislators are concerned, probably the main reason is that they are not very inclined to consider the system as a whole. Doctrine could and should play an eminent role, also in this respect.

Doing so, however, it is much more useful to surpass the mere national level. First and most importantly, because one should not invent the wheel. Comparative exercises are clearly useful. The more so in case of topics of utmost practical and theoretical importance. Secondly, both the "tortfeasors" and the "victims" are increasingly confronted with foreign law, applying to their case. Consequently, it has to be taken into account anyway. Thirdly, in the long run it is not unlikely - and as far as possible - it would in my view certainly be desirable that this part of the law will be "harmonised", as has been done in other areas. This can only be achieved on the basis of profound knowledge of the different legal systems and cultures.

With the aim to discuss major topics of liability law, a group of eminent experts has been established, most of whom contributed to this book[7]. In the meantime the group has been expanded with colleagues form other countries, now covering about the whole Western Europe and the United States of America.

Our group started off to discussing how to keep the floodgates shut. This book provides valuable information written by the members of the group for our first discussion. The introduction mentions the outcome of our first exchange of thoughts. Our intention is to continue publishing on fundamental issues of liability law. Moreover, we very much hope to be able to contribute to the reflection on

7 I should specifically mention Prof. Dr M.R. Will, University of Geneva, who played an important role in establishing the group.

future developments of liability law. Maybe "the law of tort has fallen into great confusion"[8]; the least we could do is to create confusion at a higher level.[9]

I am very grateful to my friends and colleagues for all the work they did to achieve this book[10]. We hope that the information it provides will stimulate further thinking on the fascinating topic: how to keep liability within reasonable limits.

Jaap Spier
August 1995

8 Victoria Park Recreation Grounds Co. Ltd v. Taylor (1937) 58 C.L.R. 479,505 per Dixon, C.J., quoted by Winfield, Jolowicz on Tort, 14. ed. by W.H.V. Rogers page 18 footnote 13.

9 Freely rendered from Alice in Wonderland.

10 Also to the International Chamber of Commerce (Netherlands) and the Centre for liability law of the Schoordijk Instituut which contributed to the printing costs of this book.

Contents

Preliminary observations 1
W.V.H. Rogers, J. Spier, G. Viney

1	Introduction	1
2	Is liability law (heavily) expanding?	1
3	The principle of full compensation	2
4	The tools to keep liability within reasonable limits	3
4.1	Preliminary observations	3
4.2	Duty of care and "Schutznorm"	4
4.3	Causation	5
4.4	Various heads of damages	6
4.4.1	Personal injury	6
4.4.2	Damage to property	7
4.4.3	Economic loss	8
4.5	Ceilings and caps	9
4.6	Modification	9
4.7	The degree of negligence	9
4.8	The financial capacity of tortfeasor and victim	10
4.9	Liability covered by insurance	10
4.10	Miscellaneous	10
5	How to keep liability within reasonable limits in the future?	11
5.1	Introduction	11
5.2	Global limits and ceilings	12
5.3	Strict or fault liability	13
5.4	Financial position of the parties	14
5.5	Different heads of damages	14
5.6	Causation	14
5.7	Ad hoc control	15
6	Final observation	15

Limitation and Mitigation in German Tort Law 17
Prof. Dr. Christian v. Bar

I Areas of German law in which the principle of full compensation is felt to be inappropriate 17
1 Strict liability cases 17
2 Employment relations 19
II General principles of mitigation in German law 21
1 Causation and remoteness of damage 21
2 Scope of the protected interests. 22
3 Restrictive interpretation of the duty of care principle 23
III Preference of certain systems 24

Direct and general limits on tort damages in the United States 27
Dan B. Dobbs

I General Principles 27
II Limiting Compensatory Damages 29
A Arguments for General Limitations 29
B Types of Limits Proposed and Enacted in the United States 31
III Conclusion 34
Appendix 35
Reductions and Apportionments Possibly Made to Achieve Corrective Justice 35
Reductions to Achieve a Collateral Policy Goal 38
Reductions Indirectly Imposed by Rules of Trial Convenience or Proof 39
Limits Based on Direct, Formal, and General Rules 39
Substantive Rules Eliminating a Claim for Specified Damages 40
A Miscellany of related material 41

European tort law
Hellenic National Report 43
K.D. Kerameus and Kl. Roussos

I Introduction 43
1 Illegal behaviour and negligence 43
2 Distinguishing contractual from delictual liability 44
II Limitation of damages 46
1 Statutory limitation 47
2 Restraints developed by case law 48
2.1 Scope of protected interests 48
2.2 Adequate causation 49
2.3 Computation of damages 50
3 Unknown limits to damages 51

Mitigation of Damages under Austrian Law and Ideas for Future Regulations 53
Helmut Koziol

Introduction 53
1 The System of Austrian Law of Tort 54
2 Critical Presentation of Mitigation of Damages under Austrian Law 56
3 Trends and Suggestions for Future Regulations 60
Tools to Control the Scope and Extent of Liability 62
1 Ceilings 62
2 Ad hoc mitigation 62
3 Circumstances to be imputed to the victim 62
4 Heads of non recoverable damages 62
5 Funds established either by industry or government 62
6 Schutzzweck 63
7 Duty of care 63
8 Apportionment 63
9 Schedules, scales and matrices 63
10 Thresholds 63
11 Adequate causation 63
12 The access to justice 63
13 Insurance provided by government and/or payment by treasury 64

La modération de la réparation du dommage dans le droit belge de la responsabilité civile extra-contractuelle 65
Prof. Dr. A. van Oevelen

I Introduction 65
II Le principe de la réparation intégrale du dommage 65
III Les conséquences du principe de la réparation intégrale du dommage 66
IV Exceptions au principe de la réparation integrale du dommage 68
VI L'interprétation large de la notion de dommage 72
VII Modération indirecte de l'étendue de l'indemnisation par l'application des règles concernant le lien de causalité? 73
VIII Conclusion 74

Keeping the Floodgates Shut: 'Mitigation' and 'Limitation' of Tort Liability in the English Common Law 75
W.V.H. Rogers

Terminology 75
Is there a principle or goal of full compensation? 77
Formal Limitations upon Levels of Damages 77
Ad hoc mitigation? 78
Joint and several liability 79
The assessment of damages 79
Controlling the scope liability 82
The duty of care 82
Other control devices in the substantive law 90

How to keep liability within reasonable limits? A brief outline of Dutch law 93
J. Spier

1 Background in formation about Dutch liability law 93
2 The changing scene of liability law 97
3 A Dutch tort crisis? 98
4 Piercing the corporate veil 100
II How to keep liability within reasonable limits? A brief outline of Dutch law 100
A Causation 100
B Non-recoverable damages 104
C Ad hoc control/modification 105
D Caps and ceilings 110
E "Egalité devant les charges publiques" [Equality before public burdens] 112
F Duty of care towards whom? (Schutznorm) 113
G Contributory negligence 115
H Exoneration 116
III How to keep liability law within reasonable limits: observations 117
Appendix 121
1 Liability for dangerous substances 121
2 Joint and several liability 123
3 Uncertainty about causation 124
4 Insurability 125

Modération et limitation des responsabilités et des indemnisations 127
Rapport sur le droit français, par Geneviève VINEY

I Les tendances du droit français quant au problème de la limitation des responsabilités et des indemnisations 128
II Les orientations à envisager 133

Détermination et réduction de la réparation en droit suisse 137
Pierre Widmer

I Le soi-disant principe de la réparation intégrale 137
II Facteurs d'exonération et de réduction de lege lata et de lege ferenda 143
III Autres aspects de la limitation de la réparation 158

Preliminary observations

Le droit de la responsabilité civile n'est pas le mécanisme approprié pour faire de la charité ou pour redistribuer des fortunes afin de corriger des inégalités sociales.[1]

W.V.H. Rogers, J. Spier, G. Viney

1. Introduction

The contributions to this book touch upon an important topic: how to keep liability law within reasonable limits. Or, to put it slightly differently, keeping the flood-gates shut. They provide a lot of information about the way how this goal is reached in a number of countries. Moreover, the authors put forward a number of most interesting views how modern tort law could cope with the changes caused by increasing claim-consciousness, amounts awarded and an increase of strict liabilities.

The purpose of the observations below is to provide a brief overview of a broad range of legal systems: which tools are used to prevent the burden of liability law becoming too heavy? For many more details and other most interesting observations, we refer to the respective contributions. Besides, we aim to initiate further discussion.

In the end the proof of the pudding is in the eating. Bearing this mind, it was decided to embark on a second stage of applying the various techniques to specific cases. It turns out that the outcome may well be rather different in the respective countries. The exercise, based on cases, still needs further elaboration, but to a limited extent we have drawn on this exercise in progressing this introduction. The authors hope that the material of this compilation may already serve as a source of inspiration for legislators, courts, private practice and doctrine.

2 Is liability law (heavily) expanding?

Insurers and companies alike seem to harp on the theme of increasing liabilities which could well -and indeed are already said to- cause serious difficulties. Potential defendants might well face bankruptcy. Moreover, insurers are tending to restrict cover and some major insurers have faced and are facing serious problems.

1 See Prof. Widmer's contribution.

J. Spier (ed.), The Limits of Liability, 1-15.

It seems likely these are not merely tall stories, albeit that there certainly are considerable differences between the respective countries. However, reliable statistics are hardly available (at least: not -yet- published).[2] Still, some authors draw attention to this topic.

Prof. Koziol mentions a marked trend "towards conceding injured persons more and more possibilities of passing on their damage"; the application of the traditional fault liabilty has been expanded. New strict liabilities have been created. Prof. Rogers refers to concern over damages payable by hospital trusts and health authorities, liability for the professions, the burden of claims against local authorities and employer's liability. Prof. Viney speaks of "extension de la notion de faute, multiplication de cas de responsabilité sans faute, généralisation de l'obligation au tout des co-auteurs du même dommage, générosité croissante des tribunaux pour l'indemnisation de certains dommages, en particulier des dommages corporels". This counts even more in case of "risques majeurs" and "risques de catastrophe" like ecological, nuclear and industrial risks. Moreover, full liability sometimes has far reaching consequences, "tant sur le plan économique que sur le plan social, qu'entraînent des condamnations très lourdes, lorsqu'elles ne sont pas assurées: faillites, fermetures d'entreprises, chômage". Similar developments occur in the Netherlands.

Prof. Kerameus mentions that Greek tort law tends potentially towards "delictual inflation", although one should not overestimate the same. Prof. Dobbs speaks about "political rhetoric and anecdotal evidence of ridiculous awards. Some of that evidence proved to be misleading. Public debate became a battle of empirical studies about the extent of damages awards. This debate, although interesting, was essentially a dead end." He stresses that empirical studies have not justified the idea that liabilities have generally increased.

3 The principle of full compensation

The principle of "full compensation" is often regarded as one of the fundamentals of modern tort law (See e.g. Prof. Dobbs, Prof. van Oevelen, Prof. Rogers, Prof. Viney and Prof. Widmer). Reducing the damage suffered by the injured requires a justification. However, this statement is rather vague. After all, it does not explain the meaning of "full compensation". Prof. Widmer stresses that it anyway means that the injured is not entitled to an amount in excess of the damage actually suffered.

2 See for specific data: Report of the Tort Policy Working Group on the Causes, Extent and Policy Implications of the Current Crisis in Insurance Availability and Affordability, February 1986 and the update thereto of March 1987 and B.S. Markesinis, Litigation-mania in England, Germany and the USA: are we so very different?, Cambridge Law Journal, 49(2), July 1990 pp 233-276. O.A. Haazen and J. Spier will probably provide statistics -mainly- about the Dutch situation in a prelimary report for the Dutch Lawyer's Assocation (Nederlandse Juristen Vereniging) 1996.

One could reasonably hold that reduction due to (e.g.) comparative fault, adequate causation and the like do not infringe just mentioned principle (See e.g. Prof. Dobbs). It could well be argued that the plaintiff receives full compensation of his damage. He "only" has to take for his own account the proportion caused by himself or causes to be imputed to him.

Seen from a doctrinal point of view the discussion is undoubtedly exciting. It could equally be, seen from a legislative or jurisprudential perspective. Looking at it from the latter angle, one escapes from the "necessity" to find a justification for a "reduction".

It is also open to question whether we are right to pay too much attention to the somewhat metaphysical requirement of "full compensation" in a situation where liability or non-liability may turn on small factual differences between one case and the next. Although modern tort law is inclined to create new liabilities (by stretching the concept of fault or negligence or by creating new strict liabilities) liability is still an exception, at least in terms of injured persons recovering damages through the legal process. This raises questions which go well beyond the jurisprudence of current tort law. A number of jurisdictions represented in this collection have special, non-tort regimes for certain types of accidents (e.g. labour accidents) but in New Zealand virtually all personal injury cases have been removed from the area of tort liability.

4 The tools to keep liability within reasonable limits

4.1 Preliminary observations

Legal systems almost always provide tools to keep liability within reasonable limits. At first glance, this does not seem to be the case in Belgium nor in France. The former is apparently not inclined to find ways to keep the floodgates shut. As far as the latter country is concerned, this impression is not entirely correct. French courts are prepared to keep the floodgates shut. But the way they reach that result is rather hidden. Prof. Viney put it as follows: "Toutefois, en y regardant de plus près, on s'aperçoit sans peine que ce droit n'est pas resté insensible aux objurgations de ceux qui souhaitent restreindre l'impact des responsabilités. Mais, pour y venir, on a privilégé l'emploi de méthodes indirectes et quasi-occultes".

To some extent the same goes also for Austria. According to Prof. Koziol "the reasons for limitation of damages (...) up to now has very often been imposed by courts secretly and without any argumentation".

The following mechanisms are rather more open in their operation.

4.2 Duty of care and "Schutznorm"

The phenomenon of the "duty of care" or the "Schutznorm" undoubtedly is an important vehicle in this respect. If it were possible to find general concepts to consider who has a duty of care and who has not, this would be a useful tool to moderate liability, as Prof. von Bar says.

The German Schutznorm requires that the violation of a statute is demanded by the scope of its protected interest. However, it also applies in case of violation of a non statutory duty. In the latter case this duty should aim to protect the interest in question. A similar approach is known in Austria, Greece and the Netherlands. The same is also true for Swiss law in case of economic loss which is not caused by personal injury or damage to property, unless the tort feasor acted "avec l'intention de nuire ou contrairement aux bonnes moeurs".

Prof. Koziol stresses that the rule is relevant for two reasons. The tortfeasor has to compensate only the losses of those persons which the law is intended to protect and only those losses which the violated law is intended to avoid. If the harm is on the outer limit of the scope of this rule, it could turn out that liability will only be established if the weakness of the protective purpose of the norm is made up for by a severe degree of fault.

Yet, it seems open to open to debate whether claims will often founder on Schutznorm or duty of care. The answer may well be different from country to country. The cases revealed seem to support such a posing. In the Netherlands case law is hardly available, which seems to suggest that its impact is limited. Meanwhile, one should possibly be slightly reluctant in saying so. Leaving aside that the greater part of case law is never published (at least: in many countries), it seems not beyond imagination that potential plaintiffs refrain from suing because they consider their chances too remote due to the Schutznorm.

The English duty of care concept is much more elaborated. Prof. Rogers stresses that it is "the most important and control device in the modern law". It is of specific importance in determining the situations in which the law of negligence will operate and the type of damage it will compensate. There is a wide ranging duty in respect to acts, a narrower one with regard to omissions or statements; equally, there is a wide ranging duty in respect of physical damage and a much more restricted one in respect of economic loss. It follows from abundant case law of the House of Lords that four separate elements play a role, notably: foreseeability, proximity, fairness and policy. Especially expressions like proximity and foreseeability are so vague that they give the court a good deal of leeway in coming to a decision on the question of duty.

4.3 Causation

Only those damages which can be causally imputed to the tortfeasor can be recovered. In this respect there seem to be considerable differences between the various legal systems. One may take it that a simple conditio sine qua non theory is ineffective to keep liability within reasonable limits (leaving aside whether it always is a requirement).[3]

In the United States proximate cause rules generally exclude harms that differ in kind from those risked by the defendant's conduct. Judicial explanations usually rely on the idea that some kinds of damages were not foreseeable, or that some intervening actor was the immediate cause of the harm. If the nature of the plaintiff's harm was foreseeable, the rules do not exclude any recovery of damages, merely because the harm was more extensive than could have been foreseen. (See Prof. Dobbs) The English principles are essentially similar.

In Greek law, the theory of adequate causation plays a potentially important role with respect to compensation for lost profits. They have to be compensated to the extent that they probably would have been been expected in the ordinary course of events, or according to special circumstances. Prof. Kerameus and Mr Roussos point out that the concept "is weighed on an <u>ad hoc</u> basis, taking into account several circumstances, including moral considerations". Socially acceptable negative results may not be imputed to the tortfeasor. The former ("considérations de l'ordre social") equally play a role in Swiss law, notably in disregarding a victim's predisposition.

Adequate causation also applies in Austria, albeit with two exceptions. First, the tortfeasor violates "a protective legal provision .. forbidding a certain behaviour in order to protect assets." According to some authors the same goes if the tortfeasor acted wilfully and knowingly. (See Prof. Koziol)

The French Cour de Cassation never adopted a specific theory on causation. Consequently, the courts have a considerable freedom and "il est bien évident que celle-ci est très souvent utilisée afin d'écarter certaines conséquences lointaines inattendues du fait dommageable initial, lorsque précisément ces conséquences alourdissent de façon excessive la dette du responsable". In various cases they create in fact "une obligation de mitigation imposée à la victime". In case of contractual liability there is no obligation to compensate "dommage imprévisible".

3 Two similar prolems have frequently arisen in the context of the requirement of conditio sine qua non. First "DES-cases", where the victim has been injured by a drug, but it is not possible to indentify which of a number of manufacturers made that badge. Secondly, there are cases of "perte d'une chance". In such cases it can be said that the conditio sine qua non requirement is not met, because it has not been shown that the defendant caused the condition which constituted the plaintiffs loss. Yet, some legal systems require the tortfeasor to compensate the victim either partially or in full because the loss of a chance is regarded as being damage.

According to Prof. Viney it is conceivable that this rule will also apply to delictual liability in the future "si le besoin de renforcer le pouvoir d'équité du juge sur l'ampleur des condemnations se fait sentir de manière plus pressante".

Prof. von Bar makes a distinction between fault and strict liability. In the former case the conduct has to be an adequate cause; that means one has to find out whether it significantly increased the specific risk which was actually fulfilled. If a strict liability is at stake, adequacy does not play a role. A similar distinction has to be made for Dutch law, in that courts will be more reluctant to impute damages to a tortfeasor in case of strict liability, compared with liability based on negligence. The same may be true for Switzerland; the degree of negligence may be one of the factors to be taken into account.

To some extent proportional liability -instead of joint and several- could possibly be regarded as a kind of "modification". The latter has also been stressed by Prof. Viney, "lorsque la probabilité de la causalité est forte, car on peut penser que, à défaut de ce recours à la notion de "perte de chance", les juges admettraient alors une indemnisation intégrale". See for more details Prof. Dobbs and Prof. Spier. The same counts for "value of a chance" (perte d'une chance) (see also Prof. Rogers). Prof. Dobbs mentions strong evidence that many valid claims are never presented in the United States; "the value-of-the chance rule might affect claiming behaviour".

4.4 Various heads of damages

Torts may cause different heads of damages. The principal type of damages which may be caused by a tort may be (a) personal injury, (b) property damage, (c) economic loss. One should not necessarily treat the first in the same manner as the other two. However, even with regard to personal injury there is a view that material loss is a higher priority then non material damage. See for more details 5.5 below.

4.4.1 Personal injury

Under Austrian law, in case of slight negligence the tortfeasor has only to compensate the "eigentliche Schadloshaltung", but not immaterial damage. But, in case of bodily injury this rule does not apply. Besides, the victim is entitled to "subjective disadvantage".[4]

The French Supreme Court is very reluctant to control the assesment of damages by the lower courts. Consequently, they have a considerable manoeuvring room

4 See H. Koziol, Oesterreichisches Haftpflichtrecht, Band II: Besonderer Teil, 2nd ed. p. 127. The meaning of "subjektiv-konkret" is that the victim is entitled to compensation, even if the amount is very high, due to his personal circumstances.

especially in relation to compensation for pain and suffering and different heads of vague economic losses.

In England, in personal injury cases, damages can only be awarded by a court on a lump sum basis, though the parties may settle on a periodic payment basis. The approach to capitalizing a future stream of lost income is rather conservative, in that it is based on a rather low rate of return. The amounts for pain and suffering are high by European standards. Yet, "there is no evidence that this level is insupportable in the general run of cases and in the most serious cases they are likely to be small in comparison with the damages for loss of earnings and for expenses".

In case of strict liability, the Swiss commission on the reform of tort law advocates sticking to compensation "résultant d'une atteinte à la vie ou à l'intégrité physique ou psychique d'une personne, aux choses ou à l'environnement" (see Prof. Widmer).

Unlike in case of commercial transactions, damages for personal injury have to be computed on a specific rather than an abstract basis in Greece. It is not enough for the victim to assert in capacity for work. If e.g. the victim is either infant or retired and if he would be jobless anyway, the incapacity for work would be irrelevant for purposes of assessing lost profits.

Under Dutch law there is a clear trend to find a way to award full compensation for personal injury. First by creating liability, sometimes even with an apparently retroactive effect. Secondly by stretching the concept of causation. And thirdly by disregarding contributory negligence (especially in relation to children below the age of fourteen).

Some systems show considerable caution in dealing with psychic trauma ("nervous shock"). For example, while US and English law are willing to award damages for such injury in the normal way they place certain restrictions on liability which do not apply to other forms of personal injury. A further factor which may be of vital importance in determining the overall cost of tort liability is the extent to which a legal system regards "collateral benefits" (social security payments, insurance, gifts of money or services) as replacing the loss inflicted by the defendant or the victim.

4.4.2 Damage to property

Generally speaking, in the US damages are measured objectively, by the market value of the property. Under English law, in cases of damage to property the possibility of obtaining a repair or a reasonable replacement limits the range of recoverable consequential losses more than in personal injury cases.

Damage to property has to be compensated by the market value, according to Austrian law. Generally speaking, the same counts for Dutch law.

See for environmental damage under Swiss law 4.4.1 above.

4.4.3 Economic loss

Pure economic loss probably is one of the main problems in expanding tort law.

Under American law, economic loss flowing from physical damage to the plaintiff's person or property caused by negligence is fully recoverable, whereas purely economic harm is usually not actionable, in the absence of some special relationship between plaintiff and defendant that requires the defendant to use care for the plaintiffs purely economic loss. Yet, liability may be imposed for intentional infliction or in some cases for reckless or wanton infliction of such loss. Negligent infliction may be ground for recovery in many particular instances, for instance in case of unjust enrichment of the defendant and it is matched thereby, or if it gives rise of a tort such as libel or misrepresentation that is specifically designed to protect economic or other intangible assests. A few US Courts, however, have approved liability for negligently inflicted, stand-alone economic losses in particular cases.

English law is extremely reluctant with regard to negligently inflicted[5] pure economic loss, unless a close relationship of proximity exists between the "parties", unlike Dutch law. In German law the question whether pure economic loss is recoverable depends on the legal basis for liability. It is not generally recoverable under § 823 BGB, nor in case of environmental liability. But there is wider recoverability under § 826 BGB. Austrian law shows also some reluctance in connection with pure economic loss. Compensation has to be made in case of wilful injury. The scope of the latter is probably rather well controlled, since intentional infliction is always directed to one person or a well difined group of persons. Swiss law is equally very reluctant.

According to the Greek Civil Code the award of non pecuniary damages has to be "reasonable". Prof. Kerameus and Mr Roussos point out that this will mean: less than full compensation; guidelines are not available, whereas the matter is not subject to review by the Supreme Court.

As far as French law is concerned, compensation for pure economic loss has to be made in principle, irrespective whether it has been caused by personal injury or damage to property.

5 As in the United States such loss is more easily recoverable when intentionally inflicted.

4.5 Ceilings and caps

Traditionally ceilings and caps are well known in conventions, especially in the area of transport law. They are not very popular in the respective national laws. This is true for Greek and Swiss law. The same counts for Belgium, Austria, England, Germany, the Netherlands and France, albeit with few exceptions (see for details the contributions of Prof. van Oevelen, Prof. von Bar, Prof. Koziol and Prof. Rogers). Many US State statutes place low ceilings on liability, especially when they created claims that were not previously recognized. See for more details Prof. Dobb's contribution.

Prof. Viney speaks about une "très grand méfiance qu'inspire toute tentative de limitation". French insurers offer ever more unlimited coverages for personal injury.

4.6 Modification

Dutch law provides an interesting vehicle to keep the foodgates shut. The court may mitigate the obligation to pay damages if awarding full compensation would lead to clearly unacceptable results, in the given circumstances, including the nature of the liability, the legal relationship between the parties and their financial capacity. However, modification may not exceed the amount for which the debtor has covered his liability by insurance or was obliged to do so. The relevant article entered into force in January 1992; case law is still hardly available. See for details Prof. Spier's contribution.

A more or less similar phenomenon is known in Swiss law. Art. 44 para 2 COS explicitely says: "lorsque le préjudice n'a été causé ni intentionellement, ni par effet d'une grave négligence ou imprudence, et que sa réparation exposerait le débiteur à la gêne, le juge peut équitablement réduire les dommages-intérêts". Yet, it is hardly applied, unless in case of une "faute particulièrement légère". As a general rule, it cannot be invoked if the tortfeasor is insured. (See for more details Prof. Widmer) Prof. van Oevelen points out that modification is allowed in Belgian law in specific circumstances. Prof. Koziol explains that moderation now also takes place in Austria, albeit not openly.

As already pointed out above (4.5) French law is unmistakably hostile to derogation from the principle of full compensation, at least in theory.

4.7 The degree of negligence

The degree of negligence plays a different role in the respective legal systems, if it is considered relevant at all.

It is of no importance in Greek law, unless non pecuniary damage is involved. In the latter case the degree of fault has an impact upon the extent of reasonable damages. English law does not draw any distinction between different degrees of negligence for the purpose of imposing liability or of assessing damages; with regard to the latter the position is rather different in the United States due to the wider availability of punitive damages.

By contrast, the degree of negligence plays a very significant role in Austrian law, albeit that this position has been critised. The same goes for France -albeit not openly- and the Netherlands. Swiss law is rather explicit: "le juge détermine le mode ainsi que l'étendue de la réparation d'après les circonstances et la gravité de la faute". See for details Prof. Widmer's contribution.

4.8 The financial capacity of tortfeasor and victim

Taking the financial capacity of tortfeasor and victim into account as a form of modification. This factor can be taken into account in Belgian and Dutch law. In specific circumstances it has to be taken into account in Austria (see for details Prof. Koziol).

4.9 Liability covered by insurance

As already pointed out in 4.6 above, the question whether liability is covered by insurance plays a role in the Dutch context of modification. Moreover, legal doctrine is inclined to believe that courts are less reluctant to establish liability if the defendant's liability is or is likely to be covered by insurance. This is probably true for all systems even though courts may be reluctant to accept it as a sufficient formal reason.

4.10 Miscellaneous

The above tools are offered as a non-exhaustive list of tools to keep liability within reasonable limits. Hereinafter we just "list" some other means to reach the same goal.

First there is "contributory" or "comperative" negligence, under which, having concluded that the conduct of both victim and defendant has played a causative role in the injury, the victim's damages are reduced to take account of his contribution. This phenomenon is not always linked to liability based upon "negligence". For example, US, Dutch and English law are willing to allow a reduction in cases of strict liability, where "comparative fault" is really a contradiction in terms. Prof. Widmer mentions a trend to disregard slight or even moderate contributory negligence, whereas the plaintiff has to keep the entire damage for his own account in case of very gross contributory negligence ("extrem grobes Selbstverschulden"). Prof. Viney states a trend to objectify the concept of "faute", to the benefit of the injured. The downside is - in case of personal injury, to her regret - that the same is true for contributory negligence.

Force majeure and "fait (prédominant) d'un tiers" are likely to relieve from liability in many legal systems. The latter is not the case in connection with different Dutch strict liabilities. The Swiss tort law reform suggests that they can only be invoked if they ont "contribué de manière manifestement préponderante à la survenance du dommage ou à son aggravation". Otherwise, the damage to be paid can be reduced. See for details Prof. Widmer.

The system of joint and several liability of concurrent wrongdoers wherby each is liable for the whole loss may be mitigated by judicial power to apportion the loss among them (see e.g. the English position). However, this does not help where one defendant is insolvent for his share then falls upon the others. Some American states have abolished the joint and several rule and provided that each wrongdoer only bears liability to the plaintiff in proportion to his own fault.

In the next section we outline the possibility of imposing arbitrary "ceilings" or "caps" on liability. However, under existing systems the burden of liability may be controlled by more or less conventionelized methods of fixing compensation, particularly for non-pecuniary loss. Thus in England there is in efffect a judge-made "tariff" for such losses and the same goes, albeit in an informal way, for France, Germany and Switzerland. See also the discussion of scales, matrices and valuation scenarios in Prof. Dobbs' paper.
Finally, one should bear in mind that a legal system may allow a defendant to be quit of a liability via bankruptcy, though this is likely to be a satisfactory solution neither for him nor the victim.

5 How to keep liability within reasonable limits in the future?

5.1 Introduction

The above provides an overview of different tools presently used, to a greater or a lesser extent, in the various systems to keep liability within reasonable limits. However, it seems unlikely that in any system they have been created as part of a coordinated strategy. Until fairly recently it may have been the case that no system faced very serious difficulty because the types of cases, the scale of the losses and the pattern of litigation were fairly predictable. However, factors like scientific advance, medical knowledge, increased environmental awareness, the scale of business activity and even "willingness to go to court" combine to present the possibility of a "doomsday scenario" and prompt questions (a) whether there should be a more adequate mechanism, going beyond the multiple overlapping and rather "open" concepts currently used and (b) whether those existing concepts should be modified.

5.2 Global limits and ceilings

Global limits are occasionally found; liability is limited to an amount per occurrence (e.g. in the case of unclear liability; a variant of this is also allowed by Art. 16 of the Product Liability Directive). However, while this may affect the defendant's insurance cover it raises the most acute problems of litigation management where there are - or may be - many victims. Furthermore, it may be necessary to create some sort of "reserve" or "fall back" position once the limited fund is exhausted.

An alternative approach is to use a "ceiling", i.e. to "cap" each claim on a certain level. [6] However, these also have disadvantages. First, they discriminate against persons with the worst injuries. It is extremely difficult -if not arbitrary- how to fix the amount. If it is set on a fairly moderate level, this is very much detrimental for victims, and not necessarily justified for disasters and/or big industry. On the other hand, if they are very high, they are useless for the majority of cases, whereas the "average" tortfeasor could never take advantage thereof. Selecting a particular group of defendants would be arbitrary. Moreover, one should be reluctant to focus on the defendant only. Relieving him, puts the burden on the plaintiff's shoulders without a specific quid pro quo. The only "quid" he receives is that the ceiling may be beneficial for society. (See for more details Prof. Dobbs) Prof. von Bar reveals that high ceilings could well imply that potential tortfeasors, who faced unlimited liability before, deem it appropriate to increase the insurance coverage. Prof. Dobbs does not oppose limitations as such. But "the real problem is to determine the proper, just and socially useful level of awards. If a just theory of limitation is developed fully, people will accept the resulting limitations."

Prof. Viney is of the opinion that ceilings could be "un instrument utile (en tout cas pratiquement inévitable) pour les risques de catastrophe, mais (..) il doit être manié avec beaucoup de précautions et que ces plafonds doivent être régulièrement révisés en fonction des possibilités d'assurance." Prof. von Bar would be in favour of differentiated ceilings. The criterion should be the typical danger caused by the company ("typisches Betriebsgefahr"). One should essentially focus on the potential amount of damages that could be caused.

It appeared that ceilings create specific difficulties in Germany. They are only used in connection with strict liability, but the plaintiff can also base his action on fault liability if the requirements for fault liability are met. Moreover, only fault liability can lead to payment for pain and suffering. It means that companies are not willing

6 Another variant is to require that each claim passes a certain minimum threshold, thereby eliminating small claims. See Prof. Dobbs.

to settle with respect to damages above the ceiling or for pain and suffering, because the directors of that company may be held liable in criminal law if (fault) liability is acknowledged in a settlement.

5.3 Strict or fault liability

As a general rule, liability will be based on negligence. Still, the number of strict liabilities is increasing. Should one make a distinction between the two? And, if so, should one equally discern different grades of negligence? Opinions were divided, as they are in doctrine.

German doctrine is of the opinion that liability based on fault and strict liability should be treated the same, at least in relation to ceilings. Prof. Koziol is of he same opinion. If exposure to danger is deemed to be a reason for strict liability, "it is incomprehensible for the (latter) .. to be limited by maximum amounts, whereas the liability based on fault, naturally, is not. .. There is no reason to foresee a special possibility for calculating the risks of damages in the area of strict liability. Furthermore, the economic capacity of the liable person is to be considered in the exact same way as in the area of strict liability". Prof. Rogers mentions a similar - and even more general- view of English law: "while it would be contrary to common sense to say that there are not degrees of negligence, as far as tort liability is concerned there is only one standard and it has been said that for the purposes of the civil law "gross negligence" is only negligence with the addition of a vituperative epithet. Once the defendant's conduct crosses the line which separates legal fault from non-fault he is liable to make "full" compensation in so far that is required by law". Meanwhile, Prof. Koziol points out that it may well be reasonable to pay attention to the degree of fault, or degree of danger in relation to strict liability "but this should not be the sole element taken into account. .. Rather the weight of all reasons for liability should be considered". He advocates full compensation, even in case of very remote harm, in case of wilful torts.

Prof. Viney is of a different opinion: ".. il paraît plus naturel de limiter la responsabilité sans faute ou objective que les responsabilités fondées sur la faute". Prof. Kerameus shares her view. However, Prof. Rogers mentions that the difference between both kinds of liabilty may well be of limited practical relevance, because the plaintiff could base his claim on fault just to avoid the harshness of ceilings.

Prof. Widmer speaks of an opposite effect which may arise in a situation subject to strict liability but when the defendant in fact has been guilty of fault. "(L)orsqu'il y aurait en principe lieu de réduire l'indemnité en raison d'une autre circonstance, notamment une faute concomitante du lésé, cette dernière pourra être entièrement ou partiellement neutralisée par la faute additionelle ... imputable au "responsable causal".

5.4 Financial position of the parties

Prof. Koziol suggests to take the financial position of the tortfeasor and the victim into account; in his view one should equally consider which party can best be expected to insure the risk, apparently a retro-active assesment. The latter is also true for Prof. Viney. Prof. Widmer is of a slightly different view. It follows from the motto quoted above. He adds: "la structure même du droit de la responsabilité s'y oppose puisque ces corrections n'interviendraient que de façon purement aléatoire, selon le rythme irrégulier et les coups aveugles de la fatalité. ... Ni la pauvreté ni l'abondance peuvent dès lors être admises comme critères d'imputation valables". Still, it may be justified to look at these factors in exceptional cases; the same is true for coverage by insurance. "Ce qu'il faut éviter, c'est que ces considérations métajuridiques deviennent d'un usage trop commun et qu'elles commencent à se glisser discrètement dans les fondements de la responsabilité.

5.5 Different heads of damages

Personal injury deserves special attention, according to Prof. Viney and Prof. Koziol. Prof. Viney adds that this seems "beaucoup moins indispensable en ce qui concerne les atteintes aux biens ainsi que les pertes de profits économiques. Pour ces dommages, un aménagement de la réparation dans un sens restrictif est en effet plus facilement concevable", unless "elles mettent en péril les resources essentielles pour la victime, c'est-à-dire ses moyens de vivre". With regard to compensation for pain and suffering "il serait envisageable non seulement de plafonner les indemnités, mais même de prévoir des forfaits plus ou moins symboliques".

Prof. Spier is inclined to think that one should be careful to distinguish between the different heads of damages, not being personal injury. One should take into account the consequences of full compensation (for society in general). Prof. Viney -whose view is supported by Prof. Rogers and Prof. Spier- argued that pure economic loss may well have serious consequences for the victim. Consequently, one should at least be cautious in concluding that - as a general rule - it cannot be recovered. Moreover, the difference between "material damage" and economic loss may well be arbitrary. Prof. Widmer refers to a broken electricity cable (a frequent hypothetical in the German and Anglo-American systems). One company will suffer loss of profit (pure economic loss), whereas another will suffer "material damage" caused by products which were damaged due to the fact that machinery breaks down.

5.6 Causation

It appeared that there are many similarities between the concepts of Schutznorm or duty of care and adequate causation. The results will probably be similar. In the latter case plaintiffs will not entirely be cut off from an action; the amount to be paid may be reduced. It was argued that the concept of foreseeability is rather unconvincing. Some damages are deemed to be foreseeable, although in reality no reasonable man would possibly foresee them. Clearly some concept of adequete causation is a vital component of any system. However, the openness of the concept and the considerable variations in the extent to which the juge du fond is subject to control make it an uncertain tool to limit liability.

5.7 Ad hoc control

Finally, one could consider to establish a discretionary power for courts to apply ad hoc control, more or less in line with the Dutch example, also advocated by Prof. von Bar and others, but rejected by Prof. Rogers. But one should not expect miracles by introducing such a phenomenon. For various reasons. Quoique une telle solution soit "séduisante par sa souplesse, .. elle peut aussi effrayer car elle introduit officiellement un élément d'arbitraire", as Prof. Viney put it. Yet, she would not object such an approach "au moins pour les dommages moraux et pertes de profit économique". Such a solution would be inappropriate in case of economic loss caused by personal injury. Moreover, ad hoc control could have the advantage that the courts would have to explain (in more detail) why they moderated the amount of damages.

Even if we could take it that modification would fit in the respective legal systems and/or that courts would be prepared to apply it, we have to provide criteria when and how to use this or similar tools. In this context one should bear in mind that the law as it stands may well provide sufficiently adequate means to cope with expanding liabilities. Even if that would be the case, "les techniques de limitation sont ... nombreuses et diversifiées, mais elles sont employées de manière assez anarchique, sans vue d'ensemble", thus Prof. Viney.

6 Final observation

The contributions to this book and the discussions in our group make it abudantly clear indeed that this most fascinating and important topic needs further elaboration. We aim to publish comparative case studies which will -together with this book-hopefully serve as useful material for further reflection. Not only on modification, ceilings and the like, but possibly also on other fundamentals of our modern tort law. If and to the extent the legitimate interests of victim and "tortfeasor" cannot be reconciled, one possibly has to consider other solutions as well.

Limitation and Mitigation in German Tort Law

Prof. Dr. Christian v. Bar/
Wissenschaftlicher Mitarbeiter Assessor Ingo Rogge, Osnabruck.

In German law the problems of keeping tortious liability within reasonable limits are solved by various other methods in addition to those of limitation and mitigation. If, for example the harm caused is not within the protective purpose of the rule in question (Schutzzweck der Norm) then issues of limitation and mitigation may not arise; what must first be answered is whether the conduct under consideration gives rise to liability at all. To regard the conditio sine qua non as the decisive cause of liability would be no more than a restriction.[1]
This may however merely be a particularly German view; the essential questions posed by the questionaire remain the basis of the following discussion.

I Areas of German law in which the principle of full compensation is felt to be inappropriate

1 Strict liability cases

In accordance with German legal traditions, the risks of strict liability are set off by statutory monetary limitations on awards of damages.[2] It was because of this that during negotiations over the European product liability directive the German government insisted that such limits were an essential part of all kinds of strict liability.[3] German tort law is based on the principle that there can be no liability without fault. Strict liability has been introduced in a limited number of statutory exceptions for circumstances in which permissible dangers could cause harm independently of any fault, and in which a system of fault-based compensation was therefore deemed to be unsatisfactory.[4] These exceptions have almost always included financial limits on damages awards.[5]

As an example, the Strassenverkehrsgesetz (Road Traffic Act, StVG) includes rules relating to the liability and limitation thereof of the keepers of cars:

1 Fikentscher, Schuldrecht, 8th ed. 1992, no. 444.
2 Geigel/Rixecker, Der Haftpflichtprozeß 20th ed., chapter 4, no. 166.
3 Schmidt-Salzer, VersR 1991, 12.
4 Deutsch, Unerlaubte Handlungen, Schadensersatz und Schmerzensgeld, 2nd ed., no. 355.
5 v.Caemmerer, Reform der Gefährdungshaftung (1971); v.Caemmerer, RabelsZ 78, 5 (15).

J. Spier (ed.), The Limits of Liability, 17-25.

StVG § 12 [Haftungshöchstbeträge]
"(1) Der Ersatzpflichtige haftet

1 im Falle der Tötung oder Verletzung eines Menschen nur bis zu einem Kapitalbetrag von 500.000 Deutsche Mark oder bis zu einem Rentenbetrag von jährlich 30.000 Deutsche Mark;

2 im Falle der Tötung oder Verletzung mehrerer Menschen durch dasselbe Ereignis, unbeschadet der in Nr.1 bestimmten Grenzen, nur bis zu einem Kapitalbetrag von 750.000 Deutsche Mark oder bis zu einem Rentenbetrag von 45.000 Deutsche Mark; diese Beschränkung gilt jedoch in den Fällen des § 8 a Abs.1 Satz 1 nicht für den ersatzpflichtigen Halter des Kraftfahrzeugs;

3 im Falle der Sachbeschädigung, auch wenn durch dasselbe Ereignis mehrere Sachen beschädigt werden, nur bis zu einem Betrag von 100.000 Deutsche Mark.

(2) Übersteigen die Entschädigungen, die mehreren aufgrund desselben Ereignisses nach Abs. 1 zu leisten sind, insgesamt die in Nr.2 Halbsatz 1 und Nr.3 bezeichneten Höchstbeträge, so verringern sich die einzelnen Entschädigungen in dem Verhältnis, in welchem ihr Gesamtbetrag zu dem Höchstbetrag steht".

Similar rules exist under §§ 9, 10 of the Haftpflichtgesetz (Liability Act) in respect of railways, power generators and electricity cables, and under §§ 37, 46 of the Luftverkehrsgesetz (Air Traffic Act, LuftVG) in respect of aircraft owners. Only in respect of strict liability under § 22 of the Wasserhaushaltsgesetz (Water Act, WHG) and the liability of animal keepers (§ 833 BGB) do such limits not exist.

In recent years, several new strict liability statutes have been introduced into German law, relating, in addition to product liability, to damage to the environment and to genetic engineering. In each of these areas the legislator rejected the principle of full compensation and decided instead in favour of that of financial limits. This, however, does not mean that when these statutes are applicable, it is not also possible to sue for damages on the traditional basis of fault liability. The latter course will in particular be necessary in the case of a litigant wishing to receive damages for pain and suffering as, with the exceptions of the Luftverkehrsgesetz (§ 53 III LuftVG) and the Civil Code (BGB) in respect of the liability of animal keepers, the strict liability statutes do not provide for damages for non-patrimonial damage.

The financial limitation of awards and the absence of compensation for pain and suffering have been much criticised in legal writings, the general opinion being that the availability and extent of damages should be independent of whether liability is strict or fault-based.[6] The financial limits themselves have also been criticised. The limits of DM 160 million set for the Produkthaftungsgesetz (Product Liability Act)

---

6 Kötz, Deliktsrecht, 5th ed., no. 370; v.Caemmerer, Reform der Gefährdungshaftung (1971), 23 f.; Will, Quellen erhöhter Gefahr (1980), 305 ff.

and the Umwelthaftungsgesetz (Environmental Liability Act) for example, have been discussed by Schmidt-Salzer, whose main criticism is that, by setting the limit so highly, the legislator has in fact failed to achieve any real limitation.[7] The figure of DM 160 million will only ever be reached in a few spectacular cases; even in the case of the Sandoz accident referred to by Schmidt-Salzer, the total damages awarded amounted only to SFr 71 million. In particular for smaller firms, a more sensible limit would have been in the region of DM 5 - 10 million. In cases of extreme danger, it may be appropriate to have rules providing for extreme sums but in normal circumstances, such high limits have no part to play.

A further point of criticism of the DM 160 million limit was its effect on the German insurance trade. Although German industry had traded for decades with unlimited liability, few business had felt the need to insure for sums in excess of DM 100 million. On the introduction of the DM 160 million limit however, many smaller businesses became apprehensive of the increased risk that appeared to have been established by the new law. Clearly the risk had not in fact been increased but the appearance thereof led many businesses to believe that increased insurance and hence expense, was necessary.

Strict liability limitation need not be effected solely by monetary limits. The statutes themselves often contain pre-conditions to the application of the strict liability rules. For example, under § 8 StVG, the strict liability of the keeper of a car does not apply in respect of persons inside that car. In addition, in cases in which circumstances beyond anybody's control cause a motor accident, no liability will arise.

In respect of other strict liability rules, similar means restrict the class of possible defendants. A clear example is the new environmental impairment act. Under § 1 Umwelthaftungsgesetz, liability can only arise in respect of a closed class of installations and facilities. No definition is given of what is harmful to the environment but only a list of harmful installations. By this means, only a limited class of companies operating such installations may be considered as possible defendants under the statute. The strict liability is further limited by the absence of provision for damages for economic loss caused other than by physical damage. Thus a landlord who loses tenants due to noxious fumes, cannot rely on the statute to claim damages.

2 Employment relations

a) Personal injuries.
Under §§ 636, 637 Reichsversicherungsordnung (Social Insurance Act, RVO) an employee who is injured at work has a cause of action against neither his employer,

---

7 Schmidt-Salzer, VersR 1991, 12 f.

nor his fellow employees. This is a case in which liability has been replaced by insurance. Rather than against his employer or fellow employee, the injured party has a "strict liability" claim against the employer's compulsory accident insurance.

This substitution may in certain cases result in the injured party receiving a smaller sum as compensation than he would under general fault liability rules, as again the insurance does not provide for damages for pain and suffering. The substitution is often justified as a means of preventing disruption at the place of work in the form of absences to attend trials but this is now openly doubted. It is also clearly no justification for the loss of a claim for non-patrimonial damage.[8]

b) Damage to the employer's property at the fault of his employee.
In this case there is no statutory provision according to which the ordinary rules of liability are to be substituted by insurance.

Much discussion, however, has been devoted to whether and if so, to what extent, the liability of a negligent employee towards his employee should be restricted;[9] even the most careful employee cannot always avoid negligence. As a result the German courts have created rules for the protection of employees engaged in particularly hazardous activities (gefahrgeneigte Arbeit). Originally developed in a decision of the Amtsgericht Plauen of 1936[10], a graduation of various degrees of negligence was later adopted with regard to these activities by all courts. Full compensation was only available if the defendant's conduct was voluntary or grossly negligently. In respect of "slight" negligence, no liability arose. For degrees of negligence in between, damages were awarded proportionally.[11]

The restricted scope of the limitation was widely criticised[12] with the eventual result that in 1993 the 8th Senate of the Bundesarbeitsgericht (Federal Labour Court) brought the question before the Grosse Senat to find a permanent solution. The Grosse Senat agreed to an extension of the restriction of liability for the employee, such that it is no longer necessary that the activity in question should be one that is considered to be particularly hazardous and thus likely to cause damage[13] Everything now depends on all the circumstances of the case.

c) Employee causing damage to third parties.
The personal liability of an employee for damage caused to third parties is unrestricted but his employer is obliged to take over the obligation to compensate, provided that the employee has acted with (at least) "slight" negligence as referred

8 Kötz, Deliktsrecht, no. 600; Hanau, Ist der Haftungsausschluß bei Arbeitsunfällen (§§ 636, 637 RVO) noch gerechtfertigt?, Jura 1970, 112.
9 See in greater detail: Schaub, Arbeitsrechtshandbuch, 7th ed. 1992, § 52 VI
10 AG Plauen, ARS 29, 62.
11 Blomeyer, JuS 1993, 903.
12 Arens, BB 1990, 67 ff.; Schalt, MDR 1992, 12 (15); v.Hoyingen-Huene, BB 1989, 1889 (1894 ff.); Naendrup, JuS 1984, 336 (339).
13 BAG GS NJW 1993, 1732.

to above. A question which arose before the BGH in 1989 however, was what should happen when a lorry driver caused extensive loss by slight negligence and his employer was insolvent. The lorry was acquired under a leasing contract. The driver had been sued personally for damages by the owner of the lorry. The BGH found the driver liable and granted compensation in full. There is no restriction on liability of employees in respect of third parties because this relationship is independent of the one between employer and employee.[14] The implications of this for the insufficiently insured employee are clear, with the result that many commentators believe that such a limitation should be developed.[15] Others believe that a limitation should exist at least in the case of the damaged property's having been given to the employee, together with permission to use it, from the third party, as in the above leasing case.[16] Professor Gamillscheg doubts whether the courts will persist in applying their rule in cases where the burden of damages would threaten the economic existence of the employee[17] but to date there has been no move in that direction.

II General principles of mitigation in German law

The questionaire upon which this discussion is based lists several headings to introduce general systems of limitation and mitigation. Whilst these headings represent particularly English methods of limitation and mitigation, they may be usefully be employed to categorise similar German approaches to the problem.

1 Causation and remoteness of damage

The simple conditio sine qua non test does not assist much in answering the question as to whether a person is liable for harm caused by his conduct. Referring to the term "legal cause" Professor Markesinis correctly says: "...German authors opt instead for one of the variants of the adequate causation theory. German authors make a distinction between causation giving rise to liability (haftungsbegründende Kausalität) and what we would call remoteness of damage (haftungsausfüllende Kausalität); the discussions about "adequacy" only arise under the second heading..."[18] When German law considers whether the conduct was a sufficient cause of the arisen loss, what it is in fact doing is considering whether the conduct significantly increased the risk of the type of damage that actually occured. Ultima-

14 BGH JZ 1990, 189.

15 Hanau, note under BAG AP § 611 BGB Haftung des Arbeitnehmers Nr. 53; Lorenz, ZfBW 1975, 491 ff.; Baumann, BB 1990, 1833 ff.

16 Gamillscheg, AuR 1990, 167 f.; Denck, JZ 1990, 175 ff.

17 Gamillscheg, AuR 1990, 168.

18 Markesinis, The German Law Of Torts, 2nd ed. (1990), 86.

tely it is a question of probability,[19] to be answered by a fictitious omniscient observer.

In strict liability cases, however, adequacy no longer plays a role.[20] Indeed some commentators suggest that this is the case in regard to all questions of liability,[21] and rely solely on the purpose of the rule in question as the decisive factor for the existence of liability.[22]

2 Scope of the protected interests.

German law relies on the principle that only the infringement of pre-existing rights and duties justifies a cause of action.

§823 II BGB provides for compensation on infringement of a protective statute. It is therefore necessary in cases based on that paragraph, to consider the scope of the protected interests. Liability will not arise if the mischief caused is not that intended to be prevented by the statute. A case will also fail if either the plaintiff does not belong to the class of people intended to be protected, or if the intention is only to protect general rather than indiviual interests.[23]

The scope of the protected interests may also be considered in cases under § 823 I in which no specific protective statute needs to be infringed.[24] Here what falls to be considered is whether the defendant was under a duty to act in a certain way to protect the special rights listed in that provision (life, bodily integrity, health, freedom, property and further absolute rights). This approach appears to be quite similar to that of the English duty of care principle. In this way the German courts have developed Verkehrspflichten.[25] Whilst these duties may extend liability by allowing to be based on omissions, they also have a mitigating effect. A good example can be drawn from what is known as the Grünstreifen-cases. In these, a motorist negligently causes an accident and blocks the street. In order to pass the accident, other drivers take to the grass verge, thereby damaging it. The liability of the first driver towards the owner of the grass verge (usually a public body) depends upon whether the duty which he negligently breached by causing the accident was intended to protect the owner of the grass verge as well. The duty to warn and prevent other drivers from crashing into his car is clearly within the first driver's responsibilities, so if a further faultless driver can only avoid crashing by using the verge, that is clearly the defendant's responsibility. The conduct of others

---

19 Deutsch, Unerlaubte Handlungen, Schadensersatz und Schmerzensgeld, 2nd ed. (1993), no. 52.
20 BGHZ 79, 259.
21 Münchener Kommentar-Grunsky, Vor § 249, no. 42; see, however, Schünemann, JuS 1979, 19.
22 Esser/Schmidt, Schuldrecht vol.I, part 2 (1993), § 33 II.
23 Markesinis, The German Law of Torts, 89.
24 Kötz, Deliktsrecht, no. 158.
25 Cf. v.Bar, Verkehrspflichten (1980).

who merely use the verge in order to avoid waiting, however, is not the responsibility of the defendant.[26] If, however, he leaves the car blocking the road for an unnecessarily long time, the case may again be viewed in another light.[27] There has been much discussion of these cases, both in judgements[28] and in academic writings.[29]

Other cases in which the purpose of the rule may play an important role are those involving nervous shock,[30] although in practice the courts often use principles of adequacy instead,[31] and the so-called Verfolger- oder Herausforderungsfälle. These latter are cases of pursuit or a challenge, for example where a policeman pursues a suspect, or a ticket collector a man whom he suspects of travelling without a ticket. If the pursuer sustains injury, the courts distinguish between the normal risks of life, and those specific to, or increased by, the pursuit. It is then decided which of these led to the injury. This differentiation occasionally leads to apparently very nice distinctions: the policeman who fell on wet grass chasing a young runaway had no claim, as a general risk of life led to his injury,[32] whereas the ticket inspector who fell down a staircase whilst following a man without a ticket did have a claim as his injury resulted from the aggravated risk involved in following the defendant.[33] Whilst the individual results of the examples may be subject of dispute, they do show that the purpose of particular rules or duties may be used as a means to limit liability in German law.

3 Restrictive interpretation of the duty of care principle

As previously mentioned, not every act leading to damage will give rise to a cause of action. Whether an action may be brought or not will often depend upon whether a duty of care applies between the parties. When an object of legal protection mentioned in §823 I is damaged, the first question to be asked is whether the defendant neglected his duty of care. In a judgment of 1987, the BGH denied the existence of such a duty of care on the following facts.[34] A man was employed by a security company to guard the warehouse of a second company, which the latter company used for storing furs. The furs were stolen whilst the guard slept. The guard was sued personally by the owner of the furs. No reason is given for sueing him rather than his employer. The BGH denied the existence of a duty of care owed by the guard to the owner. Although the guard had neglected his contractual duties, the contract between guard and employer did not create a tortious duty of

---

26 BGHZ 58, 162 (168).
27 Kötz, Deliktsrecht, no. 161.
28 LG Düsseldorf NJW 1955, 1013; OLG Bremen VersR 1970, 424; BGHZ 58, 162.
29 Larenz, NJW 1955, 1009; Deutsch, JZ 1972, 551; Lange, JuS 1973, 280.
30 Münchener Kommentar-Grunsky, Vor § 249, no. 53 ff.
31 RGZ 133, 270; OLG München NJW 1959, 819.
32 BGH NJW 1971, 1982
33 BGHZ 57, 25.
34 BGH ZIP 1987, 1260.

care to third persons. The BGH explained that a duty of care may arise solely as a result of the profession carried on by a person but only in the case of independent contractors and the self-employed. Simple employees owed no duty of care to third parties in situations as this. It is submitted that this is an attempt by the BGH to hold liability to reasonable limits. At the very least it shows that not every infringement of a contractual duty resulting in damage to property or other objects of legal protection belonging to third parties gives rise to tortious liability.

The precise limits of this restriction are not yet clear. In a subsequent judgment, the BGH dealt with the similar problem of a company which supplied building materials to another limited liability company (GmbH) under a contract containing a retention of title clause.[35] A further clause allowed the GmbH to sell the materials to a third party but only under condition that any claims against that third party arising from any such transfer should be conveyed to the original owner. As part of a building contract, the GmbH sold the materials to a third party, X, under a contract containing a term to the effect that the GmbH would transfer none of its rights against X arising therefrom to any other party. The GmbH then became insolvent and failed to pay the original owner. The original owner was unable to pursue X as the GmbH's right to payment against X had not and could not be transferred. Pursuing the GmbH would have been pointless due to its insolvency. Hence the plaintiff sued the managing director of the GmbH personally. Although the managing director had had nothing to do with the conclusion ot the two contracts and indeed, may not even have known of them, the BGH held that he was liable as he had neglected his own personal duty of care (Verkehrspflicht).

This latter decision appears to contradict that of the night-watchman case above at first glance only.We do not share the views of many commentators[36] that the managing director was held liable for an omission which should only have resulted in the liability of the GmbH.[37] The question to be answered in both these cases is who is to be held responsible when a person takes over the responsibilities of another person. The answer need not always be the same and may depend on principles that have not previously been made clear. We believe that one of the most important of those principles must be the extent to which the defendant inspired reliance in his ability to handle the risk, and in this respect there is an obvious difference between the position of a managing director and of a simple employee.

III Preference of certain systems

The (Nieuw) Burgerlijk Wetboek of the Netherlands introduced practical methods to ensure liability remains within reasonable limits. Under Article 6.109 NBW the

---

35 BGHZ 109, 297.

36 Mertens/Mertens, JZ 1990, 488 ff.; Krebs/Dylla-Krebs, DB 1990, 1271 ff.

37 v. Bar, Festschrift für Kitagawa (1992), 279, 290ff.

Judge is allowed to reduce the award of damages in cases in which the obligation to pay would lead to unacceptable results. All circumstances of the actual case must be taken into account, among them the financial capacity of the defendant. All Scandinavian Tort Liability Statutes provide for insurance of both parties to be considered in this respect as well. We think that a common European approach should be developed along these lines. The current German system, who still relies on the "all-or-nothing-principle" should be given up.

Direct and general limits on tort damages in the United States[**]

Dan B. Dobbs[*]

Scope. This paper considers the possibility of direct limitations on damages in the United States through application of a general principle addressed to the recovery of a judgment for damages. It thus does not address rules that require *ad hoc* determinations of damages limits for particular cases. For this reason, it does not discuss limitations achieved in particular cases through doctrines of proximate cause, cause-in-fact, comparative fault, comparative causation, or value-of-the-chance rules. These and other limitations are listed in an appendix made available to Professor Spier.

I General Principles

1. *Full compensation principle.* The laws of the fifty states differ from each other in many details, so generalizations are almost always imperfect. However, the courts in the United States generally agree that the principle by which damages are measured is full compensation, no more, no less. The rule applies in strict liability cases and in environmental cases[1] as well as in common negligence cases. There

* Regents Professor and Rosenstiel Professor of Law University of Arizona Tucson, AZ. 85721 USA.

** A paper for presentation at The Center for Liability Law, Katholieke Universiteit Brabant, Tilburg, March, 1994 *See*: Dan Dobbs, The Law of Remedies § 3.1, p. 281 (2d ed. 1992).

1 The federal Superfund Law (CERCLA) imposes liability upon present owners of contaminated land as well as those who actually caused the pollution. Liability is strict and may include not merely the diminished value of land, but the costs of cleaning it up. See 42 U.S.C.A. § 9701(a). States may impose similar liabilities. Starr v. Com'n of Environmental Protection, 226 Conn. 358, 627 A.2d 1296 (1993) (present owner, who did not contaminate, liable to state for clean-up costs necessary because prior contamination was polluting state rivers). In T & E Industries, Inc. v. Safety Light Corp., 123 N.J. 371, 587 A.2d 1249, 13 A.L.R.5th 1041 (1991) the current owner was required to move his factory off the premises and forbidden to sell the land until clean up was complete, but he was allowed to claim damages against the corporations who had sold the land to him. However, in Philadelphia Elec. Co. v. Hercules, Inc., 762 F.2d 303 (3d Cir. 1985) the court held that the present owner, who had been compelled to pay for the cost of cleaning contaminated land, was denied any recovery against persons who had sold the contaminated land. The court thought that the current owner had probably paid a reduced price as a result of the known risk that the land might be contaminated.

J. Spier (ed.), The Limits of Liability, 27-42.

are no formal exceptions of general application and there is no formally recognized discretion to reduce damages.[2]

2. *Exceptions or qualifications*. The full compensation principle is subject to a few qualifications or exceptions. Besides the possibility that the award will be enhanced by punitive damages, the qualifications can be grouped as follows. *(a) Corrective justice reductions*. The award is reduced in a number of instances, to make it commensurate with the corrective justice. Under one conception of compensation, the result is not less than compensation but is rather exact compensation. Reductions grounded in rules of comparative fault, proximate cause, or avoidable consequences are in this category. *(b) Indirect control over awards*. It goes almost without saying that, regardless of formal rules, awards may be reduced or enhanced through informal discretion of the jury or through manipulation of rules by the judges. For instance, the judge may reject some claims for damages because proof is too uncertain. *(c) Use of objective or market measures*. The measure of damages adopted in the first instance may have the effect of providing either more or less than exact compensation. A measure of damages for pollution of land, for example, might be the cost of cleaning the land or it might be the diminished market value of the land. The diminished market value measure tends to be less and thus might be regarded as a kind of limitation. *(d) Ceilings*. The most important reduction in compensation is the absolute ceiling or "cap" on certain awards. Proposals to limit damages are heavily debated in the United States. About one-half of the states have enacted statutes that do impose ceilings in personal injury cases and these will furnish one focus of this paper.

3. *Rationales*. The full compensation principle seems to be based primarily on the logic of corrective justice notions. Given a right not to have your leg broken by the defendant, the right is not vindicated by anything less than full compensation for all losses. Commentators who emphasize economics argue a different point: the correct amount of deterrence is achieved by holding defendants liable for all harms they cause. In a legal system that limits damages to less than compensation, defendants like manufacturers would find it profitable in many instances to produce

2 Courts enjoy discretion to adjust remedies that are historically considered to be "equitable" remedies such as injunctions. 1 DAN DOBBS, THE LAW OF REMEDIES § 2.4 (2d ed. 1993). Damages are not in this category. [The American Rule denying attorney fee awards to the prevailing party is a practical exception to the full compensation rule but not a formal one. Full compensation aims at compensation measured at the time and place of the loss, not at compensation for the costs of obtaining compensation. This is not to say that the rule is justified. Isolated statutes authorize discretion in reducing particular elements of damages. For instance, one state's RICO statute provides that "a court shall not award costs, including attorney fees, if the award would be unjust because of special circumstances, including the relevant disparate economic position of the parties or the disproportionate amount of the costs, including attorney fees, to the nature of the damage or other relief obtained." Ariz. Rev. Stat. § 13-2314.04 (M).]

negligently made products that cause harm, because they can pay the limited damages and still profit from the bad product.[3]

II Limiting Compensatory Damages

A Arguments for General Limitations

1. *Pragmatic arguments.* Most of the debate about limited damages in the United States has centered on pragmatic, intuitive, and self-interested arguments, for example, the argument that damages awards are too high, or too numerous, or that they will ultimately be economically destructive. These arguments seem ultimately to raise empirical questions, but empirical studies have not justified the idea that liabilities have generally increased.

2. *Situations for principled arguments.* Arguments based on corrective justice principles have not been much developed in American literature. I tentatively suggest two kinds of situations in which principled limits might be possible.

(a) *Arbitrary right-duty assignments.* The first would include any cases in which we could fairly assign rights either to the injured or to the injurer. For example, if we could justly provide that the victim of an insane person's act must protect himself and that he has no right against the insane person, then we could also justly provide that the victim has a right against the insane person for an amount of damages that is less than compensatory.

(b) *Inherently unmeasureable damages.* The second category would include all cases in which the harm done is not in fact susceptible to measurement and where, in consequence, we cannot be confident that any given sum is the "right" amount to award. Arguments and statutes in the United States have concentrated on this second category. They have been aimed principally at the claim for physical or emotional suffering. However, the category includes any inherently unmeasurable damages, such as those that arise from invasion of privacy or the violation of moral rights of artists.

3. *The moral and utilitarian arguments. (a) Unequal treatment.* Arguments based on corrective justice principles have not been much developed. However, in the case of inherently unmeasurable damages in the second category, it is possible to argue that the wide discretion afforded the decision maker violates the concept of law itself, or that it promotes biased and unfair or discriminatory decisions or even

3 Feminist jurisprudence in the United States may develop other reasons for full compensation or at least against limits on liability. See Magaret Jane Radin, *Compensation and Commensurability*, 43 Duke L.J. 56 (1993); Theresa Gabaldon, *The Lemonade Stand: Feminist and Other Reflections on the Limited Liability of Corporate Shareholders*, 45 VAND. L. REV. 1387 (1992).

that such wide discretion fails to achieve whatever compensation is truly appropriate.[4]

(b) *(i) Inefficiency of pain insurance.* Both efficiency and corrective justice arguments might be constructed by considering the possibility that one could insure oneself against the risk of pain. It would normally be inefficient for a healthy person to spend current income in premiums for insurance against pain.[5] *(ii) Lack of demand pointing to a social contract.* Whether such insurance is inefficient or not, however, people generally do not seek such insurance for injuries unconnected with tort. That might suggest that if all of us were to contract in advance about damages for pain, not knowing whether we would be injured or injurers, we might contract for careful limits on recovery for pain.[6] *(iii) Limiting liability by amounts plaintiff would provide for himself.* Perhaps independent of that idea, one might even develop a principled argument that pre-injury self-assessment of intangible damages is the most just measure.[7] The idea is that one should not be entitled to recover from others in excess of amounts he would provide for himself if he were purchasing insurance. Whether this can be developed into a substantial argument I am not sure.[8]

4 See Bovbjerg, Sloan and Blumstein, *Valuing Life and Limb in Tort: Scheduling "Pain and Suffering"*, 83 NW. L. REV. 908, 924-927 (1989). These authors list four values at risk when awards are extremely variable, although only the first is clearly based on corrective justice: fundamental fairness, erosion of confidence in justice, undermining deterrent effect of damages, and cost of operation. Lack of objective guidelines, as distinct from variability of the awards, might also lead one to doubt that a just award can be made except by happenstance. Cf. Id. at 915 ff.

5 It would usually be inefficient to purchase pain insurance because a healthy person would have unlimited uses for surplus income while an injured person suffering from serious pain would not. See II American Law Institute, Reporter's Study, Enterprise Responsibility for Personal Injury 207 (1991). Steven Shavell, Economic Analysis of Accident Law 228-31 (1987) gives calculations showing that it would always be inefficient to purchase pain insurance unless money is worth more to an individual after injury than before.

6 Cf. JOHN RAWLS, A THEORY OF JUSTICE 12 ff. (1971).

7 Saul Levmore, *Self-Assessed Valuation Systems for Tort and Other Law*, 68 Va. L. Rev. 771 (1982).

8 The comparison between the protection you would provide for yourself and that you would expect from others may not be just, because the comparison necessarily omits to put a value on your rightful autonomy. You negligently use your knife and injure yourself as a result. You have pain, but no loss in your freedom from interference. If you are injured by another person using a knife in the same way, you have the same pain plus a loss of control over your own destiny. Although that loss of autonomy may not be grounds for added damages, it might well indicate why a rational person would demand more in damages from another than he would insure for. Some other reasons why people do not in fact attempt to purchase their own pain insurance are summarized in Bovbjerg, Sloan and Blumstein, *Valuing Life and Limb in Tort: Scheduling "Pain and Suffering"*, 83 NW. L. REV. 908, 932-933 (1989). Professor Pryor attacks the whole idea in *The Tort Law Debate, Efficiency, and the Kingdom of the Ill: A Critique of the Insurance Theory of Compensation*, 79 VA. L. REV. 91 (1993) (arguing that the insurance theory is wrong in asking what level of insurance or compensation people would buy in advance, because compensation should be determined by actual needs after injury). Professor Margaret Jane Radin, *Compensation and Commensurability*, 43 Duke L.J. 56 (1993) attacks the idea in an elaborate philosophical argument. She also specifically argues that the reason why people may not buy insurance against pain is that pain and dollars are incommensurable. People might reject the idea that their own pain is a

B Types of Limits Proposed and Enacted in the United States

Most but not all proposals to limit damages in the United States have been addressed to damages for pain and emotional suffering. When limitations are imposed on pecuniary recoveries, the award may fail to provide both appropriate compensation and appropriate deterrence.

1. *Percentage limits*. Two proposals for limiting damages have so far received little support. The first, made many years ago, would limit damages for pain to some percentage of the award for physical harm.[9] The second suggests that at least some awards for pain be limited to actual expenses reasonably incurred to cope with pain except where the defendant has acted in a way that deserves punishment.[10]

2. *Caps or "ceilings"; limits fixed in a stated currency amount.*[11] *(a) Statutory characteristics*. Beginning in the 1980s, the so-called "tort reform" movement began to convince state legislatures that some kinds of limitations were required in personal injury cases. Statutes have now been enacted in more than half of states to impose flat limits or "caps" on some or all claims for personal injury.[12]

There are two major variables in the statutes. *First*, the statute may cover any kind of personal injury case[13] or only some particular kind such as medical malpractice.[14] *Second*, the statute may impose a ceiling on all damages[15] or only on nonpecuniary damages such as those for pain.[16] The common feature of the statutes is that, whatever their exact scope, they all state a flat dollar limitation on the total recovery. For example, the California statute limits awards for non-pecuniary damages against medical defendants to $250,000.

It is hard to convey a balanced impression of such statutes because under the American system, plaintiffs' attorneys are paid a percentage of the plaintiffs recovery, not by the defendant. So, realistically speaking, the pain award is

commodity reducible to monetary units.

9 Plant, *Damages for Pain and Suffering*, 19 OHIO ST.L.J. 200 (1958).

10 Ingber, *Rethinking Intangible Injuries: A Focus on Remedy*, 73 CALIF. L. REV. 772 (1985).

11 Additional material may be found in 2 Dan Dobbs, Law of Remedies § 8.8 (2d ed. 1993).

12 The 1991 Civil Rights Act amended the older statute on employment discrimination to permit recovery for emotional harms resulting from employment discrimination. In doing so, the Congress imposed a scaled limitation on the emotional harm recovery. The scale was constructed so that a higher award was available against businesses with larger numbers of employees. 28 U.S.C. § 1981a(b)(3).

13 See Md. Ann Code, Ct. & Jud. Proc., § 11-108.

14 See Cal. Civ. Code § 3333.2.

15 E.g., Colo. Rev. Stat. Ann. § 13-64-302 ($1 million cap on total damages in medical malpractice). Social programs may at some point be burdened with the excess costs; however, many individuals in the United States currently have no medical insurance at all.

16 Cal.Civ. Code § 3333.2.

necessary to achieve full compensation to the plaintiff, since otherwise the attorney's fees will come from the plaintiff's compensatory damages.

(b) *Constitutionality*. Some state courts have struck down statutes limiting the amount of personal injury damages on the grounds that the statutes violate the constitution of the particular states.[17] Courts holding that the limits are unconstitutional operate under the specific provisions of different state constitutions, but they have generally emphasized one or more of these themes:

(A) the injured plaintiff cannot be made to bear the burden of reducing insurance costs for others or for society as a whole;

(B) it is arbitrary to select the particular group of defendants (such as doctors or hospitals) for special privileges in the form of limited liability;

(C) no alternative redress or even assistance is provided for the injured plaintiff; the plaintiff shoulders the burden others are feeling without a *quid pro quo*;

(D) caps are in themselves arbitrary, especially when injuries may be quite different among those affected.

Other courts have upheld the cap statutes in their states.[18]

(c) *Criticisms*. Commentators have generally criticized the use of raw caps. Even if caps are adjusted for inflation, caps can be criticized because they discriminate against persons with the worst injuries. By limiting damages to a stated amount, the legislature can reduce the cost of insurance to defendants. But the cost of doing this is not borne by everyone alike, only by those whose injuries are the very worst. People with small injuries will be fully paid, but those whose lives are virtually ruined will not. In addition, the cap will not address the disparity in awards below the cap level. People with small injuries could still receive too much and people could still be treated differently because different decision-makers may react differently to similar injuries.

3. *Thresholds or "floors"; minimum necessary to assert any claim*. A second form of limitation sometimes proposed is the threshold. The threshold allows the injured person to recover only the portion of his loss that exceeds the stated threshold amount. If the plaintiff suffers a loss of $50,000 and the threshold is $1,000, the plaintiff recovers $49,000. The American Law Institute's Enterprise Responsibility study proposed a very general threshold to govern damages awards for pain, in effect excluding pain damages for any injuries not deemed significant.[19]

17 E.g., Lucas v. United States, 757 S.W.2d 687 (Tex. 1988).

18 Scholz v. Metropolitan Pathologists, P.C., 851 P.2d 901 (Colo. 1993); University of Miami v. Echarte, 618 So.2d 189 (Fla. 1993).

19 II American Law Institute, Reporter's Study, Enterprise Responsibility for Personal Injury 230 (1991).

Even very low thresholds could be effective in reducing total costs for defendants and their insurers because many injuries are small. Thresholds are in fact imposed in some states under no-fault automobile laws. These laws set up a system of compulsory self-insurance to cover the amounts below the threshold. The disadvantage under these laws lies in their compulsory nature and in the possibility that they reduce the appropriate level of deterrence for unsafe activities.

Thresholds may be difficult to justify on moral grounds, but if they are applied only to damages for pain or emotional injury, they probably do not discriminate against any particular group. So far, however, thresholds have not gained statutory support.

4. *Schedules.* A third kind of proposal is to provide statutory schedules of damages rather than flat caps. This idea is derived most immediately from workers' compensation statutes, which schedule or list some injuries, with specified amounts to be paid for each injury on the list.

Where the plaintiff has a provable loss, a schedule is as difficult to justify as a cap.[20] Where the plaintiff's loss is not provable in a measurable amount, as in the case of pain or distress, a schedule seems impossible to construct. Perhaps for these reasons schedules have gained no current support as a general solution to limiting damages.

5. *Scales, Profiles, or Scenarios as Guidelines. (a) Using guidelines or models of injuries generally.* A very different proposal is to use scales rather than schedules to provide limits on damages for pain and for emotional distress. Scales may also be referred to as guidelines, profiles, or injury scenarios. Scales leave room for individualized decision-making about the appropriate award, but they also set either mandatory or recommended limits to that discretion.

Many variations on this technique can be imagined. At core, the idea is to provide broad models of different injuries ("injury profiles" or "injury scenarios"). A model of a high-end injury might include an injury that reduced a young healthy person to a quadriplegic, or blinded a young child. The low-end model might involve something like a hairline fracture of a small toe that caused no work loss or medical expense and only the most transient pain. The scale would provide a money guideline for injuries in each category represented by a model or injury scenario.

(b) *Using matrices.* One form of the general idea would construct a matrix of values. Although any number of considerations could be factored into the guidelines, the most thorough study has suggested a matrix of values based on two variables only: (1) severity of injury and (2) age of the victim.[21]

20 A schedule is not quite the same as a cap for a particular injury. A stated amount recoverable for loss of a thumb not only sets a ceiling but also compels an award. So the schedule may provide too little recovery in some cases and too much in others.

21 Bovbjerg, Sloan and Blumstein, supra n. 5 at 938 ff.

The Bovbjerg-Sloan-Blumstein group recommend that injuries be classed in one of nine levels of severity and adjusted for six different age groups. They believe that past awards studied in their samples correlated well with the resulting matrix of 54 cells.[22]

The decision maker would first decide which cell of the matrix controlled by determining the severity category of the injury and the age of the victim. The cell would provide a currency measure for the injury. The measure provided could be either mandatory or merely recommendatory. It could specify a specific currency figure or it could specify a range of figures. In any event, the figures would be provided in advance by legislation. If scale system is limited to pain or other unmeasurable damages, the numbers might be politically selected on a more or less arbitrary basis. However, it would be possible to set the scale for each cell on the basis of average past awards, with appropriate calculations for inflation or cost-of-living increases.

(c) *Using valuation scenarios*. A simpler system would create a small standardized stock of basic hypothetical injury scenarios. The decision-maker would be given several of these that seemed closest to the injury claimed by the plaintiff. The scenarios would not necessarily fit the case but they would provide rough benchmarks. The decision maker would decide which scenario most closely resembled the plaintiff's case and then apply the currency values or the range of currency values associated with that scenario. The values associated with each scenario could be selected in advance in the same way as under the matrix, by comparing past awards for similar cases.[23]

Although the scale-guideline-scenario approach leaves enormous room for judgment, it meets the criticisms leveled at the caps approach. At the same time, it avoids the argument that fixed schedules for fixed injuries are too mechanical. The effort required to construct meaningful guidelines would itself represent an opportunity for clarifying dialog that could in turn make guidelines broadly acceptable.

III Conclusion

Theories for damage limitation have not been adequately developed in the United States. The initial push for limitation was generated by political rhetoric and anecdotal evidence of ridiculous awards. Some of that evidence proved to

22 Age is relevant in several ways. A permanent disabling injury to a young person with a long life expectancy will cause harm longer than a permanent injury to a person of advanced age. On the other hand, young people may overcome more moderate harms very quickly.

23 Bovbjerg, Sloan and Blumstein, supra n. 5 at 953 ff.

be misleading.[24] Public debate became a battle of empirical studies about the extent of damages awards. This debate, although interesting, was essentially a dead end. The real problem is to determine the proper, just and socially useful level of awards. If a just theory of limitation is developed fully, people will accept the resulting limitations.

Proposals and enactments in the United States may have little to offer European nations in any direct way. Yet their variety suggests that many different avenues can be usefully explored, if only to inspire quite different approaches.

Appendix

This appendix attempts to mention the topics raised in Professor Spier's questionnaire. It lists some of the ways in which an award is "reduced" under rules applied in the United States. Some reductions may be conceived as providing the plaintiff less that full compensation. Others, on the contrary, may be conceived as reductions necessary to prevent an award that exceeds just compensation. The list excludes the most obvious computational adjustments, such as those made to adjust for early payment of future losses or delayed payment of past losses. On the other hand, it includes adjustments like those for comparative fault that arguably do NOT provide the plaintiff less than full compensation but instead merely allocate responsibility for compensation in a just manner.

Reductions and Apportionments Possibly Made to Achieve Corrective Justice

1. *Proximate cause*. Proximate cause rules generally exclude harms that differ in kind from those risked by the defendant's conduct. Judicial explanations usually rely on the idea that some kinds of damages were not foreseeable, or that some intervening actor was the immediate cause of the harm. If the nature of the plaintiff's harm was foreseeable, the rules do not exclude any recovery of damages merely because the harm was more extensive than could have been foreseen. See RESTATEMENT SECOND OF TORTS § 435(1) (1965).

2. *Comparative fault reductions*. Most American states, by statute or through case law, apply some kind of comparative fault rule to negligence actions. Some also apply an analogous rule to products strict liability claims. See the next paragraph. See W. PAGE KEETON, DAN B. DOBBS, ROBERT E. KEETON,

24 See Joseph Page, *Deforming Tort Reform*, Book Review of Peter W. Huber, Liability: The Legal Revolution and Its Consequences (1988), 78 GEO.L.J. 649 (1990); Saks, *Do We Really Know Anything About the Behavior of the Tort Litigation System—And Why Not?*, 140 U.PA.L.REV. 1147 (1992).

& DAVID G. OWEN, PROSSER & KEETON ON TORTS § 67 (5th ed. 1984) (here after cited as PROSSER & KEETON).

3. *Comparative causation reductions.* When a defendant is strictly liable, comparative negligence reductions are literally impossible, since the defendant is guilty of no proven negligence that can be compared to the plaintiff's fault. Nevertheless, in some states, courts make some kind of reduction based on the fact that the plaintiff is at fault. It has been suggested that this is not comparative negligence or comparative fault but comparative "causation." The reduction may reflect, not the relative fault of the parties but thc relative significance of their causal roles in producing harm. See Strassfeld, *Causal Comparisons*, 60 FORDHAM L. REV. 913 (1992).

4. *Avoidable consequences.* The plaintiff's award must be reduced by sums representing any consequential losses the plaintiff actually avoided or could have avoided with reasonable effort. This is not a comparative fault reduction. The reduction is not based on the relative fault of the plaintiff and defendant. It is instead a causal apportionment, reducing the plaintiff's damages by 100% of all losses he could have reasonably avoided. 1 DAN DOBBS, THE LAW OF REMEDIES § 3.9, pp. 385-86 (2d ed. 1993).

5. *Value of the chance/proportional causation.* (a) *Value of the chance and proportional causation.* The traditional rule holds that the plaintiff must prove his injury by a more-likely-than-not standard. To put it in numbers, the plaintiff must show that he suffered injury as a result of the defendant's tort by a probability of more than 50%. If he does show that, he recovers the full 100% of damages. If he does not, he recovers nothing.

A few courts have allowed the plaintiff to recover even though the probability that the defendant caused the plaintiff's loss is less than .50. In such cases, the damages will be reduced ratably. For example, in *Wollen v. DePaul Health Center*, 828 S.W.2d 681 (Mo. 1992) Mr. Wollen had gastric cancer. If he had been given proper medical treatment, he would have had only a 30% chance of survival. Because the medical defendants were negligent, he was NOT given proper treatment and he died. More likely than not, he would have died even with perfect medical treatment. Traditional rules denied all liability on the ground that the defendants were not proven to have caused harm. The court allowed a recovery, however, saying that Mr. Wollen had lost the chance and suggested that its value would be based on the extent of that chance. In this case the chance was 30% and damages would thus be reduced to 30% of normal damages. Several other courts in medical situations have adopted such a view in similar medical cases. All of them arc dcrivcd from Joseph King, *Valuation of the Chance in Personal Injury Torts Involving Pre-existing Conditions and Future Consequences*, 90 YALE L. J. 1353 (1981). A prestigious study has favored of a similar approach in environmental cases where the defendant's toxic pollution might be a cause of harm but where the harm could also have resulted from other factors. See II American Law Institute, REPOR-

TER'S STUDY OF ENTERPRISE RESPONSIBILITY FOR PERSONAL INJURY 370 ff. (1991).

(b) *Proportional causation as a reduction or not.* Should the rule be regarded as a reduction in damages? From the individual plaintiff's viewpoint, he gets less than necessary to make him financially whole, but more than he would have obtained under the traditional rule. From the individual defendant's point of view about this particular case, the rule does not reduce damages but increases them. From the defendant's institutional point of view, however, the value-of-the-chance rule may make no difference at all. The defendant or its insurer in the past paid 100% to some and zero to others. If the value-of-the-chance rule is extended to cover all cases, including those in which the plaintiff proves a 90% probability that defendant caused his harm, then the defendant will almost never pay 100%. If all cases go at a discount, then the defendant may end up paying, overall, the same amounts of money, albeit to more people.

However, it is also possible that the rule could reduce overall payments by defendants or their insurers. Evidence is now strong that many valid claims are never presented at all in the United States. The value-of-the-chance rule might affect claiming behavior. One cannot be certain whether it would increase or decrease claims. If it reduced claims, then the insurers' ultimate liability would be less.

Perhaps more fundamentally, if we take into account that many claims are not made at all, we cannot be sure that the defendants-insurers are presently paying sums equal to the "average" of all percentage liabilities. Suppose, for example, that an insurer presently has before it two claims, one for 100,000 and one for 50,000. The plaintiff can prove 60% probability in the larger claim but only 50% in the smaller. Under present or traditional law the insurer would pay the full 100,000 on the larger claim and zero on the smaller. If the value-of-the-chance rule applied to both claims, the insurer's payment would be only 85,000 (60,000 representing 60% of the first claim and 25,000 representing 50% of the second claim).

What this example shows is that if the high-end claims tend to be more successful under the traditional rule, the defendant-insurer may see an overall reduction of its liabilities under the value-of-the-chance rule. The question is an empirical one and we cannot give an answer with any certainty at this point. However, we can say that the chance of reducing overall liabilities depends on application of the value-of-the-chance rule across the board, to those claims in which the plaintiff has strong proof of injury as well as to those in which the plaintiff has only weak proof.

6. *Market-share theory.* Market-share theory is similar to the value-of-the chance theory, although the reasons for causal uncertainties are different. Ten manufacturers produce a standardized product. All such products are identical in form as well as function. One of the products injures the plaintiff, but it is impossible to determine which manufacturer produced it. Some courts have

held that in such a case each manufacturer is liable, but only for a percentage of the plaintiff's damages equal to its market-share. Since this is the most probable means of estimating proportional causation, the rule can be regarded as a special case of the value-of-the-chance rule. This particular idea originated in Comment, *DES and a Proposed theory of Enterprise Liability*, 46 FORDHAM L. REV., 963 (1978). An application can be seen in *Hymowitz v. Eli Lilly and Co.*, 73 N.Y.2d 487, 541 N.Y.S.2d 941, 539 N.E.2d 1069 (1989).

7. *The collateral source rule.* The traditional rule held that the plaintiff recovered fully for all losses as originally suffered, even if he was compensated for some of them by payments from sources unrelated to the defendant, for instance, from the plaintiff's own insurance. A number of states have been enacting statutes that require or permit the decision maker to reduce the plaintiff's award to account for collateral payments. 1 DAN DOBBS, THE LAW OF REMEDIES § 3.8 (2d ed. 1993).

8. *Joint and several liability; tort reform statutes.* When two or more person act tortiously and cause an injury that cannot be allocated or apportioned between them, all the tortfeasors are liable and the plaintiff may collect damages from any one or any combination of them. The effect of this rule is that if one tortfeasor is insolvent, the other must bear the insolvent's share of liability. So-called "tort-reform" statutes have abolished the joint and several liability rule in some states. E.g., CAL.CIV.CODE § 1431.2. The effect of this in some cases is that a tortfeasor is liable for only a percentage of the plaintiff's damages equal to the percentage of his fault. This may be so even if the tortfeasor's act, standing alone, was sufficient to cause all of the plaintiff's injury. Federal law, however, has expressly retained joint and several liability for certain kinds of environmental damage. 42 U.S.C. § 9607 (CERCLA or the "Superfund" statute).

Reductions to Achieve a Collateral Policy Goal

9. *Libel rules.* The United States Constitution protects the right to free speech. This has been interpreted to require the libel suit plaintiff to prove a knowing or reckless falsehood when the plaintiff is a public official or public figure. When the plaintiff is a private person but the libel bears on issues of public concern, the plaintiff must prove "actual" damages; the decision-maker cannot award presumed damages or damages based on some general estimate of reputation loss. *Gertz v. Robert Welch, Inc.*, 418 U.S. 323, 94 S.Ct. 2996, 41 L.Ed.2d 789 (1974). Emotional harm damages, however, can be recovered. States also limit damages in certain kinds of cases; they require pecuniary loss in many cases of slander and in such cases emotional harm is not enough. State statutes also frequently limit the recovery to pecuniary losses when the defendant retracts a libel.

Reductions Indirectly Imposed by Rules of Trial Convenience or Proof

10. *Objective damages measurements.* When damages are measured objectively, by the market value of property, the plaintiff receives no compensation for any additional value he attaches to the property over and above the market value. The market or objective measure of course excludes recovery for the plaintiff's emotional attachment to the property; but it also excludes the plaintiff's own economic valuation. In many instances, loss is measured by reference to the market value, both in tort and in contract cases. See, among many references to this idea, 1 DAN DOBBS, THE LAW OF REMEDIES §§ 3.2, 3.3 (6) (2d ed. 1993).

11. *Uncertainty rules; profits.* States uniformly recognize that proof about future losses must be made with reasonable certainty. As a practical matter, this rule excludes recovery for loss of future profits in a number of cases. However, where the plaintiff provides reasonable evidence as to the amount of future profits he would have made, the profit loss is fully recoverable.

Limits Based on Direct, Formal, and General Rules

12. *Conventionalized damages awards and those specified by a statute in the absence of proof.* Under a few statues applicable only in limited situations, courts are told to make an award ranging between a stated minimum and a stated maximum amount. The effect is that the court has discretion as to the amount awarded, provided that it is within the range specified. The copyright statute is an example. 17 U.S.C.A. § 504(c)(1) (judge to award just amount between $500 and $20,000). Other statutes specify a given amount that can be awarded when the plaintiff cannot prove actual damages in a larger sum. Invasion of privacy by wiretapping or by secretly receiving telephone communications is an example. 18 U.S.C.A. § 2520 permits recovery of actual damages if proved, otherwise "the greater of $100 a day for each day of violation or $10,000". These seem more like minimum awards than limitations. In any event, these statutes do not authorize reductions from an amount *known* to be compensatory.

13. *Caps.* (a) Many state statutes create a claim or right that was not previously recognized as a valid claim, then at the same time place a low ceiling on liability. Statutes imposing liability upon parents for acts of children are examples. E.g., CONN. GEN. STAT. § 52-572 ($5,000 limit on parental liability for child's acts).
(b) More than one-half of the 50 states have enacted *some* kind of cap or fixed ceiling on damages for *some* kinds of traditionally recognized claims. Some caps applied only in medical malpractice claims, some only to claims against governmental entities. Others apply only when comparative fault principles are invoked. A second variable in the statutes concerns the kind of

damages capped. A few statues apply to all claims, pecuniary and non-pecuniary. Most commonly, however, statutes cap only the non-pecuniary claims, such as the claim for pain and suffering or emotional distress. Illustrative statutes include CAL.CIV.CODE § 3333.2; MD. CODE COURTS & JUDICIAL PROC. § 11-108. Caps are especially significant in the United States because attorneys for the plaintiff are normally paid by a percentage of the recovery; the loser does not pay the winner's attorney fee. When the damage is capped, therefore, the plaintiff not only recovers less but the attorney's fee becomes more limited and that may reduce the economic feasibility of the case.
(c) Caps are indirectly applied in cases that are removed from the tort system and determined instead under workers' compensation laws, under the National Childhood Vaccine Injury Act, 42 U.S.C. § 300aa-1, or under insurance schemes.

14. *Scales and schedules*. Scales and schedules are not currently in use in tort cases. Scheduled injuries have long been a feature in workers' compensation claims, e.g., a fixed amount is recoverable for loss of a thumb, a different fixed amount for loss of the first finger and so on. Scales have been seriously proposed for limiting nonpecuniary injuries. Scales of various kinds work by classifying injuries in categories and prescribing appropriate sums for the categories. Many variables can be included to give detailed guidance. Scales may be mandatory or merely taken as good guides.

Substantive Rules Eliminating a Claim for Specified Damages

In some instances the legal rule provides that the defendant is under no duty whatever with respect to specified kinds of harm. The rule is not usually considered to be a rule reducing damages but rather a substantive rule that denies a right in the plaintiff or a duty in the defendant.

15. *Emotional harm*. American states usually allow the plaintiff to recover for emotional harm that results from a physical injury or from some other tort such as a libel or a privacy invasion. However, most states recognize claims for emotional harm standing alone only under the most limited circumstances. For example, the plaintiff who is emotionally disturbed by seeing the defendant driving at a very dangerous speed is frequently not entitled to recover for emotional harm unless the plaintiff herself or a family member was endangered.

16. *Economic harm*. Subject to the rules generally applicable to torts, negligently inflicted economic harm is fully recoverable when (a) it is adequately proven and (b) it is the result of some actionable tort such as personal injury. Economic harm is also fully recoverable when it results from infringement of intellectual property interests. Otherwise, negligently inflicted economic harm standing alone, without other tort, is not usually actionable at all in the absence

of some special relationship between the plaintiff and defendant that requires the defendant to use care for the plaintiff's purely economic interests. The two strongest examples of such a relationship are cases of attorneys who negligently cause their clients economic harm and cases of parties involved in an economic transaction who make a negligent misrepresentation to one of the other parties. Liability for negligence is imposed in such cases. In the absence of some such relationship, only three American states have said they would impose liability for negligence causing only economic harm.

17. *Other typical substantive limits*. Other important substantive rules of tort law exclude liability altogether in a number of instances. The duty and hence the liability to the plaintiff is frequently limited or nonexistent in these cases among others: (a) the plaintiff is an unexpected entrant upon the defendant's land; (b) the plaintiff is a public servant injured in the course of his or her duty by the defendant's negligence, e.g., a firefighter; (c) the defendant is a family member living in the same household; (d) the defendant is a charity; (e) the defendant is a governmental entity; (f) the plaintiff suffers harm because of the defendant's acts before the plaintiff was born or even in some cases before the plaintiff was conceived; (g) the plaintiff suffers harm because the defendant, who was in no special relationship to the plaintiff, failed to act to rescue or protect the plaintiff from others or from danger not caused by the defendant; (h) the defendant puts another person in position to harm the plaintiff by providing substances that impair the other person or by providing instrumentalities that increase the risk and the plaintiff is in fact harmed as a result. Most of these are represented, in approximately the same order, in DAN DOBBS, TORTS AND COMPENSATION: PERSONAL ACCOUNTABILITY AND SOCIAL RESPONSIBILITY FOR INJURY 315-537 (2d ed. 1993)(a casebook).

A Miscellany of related material

18. *Shareholder immunity*. Shareholders in corporations are not liable to corporate creditors and thus not liable to pay any judgment against the corporation, even if it is grounded in a corporate tort. Some commentators have favored imposing liability upon shareholders rather than retaining the present limited liability. See, reviewing the literature and taking a moderate position, Theresa Gabaldon, *The Lemonde Stand: Feminist and Other Reflections on the Limited Liability of Corporate Shareholders*, 45 VAND. L. REV. 1387 (1992).

19. *Admiralty*. By statute, shipowners are placed in a situation similar to investors in corporations. They enjoy a limit on their liability equal to the value of the ship plus accrued claims against shippers for freight charges. This limitation does not apply to all ships, only "sea-going" vessels, and does not apply to all claims, only to those involving loss to goods on the ship, losses from collision, and losses incurred "without the privity or knowledge of such owner." 46 App. U.S.C. § 183.

20. *Annuities for future losses*. The traditional rule imposes a single liability for past and future expected losses. In the last few years many personal injury cases have been settled by an agreement that provides the injured person, not with the traditional lump-sum payment, but with an annuity. Because the plaintiff may not live out his statistical life expectancy, the annuity (or some portion of it) may be cut short. This contingency makes it possible in some instances for the defendant to pay less for a given annuity than for a lump-sum payment. Many states have now enacted some kind of periodic payment statutes that permit a judgment as well as a settlement for an annuity. In some instances, the defendant may get the advantage of a slight reduction in the ultimate liability because the annuity is cheaper than the lump-sum payment. See 2 DAN DOBBS, THE LAW OF REMEDIES § 8.5(5) (2d ed. 1993).

21. *Bankruptcy*. The defendant's financial condition is not explicitly considered in making a compensatory award, although it is of utmost interest in making a punitive award. The defendant's limited financial position may operate to reduce the actual recovery of damages (as distinct from the formal award) in two ways. First, certain assets cannot be seized for payment of judgment. One's home, up to a certain value, is usually in this category. Second, the defendant who has more debts than assets may take advantage of bankruptcy laws. In the case of any tort that is not fraudulent or malicious, the defendant may give up all his assets to creditors, and receive in return a discharge of all liability. The result is that the injured plaintiff may be paid only a small fraction of the formal judgment.

European tort law

Hellenic National Report

CONFINES AND LIMITATION OF DAMAGES UNDER THE GREEK LAW OF TORT

K.D. Kerameus[*] *and Kl. Roussos*[**]

I Introduction

Both the existence and the amount of damages resulting from tortious activity depend, among other things, on the delimitation of the law of tort. In this respect, two issues are crucial in Greek law. First, the relationship between tortious activity and illegal behaviour; second, the separation of delictual from contractual liability.

1 Illegal behaviour and negligence

With regard to the first issue, article 914 of the Greek Civil Code (hereinafter: CC)[1] stipulates that whoever "unlawfully and culpably" has caused prejudice to another shall be liable for compensation. "Unlawfully" means obviously in a manner contrary to the law. Here arises the question: Does the tortfeasor's delictual liability depend upon his behaviour contravening a *specific* provision of law? In other words, is article 914 CC a "Blankettnorm", a mere reference to other statutory commandments whose violation may give rise to liability for damages? This issue is a real rather than a fictional one. Article 330.2 CC offers a definition of negligence by declaring that a person who does not exercise ordinary care, as normally required while conducting business, acts negligently. One may therefore wonder whether such negligence, *i.e.* deviation from what is normally required under the specific conditions of the case, may *in itself qualify* as "illegal" behaviour and, thus, establish delictual liability, regardless of any specific provision which might prohibit that behaviour.

* Professor of Civil Procedure, Athens University School of Law; Director of the Hellenic Institute of International and Foreign Law.

** Assistant Professor of Civil Law, Athens University School of Law.

1 The Greek Civil Code was promulgated in 1940 and has been in force since 23 February 1946. There is a translation into English by C. Taliadoros, *Greek Civil Code* (1982). An outline of Greek tort law in English is offered by Ph. Christodoulou, *in*: Kerameus/Kozyris (eds.), *Introduction to Greek Law*, 2d ed. (1993) 114-117.

J. Spier (ed.), The Limits of Liability, 43-52.

The classical Greek doctrine[2] and the prevailing case law tend to give a negative answer to this question. Unlawfulness is clearly distinguished from culpability. Negligence, as defined in article 330.2 CC, refers to culpability only, and neither does it create nor touch upon the lawful or unlawful character of any human behaviour. Objective elements of unlawfulness are thus separated from subjective elements of culpability, including negligence and the corresponding standard of required care.

Despite this classical and clear-cut approach, modern scholarship[3] and a growing number of recent cases seem to blur the lines of demarcation by not insisting on the search for specific provisions prohibiting the relevant behaviour and, instead, by considering the departure from normal standards of care as a sufficient feature of unlawfulness. For instance, *Areios Pagos* (the Greek Supreme Court)[4] was satisfied that the defective maintenance of the power distribution net which caused a fire to the adjacent field of olive trees was as such illegal, because it did not meet the required standard of care. In the same vein, the launching into the market of defective or dangerous insecticide boxes was also held to be illegal[5]. Reference to the rules of medical science is also increasingly resorted to in order to establish doctors' delictual liability[6].

In conclusion we note that with regard to the *unlawful character of tortious behaviour*, Greek law is probably in a state of gradual change. While in most tort cases the violated norm may easily be identified, courts are willing, in cases not covered by specific statutory provisions, to rely on the required standard of appropriate care under the circumstances. Failing to meet such standard may also satisfy, in some cases, the requirement of illegality.

2 Distinguishing contractual from delictual liability

In many cases the breach of contract may give rise to delictual liability since the damaging behaviour can be construed as unlawful in the above mentioned sense, especially when an infringement occurs of the other party's rights *in rem* or physical injuries are caused to the contract partner as a result of such a breach of the contractual rules. On the other hand, there is no place for delictual liability if

2 A. Ligeropoulos, *Elements of the Law of Obligations* (University Lectures) (1960) §241, pp. 347-354; K. Kafkas and D. Kafkas, *Law of Obligations* (A Commentary on the Articles). Special Part, 7th ed., vol. II (1993) 723; G. Mantzoufas, *Law of Obligations* (1982) (reprint of the 3rd edition, 1959) §64, pp. 522-525; J. Deliyannis & P. Kornilakis, *Special Part of the Law of Obligations*, vol. III (1992) §346, pp. 129-133, §§348b, 348c, pp. 142-149.

3 M. Stathopoulos, *Law of Obligations*. General Part, vol. A1, 2d ed. (1993) 258-263; Ap. Georgiadis *in*: Georgiadis/Stathopoulos (eds.), *Commentary to the Civil Code*, vol. IV (1982) art. 914 nos 15-26; J. Deliyannis & P. Kornilakis, *ibid.*, §346, pp. 132-133.

4 *Areios Pagos* 183-186/1987, HellDni 29 (1988) 492 (493 II).

5 *Areios Pagos* 81/1991, HellDni 32 (1991) 1215 (1216 I).

6 See *Areios Pagos* 1356/1991, HellDni 33 (1992) 1192.

the damage results from a breach of a contractual obligation which is part of the consideration.

Greek law adheres, unlike French law, to the *coexistence of delictual and contractual liability*. The latter does not discard the former. Rather it is for the plaintiff to opt for the one or the other after weighing the advantages and disadvantages of each with respect to an available venue, burden of proof, degree of fault, availability of exceptions, or length of the respective periods of limitation.

Regarding this last aspect, a much discussed opinion was delivered in 1973 by the *Full Bench of Areios Pagos*. A film distributor had assigned to another company the printing of translated subtitles on a film. The latter dealt negligently with this matter, and as a result two copies of the film were destroyed. The film distributor lodged an action for damages under the contract for work. Such action, however, had fallen victim to the six-month period of limitation specifically provided for damages under similar contracts. Thereafter, the film distributor, based on the same factual allegations, brought an action in tort which as such prescribes only after five years. The critical issue was then whether the second suit could survive the *res judicata* defence and benefit from the longer limitation period that applies to claims in tort. After conflicting opinions by two panels of *Areios Pagos*[7], the Full Bench[8] held that the claim in tort is independent from the contractual claim, therefore the *res judicata* plea is rejected and different periods of limitation apply to each claim.

A fairly recent case decided by the *Athens Court of Appeal*[9] may serve as a further example. A bank had established mortgage on a client's immovable property, in order to secure a loan claim against the latter. A dispute emerged between the parties as to the amount of the claim secured by the mortgage. The final decision held that the claim of the bank amounted to 150.000 drachmae. The client tendered this sum to the bank demanding its consent to the extinction of the mortgage. The bank declined both the offer of the money and its consent to the extinction. The client brought then a new action, this time in tort, requesting restitution of the damage he suffered for not being able to sell his piece of real estate due to the burden of mortgage. This action was dismissed on the grounds that the bank's refusal to accept the tender amounts to creditor's default (*mora creditoris*) and does not constitute tortious behaviour under article 914 CC. While one may be astonished at the result, the reasoning seems sound: the creditor is not required either by law or by common standards of diligence to accept the offer made by the debtor in fulfilment of his obligation. Despite the creditor's refusal the debtor still has the possibility to fulfill his obligation, *e.g.* by placing the money in escrow. Had the debtor done so the failure of the bank to consent to the extinction of the mortgage could safely have constituted tortious behaviour.

7 *Areios Pagos* 444/1971, NoB 19 (1971) 1240 (1241 I); 384/1973, NoB 21 (1973) 1205 II.

8 *Areios Pagos* (Full Bench) 967/1973, NoB 22 (1974) 505-506.

9 *Athens Court of Appeal* 12263/1990, NoB 39 (1991) 583 (586 II).

This leading opinion represents the actual state of Greek law regarding the concurrence of both kinds of civil liability. Undoubtedly, the Roman law heritage as well as a formalistic approach to the structural bifurcation of modern liability law must have influenced the outcome. On the other hand, we may discern an attempt to give full effect to all specific rules, including those on periods of limitation, that condition both existence and extent of the obligation to pay damages. Such concurrence of contract and tort may not, however, be taken for granted under all circumstances. Very often the breach of contractual obligations will not amount to tortious behaviour. A good example is a recent opinion of *Areios Pagos*[10] concerning a last-minute demand by the car seller to obtain additional payment, otherwise threatening not to deliver the car. The buyer conformed by paying the extra amount, took delivery of the car and then brought an action in tort to get the additional amount back. The action was dismissed on the grounds that the violation of the agreement on the price due does not constitute a tortious conduct, since its unlawful character arises from the breach of the contract and only therefrom. *Areios Pagos* reasoned that, outside the contractual arrangement of the parties, the demand of a sum of money was not open to any legal evaluation, it was therefore unqualifiable and unable to establish liability in tort.

II Limitation of damages

Both features of the Greek tort law that have been presented up to now tend potentially towards delictual inflation. Perceiving the basic provision of article 914 CC as an open-ended yardstick of illegality invites to searching almost everywhere for standards to be met and, thus, to transforming social expectations to legal duties. On the other hand, admitting the coexistence of delictual and contractual liability may well result in using tort aspects as a vehicle for making up what has been left uncovered by contractual arrangements; claims in tort could then be a functional supplement to contractual gaps and a highly efficient weapon to unobtrusively expand the scope of civil liability in general.

Such tendencies should not be overestimated. We have seen that cases resorting to the required standards of appropriate care because of missing specific statutory provisions are rather marginal. In the same spirit, the recent *Areios Pagos* opinion on the demand of extra price for a car to be delivered[11] shows that in major areas the existence of a contract does not leave room for tort considerations to come in. It would, therefore, be safe to say that the practical relevance of both issues is limited and, in any event, does not substantially alter the overall picture of Greek tort law. What is, however, more important are some built-in mechanisms which, by virtue of either statutory provisions or case-law developments, effectively limit the damages to be awarded under tort rules. Limits imposed by statute include contributory negligence and the requirement of culpability (under 1), while

10 *Areios Pagos* 754/1990, NoB 39 (1991) 1097 II.
11 *Ibidem*.

restraints developed by case law refer to the scope of protected interests, to adequate causation, to the abstract computation of damages as well as to the limited restitution of non-pecuniary loss (under 2). By contrast, neither foreseeability of loss nor purely quantitative limitation of damages are of much relevance (under 3).

1 Statutory limitation

Under article 300.1 CC, where a person has contributed of his own fault to the loss he had suffered or to the extent thereof, the court may refrain from awarding compensation or reduce the sum thereof; the same rule shall also apply where a person having suffered a loss omitted to prevent or mitigate it or did not draw the debtor's attention to the risk of an unusually large loss of which the debtor was not nor ought to have been aware. In practice, however, cases decided under this provision are rather obvious and have not given rise to extensive discussion. Two fairly recent examples are the following: A vessel engineer, who was fatally injured at an explosion in the engine room caused by irregular oil flow was held to have contributed to the accident, on the grounds that he failed to turn off the engine although he had noticed the dangerous oil flow[12]. On the other hand, a pedestrian crossing the highway was found to be partly liable for the ensuing fatal accident[13]. As far as the victim's duty to mitigate damages is concerned, most cases pertain to personal injury and require the victim to re-orientate his future professional activity in order to adapt it to his diminished or altered abilities[14]. Should this requirement not be met, the amount of damages to be awarded because of personal injury would be reduced accordingly.

In the mind of the Civil Code drafters, the tortfeasor's personal fault should constitute a fundamental element of his delictual liability. Such liability was to be construed as a subjective rather than as a strict one. In practice, however, the element of fault has not proven to be a major bar to holding for the victim of tortious activity. This is so because, to the extent that an illegal behaviour has been assessed, grounds of justification for the tortfeasor's benefit are truly rare. As a rule of thumb, in the vast majority of cases, illegality implies fault as well. The recent case-law tendency that finds illegality where appropriate standards of care have not been met[15], might also have contributed to this result, which almost amounts to a factual presumption of fault. It is no longer, in practice, an obstacle at which delictual liability might, in a sensible number of cases, stumble.

12 *Areios Pagos* 666/1986, HellDni 28 (1987) 835-836.
13 *Areios Pagos* 1102/1990, NoB 40 (1992) 70 (71/72).
14 *Areios Pagos* 1716/1985, NoB 34 (1986) 1065.
15 *Supra* text at notes 4-6.

2 Restraints developed by case law

2.1 Scope of protected interests

By contrast, case law supported by doctrinal statements[16] has been inserting significant limitations in the existence or amount of damages in tort. First among them is the search for the so-called *scope of protected interests*. Greek law, in order to sanction delictual liability, is not satisfied with the mere assertion that a statutory provision has been *in casu* violated. It is, furthermore, required that such a provision should aim at the protection of rights or interests connected to the victim of tort. It may be that at the same time both general and individual interests are protected by the same provision. However, no delictual liability would arise if the violated norm aimed at the protection of general interests or interests at large only.

Under this concept, most criminal law provisions are considered to protect individual interests as well. However, a large part of building provisions and restrictions are held to serve only the public interest. Therefore, the owner of a piece of real estate is not entitled to demand reparation from his neighbour who did not stick to the requirement of minimum space to be left open since such a requirement has been constantly and consistently construed to serve general rather than individual interests[17]. Along the same lines a private television station had put up an antenna without following the required procedure for obtaining a licence. The local union of videotape sellers, whose professional interests were affected by the operation of the television station, brought an action for damages. The action was dismissed on the grounds that the provisions on licensing television stations aim at safeguarding the constitutional principles of equality and pluralism in the diffusion of news rather than the protection of professional groups fighting for their individual interests[18]. A further case took place offshore in the Ionian Sea where, under bad weather conditions, a speedboat kept following for several miles a cruiser seeking protection from the storm. The cruiser captain misinterpreted this conduct to be a terrorist attempt and warned the port authorities which arrested and indicted the passengers of the speedboat. The latter brought an action seeking compensation for defamation. The action was dismissed. The court held that the conditions of defamation in this case cannot fit into the goal served by the provision invoked, *i.e.* the protection of personality against slander[19].

In summary, the scope of protected interests makes up a major area where, by interpreting each time the goals and perspectives of various norms, courts may well expand or restrict the field of delictual liability.

16 G. Balis, *General Principles of Civil Law*, 8th ed. (1961) §171.1, 448-449; K. and D.C. Kafkas, *supra* note 2, pp. 725-726; J. Deliyannis & P. Kornilakis, *supra* note 2, §348a, pp. 140-142.

17 *Athens Court of Appeal* 12757/1987, HellDni 30 (1989) 1193/1194.

18 *Agrinion First Instance Court* 66/1991, HellDni 32 (1991) 840/841.

19 *Patras Court of Appeal* 1341/1990, HellDni 32 (1991) 1335-1337.

2.2 Adequate causation

The other major area of potential limitation is *adequate causation*. The concept is to be found in article 298.2 CC with respect to compensation for lost profits. Such lost profits are to be restored to the extent that they would probably have been expected in the ordinary course of events or according to the special circumstances, especially in the light of arrangements made. This notion of adequate causation had been developed by the Greek doctrine even before the Civil Code came into force[20]. Under the Civil Code, the courts have been resorting very often to adequate causation in order to delineate precisely the scope of delictual liability. The notion, as refined and implemented in Greece, is accompanied by at least two advantages. First, it is flexible, in the sense that it bears upon both the existence and the extent of damages in tort. Second, it has been constantly regarded as a notion of law rather than of fact, with the result that even a final appeal to the *Areios Pagos* may be founded thereon[21].

Fairly recent examples of adequate causation may be identified in the following cases:

a. A witness deposition of false and defamatory facts against a judge was followed by his promotion being delayed for three years. The judge brought an action against the tortfeasor seeking compensation for the moral harm he suffered and also for the difference between the salaries of the lower and the higher judicial rank. The action was dismissed on the grounds that the tort committed (slander) cannot be causally linked to the decision of the Supreme Judicial Council on non-promotion, since the latter in essence depended on the Council's authority and discretion which is not subject to judicial review[22].

b. *Areios Pagos* held that the overtime work of a seaman for a long period, under extraordinary conditions and beyond the usual overtime schedule defined by law, may constitute an adequate cause for the latter's heart attack[23].

c. A collision of cars caused a lamp post to dangerously bend. It finally collapsed about 40 minutes later, injuring a bystander who had been there ever since the collision watching what was going on. Is this injury adequately connected to the collision and the initial damage to the lamp post? The *Court of Appeal* gave a negative answer, *Areios Pagos* an affirmative one[24]. It is, however, worth wondering whether the bystander's negligent persistence on walking around a manifestly dangerous place would not interrupt, under the circumstances of the case, the causal chain of events.

20 K.D. Triantaphyllopoulos, *Greek Law of Obligations*, 2d ed. (1938) §6 III, pp. 84-192.
21 *Areios Pagos* 317/1977, NoB 25 (1977) 1332.
22 *Athens First Instance Court* 4175/1983, NoB 32 (1984) 106-108 with a note by D. Papadopoulou, *ibid.*, pp. 108-111.
23 *Areios Pagos* 1929/1988, NoB 37 (1989) 1036 (1038).
24 *Areios Pagos* 1948/1986, NoB 35 (1987) 1228 (1229).

d. The construction of an artificial lake at a rural area impeded the communication of neighbouring villages; a contractor had thus undertaken the construction of a detour. However, due to delays in the work, the inhabitants of the villages used to cross the lake by boat, which was dangerous. Once a boat capsized and many of the passengers drowned. Although the accident was partly ascribed to fault of the ferryman and partly to the overcharge of the boat, *Areios Pagos*[25] did not accept that the adequate causation had been interrupted and held the contractor responsible for the accident, considering that the latter was the adequate consequence of the delay in the construction of the deviation, the filling of the lake prior to the construction of the road and the absence of exercise of control on the sailing conditions.

e. The leading opinion in recent years on issues of adequate causation was delivered by the Full Bench of *Areios Pagos*[26] on a widely publicised case. A pedestrian was hit by a car and abandoned helpless by the driver. A bystander who stepped on the road and by waving and gesticulating tried to stop the oncoming cars, was hit by one of them during the attempt at rescuing the victim. After conflicting opinions by two panels of *Areios Pagos* on the issue of adequate causation between the first driver's behaviour and the second victim's damages, the Full Bench by a vast majority of its members gave an affirmative answer. Regardless of whether the second victim, by running onto the highway without taking any account of traffic conditions, might have contributed to his own injury, such behaviour was not able to interrupt the adequate causation. The opinion, in order to highlight the adequate link, indicates that the second victim was morally expected and legally required to offer assistance.

The previous cases are not apt to establish a reasoned and cohesive line of thought. Rather, adequate causation is weighed on an *ad hoc* basis, taking into account several circumstances, including moral considerations. The last two cases in particular, dealing as they do with fatal injuries of weak and innocent persons, hardly dissimulate a drop of morality injected into the law of tort. This is perhaps for the better. All things considered, tort law seems to be a preferential vehicle for activating value judgments in the legal treatment of everyday common events.

2.3 Computation of damages

Computation of damages under the Greek tort law is, as a rule, specific, as opposed to the abstract computation that is often admitted in commercial transactions[27].

25 *Areios Pagos* 854/1974, NoB 23 (1975) 479 (481/482).

26 *Areios Pagos* (Full Bench) 23/1988, HellDni 30 (1989) 1150/1151. However, the depressed wife's suicide, several months after her husband's death in a car accident, was not held to be adequately connected to the latter: *Athens Court of Appeal* 10796/1988, HellDni 34 (1993) 603-604, note by A. Kritikos.

27 *Areios Pagos* (Full Bench) 790/1958, NoB 7 (1959) 422.

Then, in order to claim damages because of personal injury, it is not enough for the victim to assert incapacity for work. If, *e.g.*, the victim is either under age or retired, or if he would be jobless anyway, the incapacity for work would be irrelevant for purposes of assessing lost profits. Under this point of view, the insistence on specific calculation of damages could also be regarded as an instance of limitation of liability as opposed to an eventual award of general and non-individualised damages.

As a rule, damages for non-pecuniary loss may be awarded as a result of any tort. However, article 932 CC allows only the award of a reasonable amount of money. "Reasonable" damages are generally considered in Greek law as lower than "full" or "regular" damages. In fact, most cases tend to keep the level of damages for non-pecuniary loss down. In any event, there are no official or unofficial guidelines providing for a specified sum or a range of sums with regard to various types of tort. The quantification of such damages is not subject to review by *Areios Pagos* sitting on a final appeal.

It should be pointed out that even in the case of property damage, Greek tort law provides compensation for non-pecuniary loss resulted therefrom.

3 Unknown limits to damages

Other limits to damages, appearing in several legal systems, are not familiar in Greece. Thus, the *degree of fault* on the tortfeasor's part is generally irrelevant[28]. While delictual liability requires culpability, *i.e.* a *faulty* behaviour (including omission), neither the existence nor the amount of a claim for damages depend on the degree of fault. Therefore, even if only slight negligence has been assessed the amount of damages to be awarded will not be diminished. Only with regard to non-pecuniary loss may the degree of fault have an impact upon the extent of reasonable damages.

Further, *foreseeability* as such is not a distinctive element of delictual liability. The existence or the degree of foreseeability do not have a direct bearing upon delineating or delimiting the amount of damages. An exception is statutorily admitted with respect to lost profits: only those are to be awarded, under article 298.2 CC, that could probably have been expected in the ordinary course of events or according to the special circumstances, especially in the light of preparations and arrangements made. It should be added that, with regard to any damages, foreseeability may have an indirect impact, namely with regard to the issue of negligence[29].

28 J. Deliyannis and P. Kornilakis, *supra* note 2, §350 at p. 159.

29 Michaelides-Nouaros, *Interpretation of the Civil Code. A Commentary* (ErmAK): *Law of Obligations*, vol. II (1949) art. 330 nos 27-30.

Finally, there exist no statutory provisions about *maximum amounts of tort damages*. By contrast, such limits may sometimes be found in certain areas of contractual liability.

Mitigation of Damages under Austrian Law and Ideas for Future Regulations

Helmut Koziol, Wien

Introduction

In the last few decades there has been a marked trend, not only in many other legal systems, but also in Austrian Law, toward conceding injured persons more and more possibilities of passing on their damage to other persons or institutions. This has led to considerable extension not only of the social security system, but also of the liability of third parties. In the law of damages, on the one hand, the field of application of traditional fault liability has been expanded by making the duties to take due care more stringent. One should bear in mind the acknowledgment of far-reaching "Verkehrssicherungspflichten"[1], for our purpose I will refer to it as legal duties to maintain safety.[2] Also worth mentioning are the duties of care in the course of business activities (culpa in contrahendo, positive Forderungsverletzungen, i.e. positive breach of contract).[3] On the other hand, liability regardless of fault has been extended by creating both new provisions of strict liability for dangerous objects and strict liability independent of a special danger, the latter referring to product liability.[4]

This extension of liability is indeed favourable to injured persons; on the other hand, it inspires the fear that the tortfeasor is exposed to an unreasonable burden. Up until now this consideration has not led to any reduction in the creation of liability, although thought has been given as to whether limiting the compensation would provide a reasonable solution.

Consequently, a contradictory development can be seen: extension of liability on the one hand and limitation of the extent of liability on the other. This development should not be rejected on principle, because it may be reasonable for the injured

1 Koziol, Österreichisches Haftpflichtrecht, 2nd ed, II (1984) 57 ff; Reischauer in Rummel, ABGB, 2nd ed, II (1992) § 1294 margin note 4.
2 Markesinis, A Comparative Introduction to the German Law of Torts, 3rd ed (1994) 75, says, that the term "Verkehrssicherungspflichten" is not easy to translate, but that "its meaning could be summarized by saying that whoever by his activity or through his property establishes in everyday life a source of potential danger which is likely to affect the interests and rights of others, is obliged to ensure their protection against the risks thus created by him."
3 Koziol/Welser, Grundriß des bürgerlichen Rechts, 10th ed, I (1995) 204 ff, 267 ff.
4 Produkthaftungsgesetz 1988.

J. Spier (ed.), The Limits of Liability, 53-64.

person to receive reparation for only a portion of the damage suffered. But I think it should be seriously considered whether, in some cases, the reasons for responsibility are already so exaggerated that the liability for damages should be rejected altogether.

Which reasons are relevant for the mitigation of damages is a puzzling question. In the following, I would like to show you the solution offered by the Austrian Law in force, our experience with it thus far and the potential for future regulation.

But before doing that, let us to take a look at the rules of liability in Austrian Tort Law. The significance of mitigation of damages can only be ascertained if you know under which conditions liability is established under Austrian Law.

1 The System of Austrian Law of Tort

a) Liability for fault

Similar to the French code civile, the Austrian Allgemeines bürgerliches Gesetzbuch (General Civil Code, ABGB) establishes a general rule (§ 1295 subsection l): Everyone is entitled to demand compensation of the person who did him harm by fault; the harm may be caused by breach of contract or may have no relation to a contract.

As fault requires illegality of the conduct (compare § 1294 ABGB), in the area of Tort Law the decisive question arises as to which behaviour can be qualified as illegal. In answering this question, it is essential that the law acknowledges absolute rights. Among these are, above all, personal rights, as well as intangible property rights and rights in rem. Other persons have to respect these rights, which means that they must not endanger them as far as can be reasonably expected. The protection of absolute rights is strengthened by the "Verkehrssicherungspflichten"[5], i.e the legal duties to maintain safety. According to these legal obligations, not only is such conduct forbidden which is dangerous solely in the abstract sense, one is also required to actively safeguard others from harm.

In the area of Tort Law, the pure economic interests, as such, do not enjoy such extensive protection. But the statement[6] that § 1295 subsection 1 ABGB only protects absolute rights is not correct. It is commonly accepted that, from the beginning of a business contact, the parties are obliged not to endanger each others economic interests.[7] Therefore, in the case of culpa in contrahendo, the tortfeasor must also compensate pure economic loss. Furthermore, an expert is liable for pure economic loss if, in providing an expert opinion, he negligently declares false

5 Koziol, Haftpflichtrecht II 57 ff.

6 Supreme Court, Österreichisches Bank-Archiv 1994, 400.

7 Frotz, Die rechtsdogmatische Einordnung der Haftung für culpa in contrahendo, Gschnitzer-Gedenkschrift (1969) 163; Welser, Vertretung ohne Vollmacht (1970).

information and his report is intended for third parties as a basis for their business decisions.[8] A famous example is the liability for a prospectus meant for investors.[9] Finally, a wilful injury of pure economic interests establishes liability if there is no justified interest on the side of the tortfeasor.[10] Therefore, the intentional injury by fair competition establishes no liability, but the wilful misleading of third parties is unlawful (compare §§ 874, 1300 ABGB). For that reason it is wrong to say that in Tort Law pure economic loss does not have to be compensated.[11] It can only be stated that pure economic interests are more protected the closer the relationship between the parties is and the greater the possibilities are of endangering the economic interests of the partner.[12]

§ 1295 subsection 1 ABGB is supplemented by § 1311, 2nd sentence, case 2 ABGB, which provides liability for damage arising by transgression of a law that intends to guard against "accidental" injuries. In so doing, § 1311 ABGB refers to the so-called "Schutzgesetze" (protective laws).[13] The essential consequence of these laws is that, on the one hand, the injury of goods which are otherwise not protected is unlawful; on the other hand, they strengthen the protection by prohibiting even an abstract endangerment. Furthermore, the fault only needs to relate to the transgression of the law and not necessarily to the harmful result.

Finally, § 1295 subsection 2 ABGB provides that those persons are liable, who are acting contra bonos mores and wilfully inflict damage.

b) Liability without fault

The ABGB only provides for liability without fault in exceptional cases. It should be mentioned that a person who causes damage in an emergency situation is obligated to render compensation (§ 1306a ABGB). Furthermore, it is possible that a person who, in general, is not capable of tortious liability may have to indemnify if the injured party is not able to gain compensation from the persons liable for supervising the tortfeasor. He has to indemnify above all if the judge, in considering the financial position of the wrongdoer and that of the injured party, ascertains that it is much easier for the tortfeasor to bear the loss (§ 1310 ABGB). And finally, vicarious liability (§§ 1313a, 1315 ABGB) is also a liability without fault of the liable party.

There are a great many supplementary statutes providing for strict liability of the keeper of dangerous objects, e.g. nuclear plants, motor vehicles, railways, electrical

8 Welser, Die Haftung für Rat, Auskunft und Gutachten (1983) 80 ff.

9 Brawenz, Die Prospekthaftung nach allgemeinem Zivilrecht, 2nd ed (1992); Koziol in Avancini/Iro/Koziol, Österreichisches Bankvertragsrecht (1993) margin note 6/64 ff; Supreme Court, Entscheidungen des österreichischen Obersten Gerichtshofes in Zivilsachen (SZ) 63/136.

10 Koziol, Haftpflichtrecht II 20 ff.

11 Karollus, Funktion und Dogmatik der Haftung aus Schutzgesetzverletzung (1992) 48 ff.

12 Koziol, Delikt, Verletzung von Schuldverhältnissen und Zwischenbereich, Juristische Blätter 1994, 209 ff.

13 Karollus, Schutzgesetzverletzung 91 ff.

distribution networks, pipelines and mines. An Environmental Liability Act is in preparation.[14] It has to be stressed that in Austria it is generally accepted that the strict liability acts can be applied analogously.[15]

Another type of strict liability is product liability. The producer of goods which are put into circulation is liable without fault, but this liability is not based on the particular dangerousness of the goods.[16]

2 Critical Presentation of Mitigation of Damages under Austrian Law

a) Relation between fault and liability

According to § 1324 ABGB (Austrian General Civil Code), the tortfeasor who causes the harm by slight negligence is only obliged to pay the "eigentliche Schadloshaltung". This means he only has to compensate the "actual loss", but neither the lost profits nor the immaterial damage (§ 1324 ABGB). Furthermore, in the case of property damage, the damaged goods are to be valued at the market price (§ 1332 ABGB). We call this an objective-abstract adjustment, that is, a valuation without taking into consideration the value for the actual owner.[17]

In cases of bodily injury, however, there is scarcely any mitigation of damages if the wrongdoer only acts slightly negligently: He has to indemnify the injured person for costs of medical care and loss of earnings; in addition, he must pay damages for pain and suffering. Thus far there is no difference to the general rule, as the costs of medical care are part of the actual loss and even the loss of earnings is understood as an injury of an existing asset, namely of the ability to work, and therefore is also part of the actual loss. It is significant, however, that the injured person is not limited to objective-abstract adjusted damages, but is able to claim subjective disadvantage.[18] It is also important that the tortfeasor always has to pay damages for pain and suffering, that is, compensation for immaterial damage.

It is generally accepted as just that the degree of negligence of the tortfeasor has an influence on the extent of compensation. However, the inflexibility of the regulation is criticised.[19] It is pointed out that the graduation of the compensation is not reasonable, because in many cases the loss of an expected profit is a more hurtful and heavier damage than the loss of an already existing asset.

14 Rummel/Kerschner, Umwelthaftung im Privatrecht (1991); Gimpel-Hinteregger, Umwelthaftungsreform (1992).

15 Supreme Court, Juristische Blätter 1993, 113; Koziol, Umfassende Gefährdungshaftung durch Analogie ? Wilburg-Festschrift (1975) 173; Posch, Zum Stand der Reform der Gefährdungshaftung, Wertung und Interessenausgleich im Recht (1975) 165.

16 Koziol, Grundfragen der Produktehaftung (1980) 17 ff, 53 ff.

17 Koziol, Österreichisches Haftpflichtrecht, 2nd ed, I (1980) 24 ff.

18 Koziol, Haftpflichtrecht II 127.

19 Wilburg, Die Elemente des Schadensrechts (1941) 250.

It should be mentioned that a trend has recently emerged towards precluding liability for slight negligence. For example, the regulation of the Dienstnehmerhaftpflichtgesetz (Employees Liability Act) of 1965: If an employee injures his employer, he is not liable for "entschuldbare Fehlleistung", i.e. for the slightest degree of negligence. At the next level of negligence of the employee, if said negligence is slight, the judge is allowed to release him from damages on equitability. In such a case, the judge has to consider the degree of fault, on the one hand, and the reasons for mitigation, on the other. In cases of gross negligence, the judge is only allowed to mitigate the compensation. The reasons given for favouring the employees are that the employer is, to some extent, able to control the risks and can also insure himself against the risk[20].

§ 1319a ABGB rules that the keeper of a road is only then liable, when the defective condition of the road that has caused the accident is due to gross negligence[21]. This rule in particular - which especially favours the public sector - is very dubious, as it is also applicable to bodily injury. The asset of highest value, i.e. physical well-being, is thus without protection.

The rule on liability limitation stated in the Kapitalmarktgesetz 1992 (Capital Market Act), only refers to financial loss: The inspector of the prospectus and the agent must only account for gross negligence. It is an incomprehensible and much criticised exception to the general rule to be liable for every grade of negligence[22].

b) Immaterial damage

The Austrian Law of Torts is very restrictive as far as the compensation for immaterial damage is concerned. If property is damaged, the tortfeaser only has to pay for the sentimental value if he intentionally violated criminal law or inflicted wanton damage or acted with malicious intent. But even if personal rights are violated, the injured person is not always awarded compensation for immaterial damage. Up until a few years ago, the Austrian Supreme Court[23] held the opinion that immaterial damage is to be compensated only if the law provides for it explicitly. Based on this premise, the Supreme Court did not approve compensation for immaterial damage in the case of unlawful detention. Now the Supreme Court[24] takes the view, - just as the doctrine does[25] - that, in principle, the tortfeasor has to pay immaterial damage if he acted with gross negligence or intent, unless the law explicitly excludes this. Such an exclusion by law is found in the

20 Dirschmied, Dienstnehmerhaftpflichtgesetz (1992) 22 ff; Kerschner, Dienstnehmerhaftpflichtgesetz (1992) 45.

21 Posch, Marginalien zur Wegehaftung, Juristische Blätter 1977, 281.

22 Koziol, Die Konkurrenz zwischen allgemeinem Zivilrecht, KMG und BörseG bei der Prospekthaftung, Österreichisches Bank-Archiv 1992, 886.

23 Juristische Blätter 1952, 465; Evidenzblatt 1962/161.

24 Juristische Blätter 1975, 645; Juristische Blätter 1980, 372; Juristische Blätter 1982, 263; Juritische Blätter 1990, 456.

25 F. Bydlinski, Der Ersatz ideellen Schadens als sachliches und methodisches Problem, Juristische Blätter 1965, 173 and 237.

cases of insult (§ 1330 ABGB) and of inducing a woman to extramarital sexual intercourse by malice, threat or abuse of dependent condition (§ 1328 ABGB).

Caution with regard to compensation of immaterial damage is considered, in principle, to be reasonable: Immaterial damage can only be proved and measured with difficulty, unless some objective clues are given, as is the case for bodily injury or unlawful detention. But the limitation under present law is considered too far-reaching and there have been attempts to provide for compensation of immaterial damage in all cases of serious violations of personal rights.

c) Adequate causation

The tortfeasor must compensate the adequate damage, but not the remote. An exception must be made, however, if a protective legislative provision exists forbidding a certain behaviour in order to protect certain assets: The wrongdoer who violates this law must indemnify even remote damage of a protected asset. Some hold that this limitation is also not applicable if the tortfeasor acts wilfully and knowingly[26].

d) Protective purpose of the law

§ 1295 subsection l ABGB is worded too loosely when it entitles "everyone" to file a claim against the tortfeasor[27]. Today, it is commonly accepted that the tortfeasor only has to indemnify those injured persons whom the violated law is intended to protect. Therefore, the "Rechtswidrigkeitszusammenhang", or the more general "Schutzzweck der Norm" (the protective purpose of the norm), is decisive in determining who is entitled to make a claim[28]. For example, if a solicitor is injured, he is the only one who has a claim for compensation; his client, whom he was not able to advise and who consequently suffered a loss, has no claim. § 1327 ABGB constitutes an exception to this rule, providing only for the case of killing a person under duty to provide maintenance: The person entitled to be maintained has a claim against the tortfeasor.

The doctrine of "Rechtswidrigkeitszusammenhang" is especially applied in cases of violation of laws with protective purpose (§ 1311 ABGB). Furthermore, the purpose of the law also has to be taken into consideration if the law provides strict liability: It must be examined if there is a connection between the particular danger justifying strict liability and the damage caused.

The scope of the rule is relevant in regard to two aspects: The wrongdoer has to compensate only the losses of those persons which the law is intended to protect and only those losses which the violated law is intended to avoid.

26 Koziol, Haftpflichtrecht I 148 f.

27 Koziol/Welser, Bürgerliches Recht I 465.

28 Supreme Court, Juristische Blätter 1987, 720; Zeitschrift für Verkehrsrecht 1990/119 and 129; Juristische Blätter 1993, 788; Rabel, Das Recht des Warenkaufs I (1936) 495 ff; Wilburg, Elemente 244 ff; Bydlinski, Probleme der Schadensverursachung (1964) 63 f.

This limitation of liability is a result of the generally accepted method of interpreting the law according to its purpose ("teleologische Interpretation")[29].

e) Consideration of the pecuniary circumstances
If the wrongdoer enjoys the privilege of necessity or if he is a minor or mentally incompetent person, the judge has to consider the financial position of the wrongdoer and of the injured party. In consideration of the pecuniary circumstances, he can order the wrongdoer to compensate the entire loss or an equitable part thereof (§§ 1306a, 1310 ABGB).

The Austrian Supreme Court also considers the financial position of the employee when it has to determine the mitigation of liability according to the Employees Liability Act[30].

f) Maximum amounts of liability
In the area of liability based on fault, there are no maximum amounts under Austrian Law. The one exception that I am aware of is found under § 275 of the Commercial Code and concerns the liability of the auditor of annual accounts[31]. As regards the area of strict liability, the Civil Code itself does not state any maximum amounts of liability, even in the rare cases in which it provides liability without fault (compare § 1318 ABGB).

The situation is quite different, however, in the field of supplementary statutes: Most of the rules which provide for strict liability limit the responsibility by setting maximum amounts. That is, for example, the case for the liability of the keeper of a car, railway, aircraft, pipeline or electrical or nuclear plant. In several statutes the maximum amounts are determined very differently. It should be stressed that maximum amounts are also in force in the case of bodily injuries. I consider it very objectionable, for instance, that the Eisenbahn- und Kraftfahrzeug-Haftpflichtgesetz (that is, the statute that provides strict liability for the keeper of railways and motor vehicles) severely limits the liability for bodily injuries and, consequently, no sufficient compensation can be awarded, especially in the case of injury of several persons. On the other hand, there is no limitation provided in the case of causing damage to immovable property.

As in Germany, the limitation of liability by maximum amounts is criticised in Austria[32] and some advocate unlimited liability, as is the case in Switzerland. If it is acknowledged that the exposure to danger is a reason for liability, just as negligence is, then it is incomprehensible for the strict liability to be limited by

29 Bydlinski, Juristische Methodenlehre und Rechtsbegriff, 2nd ed (1991) 453 ff.
30 Kerschner, Dienstnehmerhaftpflichtgesetz 93 f.
31 Referred to here are the annual accounts of "Aktiengesellschaften" and large "Gesellschaften mit beschränkter Haftung", these two legal company forms being roughly equivalent to joint stock companies and private limited companies, respectively.
32 Koziol, Haftpflichtrecht I 137 f.

maximum amounts, whereas the liability based on fault, naturally, is not. It has been convincingly proved that, for the sake of insurability, limitation in the area of strict liability is no more necessary than in the area of liability based on fault[33]. There is no reason to foresee a special possibility for calculating the risks of damages in the area of strict liability. Furthermore, the economic capacity of the liable person is to be considered in the exact same way as in the area of strict liability and liability based on fault.

In recent years there has been an inclination among legislators to provide no maximum amounts even in the sphere of strict liability. Under the Forest Law and the Mining Law the liability is unlimited; this is also the case under the Product Liability Act. There have been attempts to do away with the maximum amounts for the liability of the keeper of a nuclear plant and the Environmental Liability Act, which is in preparation, will not provide for limitation by maximum amounts either.

3 Trends and Suggestions for Future Regulations

As the criticism of the existing regulations and recent legal trends show, rigid maximum amounts are not appropriate in the mitigation of damages. Consideration of the degree of fault or the degree of danger in the case of strict liability, on the other hand, is quite reasonable, but this should not be the sole element taken into account. The same can be said about adequate causation and the correlation between illegality and damage. Rather the weight of all reasons for liability should be considered, as Wilburg[34] proposed: He aims at an elastic system in which the extent of the obligation to compensate results from a flexible interplay of the elements relevant to liability. To some extent, this idea is reflected in the Employees Liability Act (§ 2 Dienstnehmerhaftpflichtgesetz). According to this act, the liability depends on the number and intensity of the elements occurring in the respective case. This means, for example, that if the negligence of the tortfeasor is slight or the strict liability is based on exposure to a minor grade of danger, the limit of adequate causation und the correlation between illegality and damage must be very strictly laid down.

Furthermore, we should deduce from the discernible indications in existing law that the value of the injured assets is to be considered together with the weight of the elements relevant to liability. In particular, if human health is impaired, the most complete compensation possible for impairment of health has to be made.

Also to be considered is the concept found in Austrian law, according to which the financial position of thc tortfcasor must bc takcn into account, as wcll as that of the

33 Von Caemmerer, Reform der Gefährdungshaftung (1971) 23 f; Taschner, Begrenzung der Gefährdungshaftung durch Haftungshöchstsummen?, Zum Deutschen und Internationalen Schuldrecht (1983) 75.

34 Wilburg, Verhandlungen des 43. Deutschen Juristentages II/C (1960) C 3 ff.

injured person[35]. This concept should be supplemented by considering which party can best be expected to insure the risk.

It has to be stressed that the concept of a flexible system does not evoke the danger of unforeseeable and unverifiable decisions. On the contrary, the system aims to disclose the reasons for limitation of damages which up until now has very often been imposed by courts secretely and without any argumentation. Moreover, the system prevents the liability from being rejected in many cases on the grounds that full compensation is considered unreasonable for the tortfeasor. The openly accepted graduation of damages which I recommend has to be done according to given legal principles and not only according to unverifiable principles of equity.

In my opinion, first of all we have to discuss under which conditions the tortfeasor must pay full compensation. When I say 'full compensation', I mean the compensation of that damage which is generally thought to be in the scope of the rule and not too remote. Since the most relevant element for liability is negligence or, in the area of strict liability, the specific danger, in the first instance it has to be determined whether even slight negligence or a minor grade of danger leads to full compensation. Next, it has to be determined for which types of harm mitigation of compensation may take place: For example, I hold that such mitigation is permissible in the case of pecuniary loss or immaterial damage, but not if human health is impaired. Finally, those reasons must be determined which, either by themselves or in combination with others, allow us to reduce damages, for instance, negligence that is very slight, the financial position, the remoteness of the harm, and damage that is on the outer limit of the scope of the rule. On the other hand, if these elements are exceptionally strong, they justify extending the damages. For example, if the tortfeasor acts willfully, he has to compensate very remote harm as well.

35 Wilburg, Elemente 23 f; Schilcher, Theorie der sozialen Schadensverteilung (1977) 166 ff.

Tools to Control the Scope and Extent of Liability

1 Ceilings

Compare 2.f.

2 Ad hoc mitigation

In Austria this tool is not openly used. But I suspect that it is sometimes used unconsciously or unadmittedly by manipulating the affirmation of negligence or contributory negligence and of the degree of negligence. This method of proceeding is criticised, because it circumvents the law.

3 Circumstances to be imputed to the victim

In the case of contributory negligence the tortfeasor only has to compensate part of the damage (§ 1304 ABGB). If the fault of the person who suffered the loss by far outweighs the fault of the tortfeasor the latter pays no damages.

If the person who suffered loss is the keeper of a dangerous object, for which he is liable without fault, and if the dangerousness of the object contributed to the damage, the tortfeasor - just as in the case of contributory negligence - only has to compensate part of the damage (compare § 11 Eisenbahn- und Kraftfahrzeug-Haftpflichtgesetz).

4 Heads of non recoverable damages

§ 1324 ABGB foresees a general restriction of liability for pecuniary loss: The tortfeasor who caused the damage by slight negligence only has to compensate the "actual loss" , but not the lost profits (compare 2. a). That the tortfeasor often does not have to indemnify for pure economic loss is a consequence of the limited protection of pure economic interests; therefore the conduct of the tortfeasor is not illegal (see l.a). Furthermore, the protective purpose of the law - mainly of "Schutzgesetzen" - may show that the tortfeasor does not have to make up for pure economic loss.
For the limitation of compensation for immaterial damage see 2.b.

5 Funds established either by industry or government

Whether to use this system in the environmental law is currently under discussion. The last draft of the "Umwelthaftungsgesetz" in 1994 does not provide for funds.

6 Schutzzweck

See 2.d.

7 Duty of care

See 1.a.

8 Apportionment

The argument of " loss of a chance" is sometimes used in cases of unclear causality: If the tortfeasor were liable for one possible cause, but the injured person had to bear the risk of the other possible cause, the tortfeasor would only have to compensate part of the damage. This solution is derived from §§ 1302, 1304 ABGB (Bydlinski, Haftungsgrund und Zufall als alternativ mögliche Schadensursachen, Frotz-Festschrift [1993] 3; Austrian Supreme Court, Juristische Blätter 1990, 524, but compare also Juristische Blätter 1994, 540 with critical comments by Bollenberger).

Up until now, the market share theory has not been used in Austria (Posch in: Fenyves/Weyers, Multikausale Schäden in modernen Haftungsrechten [1988] 153).

9 Schedules, scales and matrices

In Austrian law legal scales do not exist.

10 Thresholds

They are used only in the Product Liability Act.

11 Adequate causation

Compare 2.c.

12 The access to justice

Under Austrian Law this tool is not used for the mitigation of liability.

13 Insurance provided by government and/or payment by treasury

Social insurance results in mitigation of the liability of the employer: He is only liable for harm to employees if he injures them wilfully (§ 333 Allgemeines Sozialversicherungsgesetz). The reason for this mitigation is that the damage caused by occupational injury is covered by social insurance and the insurance is financed by contributions made by the employer.

Currently under discussion is insurance for patients who suffer damage as a result of medical treatment in hospital (J. W. Pichler, Rechtsentwicklungen zu einer verschuldensunabhängigen Entschädigung im Medizinbereich I [1994]; Koziol, Verschuldensunabhängige Ersatzansprüche bei Behandlungsfehlern? Recht der Medizin 1994, 3).

La modération de la réparation du dommage dans le droit belge de la responsabilité civile extra-contractuelle

*Prof. Dr. A. van Oevelen**

I Introduction

1. Pour le rapporteur belge le thème de ce colloque ne pose guère de problèmes. En effet, en matière de la réparation du dommage par suite d'une responsabilité civile extra-contractuelle, le droit belge adhère au principe de la réparation intégrale. Ce n'est qu'à titre d'exception que le législateur limite l'étendue de la réparation du dommage ou qu'il attribue au juge le pouvoir de modérer l'étendue de la réparation. Le droit belge ne connaît non plus un système de modération de la réparation par l'interprétation restrictive de la notion de dommage ni par l'application des règles de la relation causale entre l'acte illicite et le dommage.
Consécutivement j'examinerai le principe de la réparation intégrale du dommage (*infra, sub* II) et les conséquences de ce principe (*infra, sub* III), les exceptions que le législateur a apportées à ce principe en limitant le montant de la réparation ou en attribuant au juge un pouvoir de modération de l'étendue de l'indemnisation (*infra, sub* IV) et l'interprétation large tant de la notion de dommage (*infra, sub* V) que de la relation causale entre l'acte illicite et le dommage (*infra, sub* VI). Dans ce rapport je me limite à la responsabilité civile extra-contractuelle. Je laisse de côté l'éventuelle modération de la réparation dans la responsabilité contractuelle et dans la matière des quasi-contrats (gestion d'affaires, enrichissement sans cause, paiement de l'indû).

II Le principe de la réparation intégrale du dommage

2. Les articles 1382 à 1386*bis* du Code civil belge, qui constituent le *sedes materiae* de la responsabilité civile extra-contractuelle, ne définissent point les termes "réparer le dommage" et ne donnent guère d'indications sur la manière dont le responsable doit réparer le préjudice. Néanmoins, le seul mot "réparer" permet déjà de formuler quelques précisions concernant cette notion. En effet, comme l'affirme la Cour de cassation dans un arrêt de 15 mai 1941, "réparer un dommage, c'est

* Université d'Anvers

J. Spier (ed.), The Limits of Liability, 65-74.

rétablir la partie qui l'a subi dans la situation où elle serait demeurée si le fait illicité dont elle se plaint n'avait pas été commis"[1].
L'absence de définition légale des termes "réparer le dommage" implique nécessairement que la réparation doit être complète et ne peut dépasser le montant du dommage, parce que si la victime devrait supporter une part quelconque du préjudice, le dommage ne serait plus "réparé". Il en est de même si la victime pourrait exiger plus que la réparation complète de son préjudice. Le responsable doit donc réparer tout le dommage qu'il a causé et rien d'autre que ce dommage, qui constitue la seule mesure de l'obligation de réparation[2]. Dans ce sens on peut dire que la réparation doit être objective, ce qui signifie que le juge, en évaluant le dommage et sa réparation, ne peut prendre en considération des éléments qui sont étrangers au dommage et par lesquels la réparation serait augmentée ou modérée[3].

La jurisprudence récente de la Cour de cassation confirme le principe de la réparation intégrale du dommage causé par un acte illicite[4]. Cette jurisprudence ne fait pas l'objet de critiques de la part de la doctrine, qui approuve au contraire ledit principe[5].
Le principe de la réparation intégrale du dommage causé par un acte illicite implique que le juge n'a pas de pouvoir de modérer l'obligation de réparer ce dommage, sauf dans les cas expressément prévus par la loi et examinés plus loin dans ce rapport (voyez *infra*, n°s 9-11).

III Les conséquences du principe de la réparation intégrale du dommage

3. La première conséquence du principe de la réparation intégrale du dommage est que le juge doit évaluer le dommage - et partant sa réparation - *in concreto*, c'est-à-dire en tenant compte des particularités propres à chaque cas qui lui est soumis, afin

1 Cour de cassation belge, 15 mai 1941, *Pasicrisie belge*, 1941, I, 192. Voyez dans le même sens: DALCQ, R.O., *Traité de la responsabilité civile*, II, *Le lien de causalité. Le dommage et sa réparation*, in *Les Novelles, Droit Civil*, V-2, Bruxelles, Larcier, 1962, p. 741, n° 4139; RONSE, J., DE WILDE, L., CLAEYS, A. et MALLEMS, I, *Schade en schadeloosstelling*, I, in *Algemene Praktische Rechtsverzameling*, Gand, Story-Scientia, 1984, p. 163, n° 220.

2 DALCQ, R.O., *op.cit., Les Novelles, Droit Civil*, V-2, p. 742, n° 4140; RONSE, J., DE WILDE, L., CLAEYS, A. et MALLEMS, I., *op.cit.*, p. 172-173, n° 230.

3 RONSE, J., DE WILDE, L., CLAEYS, A. et MALLEMS, I., *op.cit.*, p. 173, n° 230. Pour un bref aperçu de ces éléments étrangers au dommage, voyez *infra*, n°s 4-6 et les références.

4 Cour de cassation belge, 21 février 1984, *Pasicrisie belge*, 1984, I, 716; Cour de cassation belge, 15 mai 1985, *Pasicrisie belge*, 1985, I, 878; Cour de cassation belge, 29 mei 1991, *Pasicrisie belge*, 1991, I, 848.

5 DALCQ, R.O., *op.cit., Les Novelles, Droit Civil*, V-2, p. 741-742, n°s 4139-4140; RONSE, J., DE WILDE, L., CLAEYS, A. et MALLEMS, I., *op.cit.*, p. 172-175, n°s 230-234; DIRIX, E., *Het begrip schade*, Anvers, Maarten Kluwer, et Bruxelles, Ced. Samsom, 1984, p. 34-35, n° 30; SCHUERMANS, L., SCHRYVERS, J., SIMOENS, D., VAN OEVELEN, A. et SCHAMP, H., "Overzicht van rechtspraak - Onrechtmatige daad - Schade en schadeloosstelling (1977-1982)", in *Tijdschrift voor Privaatrecht*, 1984, (511), p. 606-608, n° 26, D, c); FAGNART, J.-L. et DENEVE, M., "Chronique de jurisprudence - La responsabilité civile (1976-1984)", in *Journal des Tribunaux*, 1988, p. 541, n° 132.

qu'il puisse adopter, autant que possible, exactement la réparation au préjudice souffert. Une appréciation *in concreto* du dommage s'oppose à une appréciation *in abstracto*, qui n'est pas à l'exacte mesure du préjudice subi[6]. L'obligation pour le juge d'évaluer le préjudice *in concreto* lui impose de fixer la réparation en tenant compte du préjudice réellement subi par la victime, sans pouvoir accorder à la victime ce qui constituerait une réparation "normale" de son préjudice[7].

4. Le principe de la réparation intégrale du dommage a comme deuxième conséquence que le juge, lors de son évaluation du dommage et de sa réparation, ne peut prendre en considération la *situation de fortune* et de famille des parties, sauf dans la mesure où cette situation, dans le chef de la victime, influence l'évaluation objective ou *in concreto* de son préjudice. C'est ainsi que, lorsque le juge doit évaluer le dommage matériel à cause d'une incapacité de travail temporaire, il doit évidemment tenir compte des revenus professionnels de la victime et de la composition de sa famille, mais une fois qu'il a déterminé *in concreto* le dommage réellement subi, il ne peut pas faire dépendre le montant de l'indemnisation de l'état de pauvreté ou de la situation de fortune de la victime ou du responsable[8].

5. Le principe de la réparation intégrale du dommage causé par un acte illicité a comme troisième conséquence que *l'étendue de l'indemnisation ne peut varier en fonction de la gravité de la faute*. En effet, la responsabilité civile extra-contractuelle n'a pas pour object de punir l'auteur du dommage, mais tend à indemniser la victime de l'acte illicite. Par conséquent, la faute légère comme la faute la plus lourde obligent le responsable à réparer tout le préjudice causé[9]. Après que la Cour de cassation avait déjà considéré dans son arrêt du 15 mai 1941 que, pour la détermination de la réparation qui couvre entièrement le préjudice dû à un acte illicite, "l'importance de la faute commise apparaît (...) comme un élément sans rapport avec la question à résoudre"[10], la Cour a très clairement formulé cette règle dans son arrêt du 10 octobre 1972, en décidant "que l'action en réparation d'un dommage moral n'a pas pour but d'infliger une peine privée à la partie responsable du dommage; que l'indemnité ne peut notamment être proportionnelle à la gravité relative des faits commis; qu'elle a par contre pour objet l'allègement

6 DALCQ, R.O., *op.cit., Les Novelles, Droit Civil,* V-2, p. 742, n°s 4140-4141; RONSE, J., DE WILDE, L., CLAEYS, A. et MALLEMS, I., *op.cit.*, p. 178-180, n°s 238-240.

7 DALCQ, R.O., *op.cit., Les Novelles, Droit Civil,* V-2, p. 743, n° 4143; RONSE, J., DE WILDE, L., CLAEYS, A. et MALLEMS, I, *op.cit.*, p. 184-185, n°s 244-245.

8 DALCQ, R.O., *op.cit., Les Novelles, Droit Civil,* V-2, p. 743-744, n° 4145; RONSE, J., DE WILDE, L., CLAEYS, A. et MALLEMS, I., *op.cit.*, p. 199-200, n° 265 et les références.

9 DALCQ, R.O., *op.cit., Les Novelles, Droit Civil,* V-2, p. 744, n° 4146; RONSE, J., DE WILDE, L., CLAEYS, A. et MALLEMS, I., *op.cit.*, p. 201-202, n°s 268-269; FAGNART, J.-L., *Examen de la jurisprudence concernant la responsabilité civile (1968-1975)*, Bruxelles, Larcier, 1976, p. 97, n° 118.

10 Cour de cassation belge, 15 mai 1941, *Pasicrisie belge*, 1941, I, 192.

d'une douleur, d'un chagrin ou de quelqu'autre préjudice moral et de réparer dans cette mesure le dommage subi"[11].
Certains auteurs ont observé qu'il y a un cas dans lequel l'étendue de l'indemnisation est fixée par rapport à la faute, notamment en cas de faute propre de la victime[12]. D'autres auteurs ont très justement répliqué que dans ce cas l'étendue de la réparation est déterminée, non en fonction de la gravité de la faute du responsable et de la victime, mais dans la mesure où la faute de chacun d'eux a causé le dommage[13].

6. La quatrième et dernière conséquence du principe de la répration intégrale du dommage est que le juge, lors de son évaluation du dommage et de sa réparation, ne peut prendre en considération que *le responsable a fait assurer sa responsabilité.* L'assurance de responsabilité n'apporte en effet aucune modification aux règles de la responsabilité civile extra-contractuelle, et constitue un élément étranger au dommage, la seule mesure de l'obligation de réparation[14]. Ce n'est que dans un seul jugement relativement récent qu'un juge de paix a fixé l'étendue de l'indemnisation en tenant compte du fait que le responsable avait contracté une assurance de responsabilité[15].

IV Exceptions au principe de la réparation integrale du dommage

A. Classification des exceptions

7. Le droit belge de la responsabilité civile extra-contractuelle connaît trois sortes d'exceptions au principe de la réparation intégrale du dommage. Il y a d'abord des cas dans lesquels le législateur a limité le montant de l'indemnisation; ensuite les cas dans lesquels le législateur a attribué au juge le pouvoir de modérer l'étendue de l'indemnisation; enfin les cas dans lesquels le législateur attribue à la victime une indemnisation excédant le montant du dommage.

11 Cour de cassation belge, 10 octobre 1972, *Pasicrisie belge*, 1973, I, 147; *Journal des Tribunaux*, 1973, 163, avec note de TUNC, A.

12 DALCQ, R.O., *op.cit., Les Novelles, Droit Civil*, V-2, p. 219-220, n°s 2704-2706, et p. 744, n° 4148; voyez aussi les auteurs français cités par RONSE, J., DE WILDE, L., CLAEYS, A. et MALLEMS, I., *op.cit.*, p. 203, n° 271.

13 RONSE, J., DE WILDE, L., CLAEYS, A. et MALLEMS, I., *op.cit.*, p. 203-205, n° 271. Voyez dans le même sens: Cour de cassation belge, 7 novembre 1990, *Pasicrisie belge*, 1991, I, 249.

14 DALCQ, R.O., *op.cit., Les Novelles, Droit civil*, V-2, p. 744, n° 4149; RONSE, J., DE WILDE, L., CLAEYS, A. et MALLEMS, I., *op.cit.*, p. 206, n° 273; SIMOENS, D., "Hoofdlijnen in de evolutie van het aansprakelijkheidsrecht", *Rechtskundig Weekblad*, 1980-1981, (1961) et (2025), col. 2028 e.s.; DIRIX, E., *op.cit.*, p. 34, n° 30.

15 Juge de paix de Merksem, 9 avril 1981, *Rechtskundig Weekblad*, 1981-1982, 1279, avec note de SIMOENS, D.

Tenant compte du thème de ce colloque, je laisse de côté cette dernière catégorie d'exceptions, qui a d'ailleurs un champ d'application très restreint[16]. Avant d'examiner les deux autres catégories je voudrais encore souligner qu'elles constituent de vraies exceptions au principe général de la réparation intégrale du dommage, qui est encore toujours confirmé par la doctrine et la jurisprudence.

B. Cas dans lesquels le législateur limite le montant de l'indemnisation

8. Comme la plupart des pays de l'Europe occidentale, la Belgique connaît aussi une limitation de la responsabilité du propriétaire d'un navire, actuellement régie par les articles 47-57 du Livre II, Titre II, du Code de Commerce, tels qu'ils ont été remplacés par la loi du 11 avril 1989 portant approbation et exécution de divers actes internationaux en matière de navigation maritime[17], en particulier la convention de Londres du 19 novembre 1976 sur la limitation de la responsabilité en matière de créances maritimes.

Selon l'article 3*bis*, avant-dernière alinéa, de la loi du 3 novembre 1967 sur le pilotage des bâtiments de mer, y inséré par la loi du 30 août 1988[18], le membre du personnel de l'organisateur d'un service de pilotage n'est tenu de réparer le dommage qu'il a causé par sa faute grave à un navire piloté, qu'à concurrence de 500.000 francs belges par événement dommageable. Le Roi peut adapter ce montant en tenant compte de la situation économique.

En ce qui concerne la responsabilité civile de l'exploitant d'aéronefs étrangers envers les tiers, en cas de dégâts causés à la surface du sol, la loi du 14 juillet 1966, approuvant le traité de Rome du 7 octobre 1952, limite cette responsabilité à un montant fixé forfaitairement, hormis les cas de dol ou de faute lourde[19].

L'article 7 de la loi belge du 22 juillet 1985 sur la responsabilité civile dans le domaine de l'énergie nucléaire, approuvant la Convention de Paris du 29 juillet 1960 et le protocol additionnel à cette convention du 28 janvier 1964[20], limite la responsabilité de l'exploitant d'une installation nucléaire à un montant maximal de 4 milliard de francs belges pour chaque accident nucléaire. L'article 19 de la même loi dispose que, si les dommages causés par un accident nucléaire excèdent ce montant maximal, la partie des dommages supérieure à ce moment sera réparée au moyen de fonds publics alloués à un titre différent de celui d'une couverture de responsabilité de l'exploitant.

16 Il y a trois cas dans lesquels le legislateur a porté l'indemnisation au double du dommage, notamment dans l'article 1er du titre V du décret du 10 vendémiaire de l'an IV, sur la responsabilité des communes en cas d'attentats commis sur leur territoire, à force ouverte ou par violence, par des attroupements ou rassemblements; l'article 7*bis* de la loi du 28 février 1882 sur la chasse, y inséré par la loi du 4 avril 1900, en ce qui concerne les dommages causés par les lapins (pour la région flamande cet article a été abrogé par le décret flamand sur la chasse du 24 juillet 1991); l'article 50 de l'arrêté royal du 15 septembre 1919 portant coordination des lois sur les mines, relatifs à certains dommages causés à la surface.

17 *Moniteur belge*, 6 octobre 1989, *erratum* in *Moniteur belge*, 8 décembre 1989.

18 *Moniteur belge*, 17 septembre 1988.

19 *Moniteur belge*, 27 septembre 1966.

20 *Moniteur belge*, 31 août 1985.

Selon l'article 11, § 2, dernière alinéa, de la loi du 25 février 1991 relative à la responsabilité du fait des produits défectueux[21], l'indemnisation des dommages causés à d'autres biens que le produit défectueux lui-même n'est due que sous déduction d'une franchise de 22.500 francs belges[22].
Une dernière disposition législative qui limite le montant de l'indemnisation est constituée par l'article 37, cinquième alinéa, de la loi organique du 29 mars 1962 de l'aménagement du territoire et de l'urbanisme, tel que modifié depuis lors. Selon cette disposition la diminution de la valeur d'un bien immobilier résultant d'une interdiction de bâtir ou de lotir doit être subie sans indemnité jusqu'à concurrence de 20 % de cette valeur[23].

C. Cas dans lesquels le législateur attribue au juge le pouvoir de modérer l'étendue de l'indemnisation

9. La disposition législative la plus connue en Belgique en vertu de laquelle le juge peut modérer l'étendue de l'indemnisation, est l'article 1386*bis* du Code civil, qui prévoit que "lorsqu'une personne se trouvant en état de démence ou dans un état grave de déséquilibre mental ou de débilité mentale la rendant incapable du contrôle de ses actions, cause dommage à autrui, le juge peut la condamner à tout ou partie de la réparation à laquelle elle serait astreinte si elle avait le contrôle de ses actes" et que "le juge statue selon l'équité, tenant compte des circonstances et de la situation des parties". Cet article ne modifie pas le système du Code civil en matière de capacité aquilienne, mais ouvre, sur la base d'équité, un recours à la victime dans des conditions différentes de celles du droit commun[24]. La doctrine et la jurisprudence s'accordent à dire que le pouvoir d'appréciation du juge en vertu de cet article est souverain, tant quant au principe de l'obligation de réparer que quant à son montant[25]. Les circonstances qu'il peut prendre en considération sont surtout la situation de fortune des parties et en particulier le fait que l'auteur de l'acte dommageable a conclu un contrat d'assurance de responsabilité, l'importance des soins et des dépenses qu'exige l'état de santé de l'auteur de l'acte dommagea-

21 *Moniteur belge*, 22 mars 1991.

22 L'article 11, § 3, de la même loi dispose que le Roi peut modifier ce moment afin de le rendre conforme aux déci-sions prises par le Conseil des Ministres de l'Union européenne, en application de l'article 18.2. de la directive 85/374/CEE du 25 juillet 1985 relative au rapprochement des dispositions législatives, réglementaires et administratives des Etats membres de l'Union européenne en matière de responsabilité du fait des produits défectueux.

23 Cette disposition est comme telle ne plus d'application dans les régions wallonne et bruxelloise et y est remplacée par des dispositions décrétales semblables.

24 DE PAGE, H., *Traité élémentaire de droit civil belge*, II, Bruxelles, Bruylant, 1964, p. 885-886, n° 916, A; DALCQ, R.O., *Traité de la responsabilité civile*, I, *Les causes de la responsabilité*, in *Les Novelles, Droit Civil*, V-1, Bruxelles, Larcier, 1967, p. 737-738, n° 2325; RONSE, J., DE WILDE, L., CLAEYS, A. en MALLEMS, I., *op.cit.*, p. 199, n° 265; KRUITHOF, R., "De buitencontractuele aansprakelijkheid van en voor geesteszieken", in *Revue Générale des Assurances et des Responsabilités*, 1980, n° 10.179/5-verso et n° 10.179/6, n° 20.

25 DE PAGE, H., *op.cit.*, p. 885, n° 916, A, et p. 889-890, n° 916, C; DALCQ, R.O., *op.cit.*, *Les Novelles, Droit Civil*, V-1, p. 739, n° 2330; KRUITHOF, R., *op.cit.*, *Revue Générale des Assurances et des Responsabilités*, 1980, n° 10.179/11, n° 38.

ble, ainsi que le degré plus ou moins grand de conscience de ses actes qu'il possède[26].

10. Une deuxième disposition légale, qui est généralement considérée comme autorisant le juge à modérer l'étendue de l'indemnisation, est l'article 35, 6°, des lois coordonnées sur les sociétés commerciales (formant Titre IX du Livre Ier du Code de Commerce), qui dispose que "les fondateurs d'une société anonyme, et en cas d'augmentation du capital social, les administrateurs, sont tenus solidairement envers les intéressés, malgré toute stipulation contraire, des engagements de la société dans une proportion fixée par le juge, en cas de faillite, prononcée dans les trois ans de la constitution, si le capital social était, lors de la constitution, manifestement insuffisant pour assurer l'exercice normal de l'activité projetée pendant une période de deux ans au moins"[27]. La doctrine et la jurisprudence déduisent des termes "dans une proportion fixée par le juge" que le juge dispose d'un pouvoir de modération par rapport à l'étendue de la condamnation des fondateurs ou des administrateurs à l'accomplissement des obligations de la société déclarée faillite. Puisque la loi ne contient aucun critère à ce propos, le juge exerce ici un pouvoir souverain d'appréciation[28].

11. La dernière disposition légale qui autorise le juge à modérer l'étendue de l'indemnisation, est l'article 11 des lois coordonnées sur le Conseil d'Etat (arrêté royal du 12 janvier 1973), qui prévoir que lorsqu'il n'y a pas d'autre juridiction compétente, la section d'administration du Conseil d'Etat se prononce par équité et en tenant compte de toutes les circonstances d'intérêt public ou privé, par voie d'arrêt des demandes d'indemnités relatives à la réparation d'un dommage exceptionnel, tant moral que matériel, causé par une autorité administrative. Cette disposition est basée sur l'équité et trouve son fondement juridique dans la théorie française de l'égalité des citoyens devant les charges publiques.
Les termes "par équité" impliquent que l'indemnité qui est attribuée ne doit pas contenir une réparation intégrale[29]. Le Conseil d'Etat dispose d'un pouvoir souve-

26 DE PAGE, H., *op.cit.*, p. 889-890, n° 916, C; DALCQ, R.O., *ibid.* et les références; KRUITHOF, R., *op.cit.*, *Revue Générale des Assurances et des Responsabilités*, 1980, n° 10.179/11, n°s 39-43 et les références multiples à la jurisprudence.

27 Cette disposition est aussi applicable aux sociétés privées à responsabilité limitée (article 123, 7°, des lois coordonnées sur les sociétés commerciales) et aux sociétés coopératives à responsabilité limitée (article 147*ter*, 4°, des lois coordonnées sur les sociétés commerciales).

28 VAN BRUYSTEGEM, B., "Oprichtersaansprakelijkheid wegens kennelijk ontoereikend kapitaal", in *Belgische Rechtspraak in Handelszaken - Jurisprudence Commerciale de la Belgique*, 1982, (139), p. 143, n° 11; PARMENTIER, C., "La responsabilité des dirigeants d'entreprises en cas de faillite", in *Revue de Droit Commercial Belge - Tijdschrift voor Belgisch Handelsrecht*, 1986, (741), p. 767, n° 35 et les références; SMIT, E., "Le capital social et la responsabilité des fondateurs", in *Droit des Affaires - Ondernemingsrecht*, 1991, n° 18, (9), p. 12; GEENS, K. en LAGA, H., "Overzicht van rechtspraak - Vennootschappen (1986-1991)", in *Tijdschrift voor Privaatrecht*, 1993, (933), p. 1026, n° 107 et les références.

29 DALCQ, R.O., *op.cit.*, *Les Novelles*, *Droit Civil*, V-1, p. 505, n° 1535; CHABOT-LEONARD, D., "Le contentieux de l'indemnité devant le Conseil d'Etat", in *Annales de la Faculté de Droit de Liège*, 1971, (189), p. 238-239; SOMERHAUSEN, M. et REMION, F.-M. (editors), *Le Conseil*

rain d'appréciation tant quant au principe d'allouer une indemnité que quant à son montant[30]. Les circonstances d'intérêt public et privé que le Conseil d'Etat prend en considération sont surtout les conséquences financielles d'un arrêt allouant une indemnité pour l'autorité administrative et la situation de fortune du requérant[31].

VI L'interprétation large de la notion de dommage

12. L'on pourrait se demander si le droit belge de la responsabilité civile extra-contractuelle connaît éventuellement une façon indirecte de modération de l'étendue de l'indemnisation par l'interprétation qui y est donnée à la notion de dommage. La réponse à cette question me paraît clairement devoir être négative, en premier lieu parce qu'en droit belge le dommage est une notion de fait, consistant dans la perte totale ou partielle d'un bien que l'on possédait ou l'enlèvement d'un avantage que l'on pourrait attendre[32]. Pour la recevabilité d'une action en dommages-intérêts à cause d'un acte illicite, il n'est pas nécessaire d'alléger la lésion d'un droit subjectif, mais suffit-il l'atteinte à un intérêt légitime[33]. Une deuxième raison pour répondre négativement à la question posée dans l'alinéa précédente, est que le droit belge rejette la théorie connue aux Pays-Bas comme celle de "l'illicéité relative" et en Allemagne comme la "*Schutznormtheorie*", non seulement parce que la doctrine et la jurisprudence sont d'avis que le but poursuivi par cette théorie peut être mieux atteint par l'application des règles du lien de causalité, mais aussi et surtout parce qu'elle ajoute une condition aux articles 1382 et 1383 du Code civil belge que ces deux articles ne contiennent pas[34]. La théorie de "l'illicéité relative"

d'Etat, in *Les Novelles, Droit Administratif,* VI, Bruxelles, Larcier, 1975, p. 204, n° 725; VAN OEVELEN, A., *Schadevergoeding bij rechtmatige overheidsdaad in België*, Zwolle, Tjeenk Willink et Anvers, Kluwer rechtswetenschappen, 1984, p. 98, n° 61.

30 CHABOT-LEONARD, D., *op.cit.*, *Annales de la Faculté de Droit de Liège*, 1971, p. 238; VAN OEVELEN, A., *ibid.*

31 DALCQ, R.O., *op.cit.*, *Les Novelles, Droit Civil,* V-1, p. 505, n° 1535; SOMERHAUSEN, M. et REMION, F.-M. (editors), *op.cit.*, *Les Novelles, Droit Administratif,* VI, p. 204-205, n° 727; VAN OEVELEN, A., *op.cit.*, p. 99, n° 61 et les références au jurisprudence du Conseil d'Etat.

32 Cour de cassation belge, 2 mai 1955, *Pasicrisie belge*, 1955, I, 950; *Journal des Tribunaux*, 1955, 695, avec note de GREGOIRE, C.; *Revue Générale des Assurances et des Responsabilités*, 1956, n° 5677, avec note de FONTEYNE, J.; *Revue critique de jurisprudence belge*, 1957, 99, avec note de RONSE, J.; Cour de cassation belge, 31 mars 1969, *Pasicrisie belge*, 1969, I, 676; Cour de cassation belge, 4 mars 1975, *Pasicrisie belge*, 1975, I, 681.

33 Voyez, outre la jurisprudence citée dans la note précédente: Cour de cassation belge, 16 janvier 1939, *Pasicrisie belge*, 1939, I, 25; *Revue Générale des Assurances et des Responsabilités*, 1939, n° 3002, avec note de FONTEYNE, J.; Cour de cassation belge, 19 décembre 1978, *Pasicrisie belge*, 1979, I, 472; DALCQ, R.O., *op.cit.*, *Les Novelles, Droit Civil,* V-2, p. 286-287, n°s 2915-2916; RONSE, J., DE WILDE, L., CLAEYS, A. et MALLEMS, I., *op.cit.*, p. 18-24, n°s 13-18, et p. 26-32, n°s 22-27; DIRIX, E., *op.cit.*, p. 22-26, n^{os}, 12-18.

34 RONSE, J., DE WILDE, L., CLAEYS, A. et MALLEMS, I., *op.cit.*, p. 25-26, n°s 20-21; VANDENBERGHE, H., VAN QUICKENBORNE, M. et HAMELINK, P., "Overzicht van rechtspraak. Aansprakelijkheid uit onrechtmatige daad (1964-1978)", in *Tijdschrift voor Privaatrecht*, 1980, (1139), p. 1152-1154, n° 7; Cour de cassation belge, 28 avril 1972, *Pasicrisie belge*, 1972, I, 797.

revient en effet à limiter le cercle de personnes qui peuvent intenter une action en dommages-intérêts.

VII Modération indirecte de l'étendue de l'indemnisation par l'application des règles concernant le lien de causalité?

13. L'on pourrait enfin se demander si le droit belge de la responsabilité civile extra-contractuelle applique éventuellement de façon indirecte une modération de l'étendue de l'indemnisation par le biais des règles régissant le lien de causalité entre l'acte illicite et le dommage.
A cette question la réponse me paraît aussi devoir être négative, parce que le droit belge, en comparaison avec le droit d'autres pays de l'Union européenne, adhère à une théorie du lien de causalité assez large[35]. La jurisprudence fait en effet application de la théorie qui est connue sous le nom de "l'équivalence des conditions", ce qui signifie qu'il y a un lien de causalité entre l'acte illicite et le dommage lorsque sans cet acte, le dommage, tel qu'il s'est présenté *in concreto*, ne se serait pas réalisé[36]. Depuis quelques années la Cour de cassation a apporté cette restriction à cette théorie que la relation causale est rompue lorsqu'il s'interpose une cause juridique propre entre l'acte illicite et le dommage, tel l'accomplissement d'une obligation légale, réglementaire ou contractuelle qui est en soi suffisant pour justifier les dépenses qualifiées comme "préjudice", sauf si cette obligation légale, réglementaire ou contractuelle n'est que secondaire en rapport avec l'obligation de l'auteur de l'acte illicite de faire cesser la situation dommageable qu'il a créée[37]. Dans l'état actuel des choses cette jurisprudence n'est qu'une mince restriction à la théorie de l'équivalence des conditions.

35 Voyez e.a. STORME, M., "Quelques aspects de la causalité en droit des obligations et des assurances", *Bulletin des Assurances*, 1990, p. 444-461.

36 Consultez à propos de cette théorie surtout: DALCQ, R.O., *op.cit.*, *Les Novelles*, *Droit Civil*, V-2, p. 102-106, n°s 2352-2357 et 2363-2365, et p. 125-127, n°s 2426-2432; VAN QUICKENBORNE, M., *De oorzakelijkheid in het recht van de burgerlijke aansprakelijkheid*, Gand, Elsevier, et Bruxelles, Sequoia, 1972, p. 198 e.s., n°s 341 e.s., et p. 233-242, n°s 406-419.

37 Cour de cassation belge, 13 avril 1988, *Pasicrisie belge*, 1988, I, 943, avec conclusion de l'avocat général JANSSENS DE BISTHOVEN; *Jurisprudence de Liège, de Mons et de Bruxelles*, 1988, 764, avec note de HENRY, P.; *Revue critique de jurisprudence belge*, 1988, 631, avec note de GLANSDORFF, F. et DALCQ, C.; Cour de cassation belge, 15 novembre 1990, *Pasicrisie belge*, 1991, I, 282; *Jurisprudence de Liège, de Mons et de Bruxelles*, 1991, 866, avec note de SCHAMPS, G.

VIII Conclusion

14. De ce qui précède il résulte que la doctrine et la jurisprudence belge confirment fortement le principe de la réparation intégrale du dommage. Les exceptions que le droit belge accepte à ce principe sont assez restreintes et peuvent être divisées en deux catégories. D'une part le législateur limite parfois directement le montant de l'indemnisation. Il s'agit là le plus souvent des cas de responsabilité objective, basée sur l'idée de risque (voyez *supra*, n° 8). D'autre part le législateur attribue dans certains cas spécifiques au juge le pouvoir de modérer l'étendue de l'indemnisation. Il s'agit là surtout des cas de responsabilité objective basée sur l'équité (voyez *supra*, n°s 9-11). A la fin de ce rapport j'ai tenté de démontrer qu'il n'y a pas en droit belge une modération indirecte de l'étendue de l'indemnisation par le biais de l'interprétation de la notion de dommage ou l'application des règles du lien de causalité entre l'acte illicite et le dommage (voyez *supra*, n°s 12-13).

Keeping the Floodgates Shut: 'Mitigation' and 'Limitation' of Tort Liability in the English Common Law

W.V.H. Rogers

Terminology

We were in no doubt in the symposium which was the origin of this collection that we were concerned with mechanisms to keep the burden of legal liability within tolerable bounds. However, as is so often the case in comparative law we encountered an immediate minor problem of terminology in the use of the terms 'mitigation' and 'limitation'. A common lawyer who, in pursuit of his research, found these words in a bibliography would probably first be put in mind of two different matters. We normally use mitigation[1] to mean the 'duty' of the plaintiff to minimize his loss by taking whatever steps are reasonable after the initial injury has been suffered (for example, receiving proper medical treatment in a case of personal injury or hiring a substitute in the case of damage to a profit-earning chattel). Though we are familiar with 'limitation' in the sense of a ceiling on damages in certain contexts imposed by statute (for example, the Warsaw Convention) or by contract, to us the primary meaning of the word is probably the legal institution by which claims are barred after the passage of time. While most of the rest of the world uses 'prescription,' we tend to confine that to the *acquisition of rights* by long user, rather than the merely negative process of barring a claim for damages by the passage of time.

It would also be as well to note two important points about the nature and purpose of tort liability, since they would not necessarily apply in all systems.

The first is that inEngland we are fairly tolerant about '*cumul des obligations*,' so that the scope of tort is rather wider than it would be in some jurisdictions. If a passenger on a bus is injured as a result of negligent driving we accept that he has concurrent claims in contract and tort; similarly in the case of professional negligence by a solicitor, so much so in this case that one can sometimes read cases and be uncertain in respect of which head of liability the court is speaking. In the great majority of cases it makes no difference: the plaintiff cannot recover judgment

1 The word is also used, though in a different sense, in the penal context of sentencing. In fact its use in that context is rather closer to the sense in which it was used by some participants in the symposium, since the standard criminal penalty would be reduced by reference to the special circumstances of the case.

J. Spier (ed.), The Limits of Liability, 75-92.

twice over and, at least where the contract concerns services, the content of the duty is the same (though in some contracts of course there is a higher *obligation de resultat* or *de garantie* — for example in sales of goods). Though it has required some bold statutory interpretation the courts have held that where there are cumulative claims based on the tort of negligence and an equivalent contractual duty to take care the apportionment provisions of the Law Reform (Contributory Negligence) Act 1945 apply to the contract claim as much as to the tort one.[2] Where there has been more serious difficulty is (a) over limitation/prescription and (b) over cases where plaintiffs try to outflank established restrictions on implied duties in contract by an appeal to broad principles of the tort of negligence. In the case of limitation, time starts to run in most tort cases when damage has been suffered but in contract at the time of the breach. Furthermore, the Latent Damage Act 1986, which allows the plaintiff to base the running of time from the point when he had actual or constructive knowledge of his claim, is applicable to tort but not to contract.[3] On the other issue, claims have by and large been rebuffed.[4]

The second point is that it is a gross over-simplification, at least from a theoretical point of view, to regard the law of torts as concerned solely with compensation in the sense in which that term is usually understood. Over a limited range of torts (particularly defamation and false arrests and assaults by the police) the plaintiff may recover exemplary damages, the purpose of which is to punish the defendant, to vindicate the law and to deter others, to teach that 'tort does not pay.' In addition, damages for intentional wrongs may be 'aggravated' by the fact that the defendant's behaviour causes the plaintiff mental distress. In theory, these damages are compensatory, but in practice they are hard to separate from the exemplary category. In any event, even when there is no element of punishment or of aggravation it is accepted that damages for some intentional torts may have to be substantial in order to vindicate the interest (e.g. reputation, liberty) protected. One has to accept that 'compensation' for libel is a different animal from compensation for personal injury or property damage. There is also a cluster of rather ill-coordinated categories in which the plaintiff can claim damages on a restitutionary basis with a view to recovering from the defendant the profits of his wrongdoing.[5]

2 But apportionment is inapplicable to strict contract duties and the Law Commission has recommended that this state of affairs should continue.

3 This was why in *Henderson v Merrett Syndicates Ltd* [1994] 3 WLR 761 the "direct names" at Lloyd's wished to establish that their underwriting agents, who clearly owed them a duty in contract, also owed them one in tort. The decision of the House of Lords in this case in favour of concurrent liability reversed what some saw as a drift of decisions towards some doctrine of *non cumul des obligations.* Acceptance of a general doctrine of *non cumul* would cause us some difficulty: for example, an employer's duty to take care for his workers' safety clearly sounds in contract but for a century and more we have got used to thinking of it generally and primarily in terms of tort, a convenient approach since such claims are often coupled with claims for breach of statutory duty, which are clearly not contractual.

4 See e.g. *Tai Hing Cotton Mill v Liu Chong Hing Bank* [1986] AC 80.

5 A full account of these areas may be found in the Law Commission's Consultation paper No 132 (1993).

Still, at the end of the day it has to be admitted that in terms of actions coming before the courts (predominantly for negligence) compensation is the aim.

Is there a principle or goal of full compensation?

The existence of such a principle has been stated in many cases. Perhaps the most famous example is that of Lord Blackburn in *Livingstone v Rawyards Coal Co*[6]:

> '[The measure of damages is] that sum of money which will put the person who has been injured, or who has suffered, in the same position as he would have been in if he had not sustained the wrong for which he is now getting his compensation or reparation.'[7]

It is true that in the context of personal injury there are a number of statements to the effect that compensation should be 'fair' rather than 'full.' However, these are not intended to contradict Lord Blackburn's view — they merely reflect the limitations inherent in an award of monetary damages as compensation, particularly in the context of the non-financial consequences of personal injury.

Formal Limitations upon Levels of Damages

Instances of fixed legislative limits on the quantum of damages are fairly infrequent in English law and tend to be confined to matters where there are international conventions which produce a fair degree of international uniformity, for example in the areas of transport and liability for nuclear installations. We excluded these areas from our deliberations.[8] In line with this general approach was the English decision not to adopt the global limit on claims allowed for by the Product Liability Directive (implemented by the Consumer Protection Act 1987). Individual limits per claimant may, unless set very low and unless the number of claimants is predictable, not offer much protection to the defendant's insurers in assessing the risk; global limits raise formidable problems about disposing of claims which may arise over a very long period of time. There is currently a limited degree of strict civil liability for damage caused by waste under the Control of Pollution Act 1974 and the Environmental Protection Act 1990 and there is again no limitation of liability. Similarly, there is no limit on the damages for the common law strict liability under nuisance and the rule in *Rylands v Fletcher*[9] It remains to be seen what will

6 (1880 5 App Cas 25,39. See also *The Albazero* [1977] AC 774,841.

7 It will be observed that the formula is applicable to both tort and contract; but in the first case the wrong is the commission of the tort, in the second the non-performance of the contract.

8 But some of them are very controversial. For example the Warsaw Convention limits were forged at a time when it was necessary to protect the infant air transport industry. Now many countries and carriers set higher limits.

9 (1868) LR 3 HL 330.

happen if and when we have a general strict liability for pollution damage but that is probably still some way off. However, the quantum of damages is determined in many cases by fairly well defined principles established by case law so there is a good deal of semi-covert limitation in this way. This is discussed below. Though not strictly part of Tort Law since payments come from state funds, the Criminal Injuries Compensation Scheme offers an instance of a recent and highly controversial attempt to move to fixed amounts of compensation. As established in 1964 the Scheme was based upon the levels of common law damages for the injury in question with limitations upon the sums recoverable for financial loss by higher income earners and rather less generous rules on collateral benefits. The Conservative government has attempted to replace this by a fixed tariff system with no compensation for individual financial loss but the new scheme has been declared *ultra vires* by the House of Lords. Although the new scheme has been presented as providing speedier and more efficient compensation there is no doubt that the principal motive of the government is to reduce the growing burden upon public funds.

Ad hoc mitigation?

Apart from cases where damages are reduced on account of the plaintiff's contributory fault, there is no sense in which English law recognizes mitigation in the sense used by Professor Stoll in the International Encyclopaedia of Comparative Law,[10] or Art. 6:109 of the Dutch BW, that is to say of allowing the judge to modify strictly compensatory damages according to the defendant's conduct, the defendant's means or the circumstances of the case. Indeed, while it would be contrary to common sense to say that there are not degrees of negligence, as far as tort liability is concerned there is only one standard and it has been said that for the purposes of the civil law 'gross negligence' is only negligence with the addition of a vituperative epithet. Once the defendant's conduct crosses the line which separates legal fault from non-fault he is liable to make 'full' compensation in so far as that is required by law. Of course, if a particular defendant has no liability insurance or inadequate cover it may be questionable whether the plaintiff will consider the suit worthwhile, but if he does then all the defendant's assets are available to satisfy judgment, subject to the limited protection offered by the insolvency law. In the case of individuals we have generally tended to be rather dismissive of the risk to the uninsured defendant, the 'man of straw.' There have, however, been a number of cases of civil suits against wilful (and hence uninsured) criminal wrongdoers in respect of criminal assaults, attempted homicides and child abuse. In the case of corporate defendants insolvent liquidation is likely to close off any hope of compensation, particularly where the defendant is a 'sacrificial' subsidiary.[11] It is true that in some cases the court may 'lift the veil' of incorporation and go behind the

10 Vol XI, Torts, Chap 8, II and *Supplement* 8-23 (Scandinavian systems).

11 The court has power to restore the company to the register to enable an action to be brought, so the claim may be worth pursuing if there is insurance cover.

corporate form so as to give effect to the realities of the situation but it seems most unlikely that this could be applied in this situation. The Court of Appeal in *Adams v Cape Industries plc*[12] (which arose out of the American asbestosis litigation) remarked that

> 'We do not accept as a matter of law that the court is entitled to lift the corporate veil as against a defendant company which is a member of a corporate group merely because the corporate structure has been used so as to ensure that the legal liability (if any) in respect of particular future activities of the group (and correspondingly the risk of enforcement of that liability) will fall on another member of the group rather than the defendant company. Whether or not this is desirable, the right to use a corporate structure in this manner is inherent in our corporation law.'

Joint and several liability

'Full compensation' is carried to considerable lengths in the case of multiple defendants for if the actions of all of them contribute to one indivisible harm then each is liable for the whole loss, subject to their right of contribution *inter se* under the Civil Liability (Contribution) Act 1978.[13] In a sense this contribution system operates as a modified form of mitigation in that if there are tortfeasors A, B and C, and C has played only a subsidiary or innocent part, the court may apportion the loss, say, 45% to A, 45% to B and only 10% to C. But this only benefits C if A and B are solvent and can satisfy P's judgment: if they are not, he pays P 100%. Though this rule has been modified in some common law jurisdictions it has not so far been challenged in England.

The assessment of damages

Aside from defamation, fraud and certain actions against the police for infringements of personal liberty, civil trial by jury has effectively [14] disappeared in England. This has led to a substantial increase in the enunciation of detailed principles on the assessment of damages and it is no longer necessary that an award should be 'irrational' before the appeal court will interfere with it. Of course a trial judge retains a significant 'margin of discretion' if only because many cases involve

12 [1990] 2 WLR 657. It is true that there are now provisions in the insolvency legislation imposing personal liability on directors where they allow the company to go on trading in circumstances in which they know or ought to know it cannot pay its debts, but this would not be applicable in this situation provided the subsidiary was wound up when major claims began to come in.

13 This is of course overridden by any contractual provisions for indemnity which may exist among the defendants.

14 There is still a discretion to award a jury in all cases but it is now very unlikely to be exercised outside the areas mentioned. See, e.g. *H v Ministry of Defence* [1991] 2 QB 103.

difficult assessments of future contingencies based upon the totality of the evidence, but that margin is very much smaller than would have been allowed to a jury.

If we take first personal injury cases, damages can only be awarded by a court on a lump sum basis, though there is nothing to prevent parties settling on a periodic payments basis and so long as at least as the form of an instalment payment of a lump sum debt is adhered to there are fiscal advantages which can give a built-in inflation protection to the plaintiff and secure some degree of discount for the defendant's insurers.[15] However, such 'structured settlements' are at present negotiated against a background of what a court would award as a lump sum. The English approach to capitalizing a future stream of lost income (multiplicand of net annual loss and multiplier based on — but not equal to — working life expectancy) has in effect tended to assume a rate of return of about 4.5% on capital and there is a widespread view that this is too high to secure reasonable inflation protection.[16] With no special circumstances a male aged 40 at the time of permanent disablement with a net income of £20,000 p.a. might expect an award £275,000 to £300,000 for loss of earnings, though the figure might be pushed up dramatically by medical, nursing and other expenses. For non-pecuniary loss (loss of amenities and pain and suffering are usually lumped together) there is in effect an absolute ceiling for quadriplegia of about £125,000 in today's money, lesser injuries attracting what are deemed to be proportionate sums (e.g. £38,000 to £55,000 for loss of an arm, depending on whether dominant arm etc., £16,000 for total loss of taste and smell). Most claims are of course for much smaller amounts since the plaintiff recovers from the injury. In effect therefore there is a tariff (or perhaps a collection of scenarios) though it is set by the judges not by the legislature and leaves room for a considerable degree of discretion. For example, the standard figures assume a plaintiff with a significant remaining life expectancy during which the effects of the injury will be felt and there would be a reduction in the case of advanced age. Furthermore, some descriptions of injury cover such a range of seriousness that no real tariff can be stated — facial scarring and sterility are good examples.[17] Although it has several times been said that awards for non-pecuniary loss should keep pace with inflation it is probably the case that the real value of awards in the most serious cases has fallen since the 1960s.[18] As to benefits from 'collateral sources' the proceeds of insurance (including a retirement disability pension) or

15 The normal arrangement is that the defendant's liability insurers buy an annuity on the plaintiff's life, payable to them, which they use to satisfy the "debt." This is not treated as income of the plaintiff so he does not have to pay tax on it. Law Commission Report No 224 (1994) proposes various rationalizations of the system, including the ability to make the annuity payments directly to the plaintiff.

16 The Law Commission's Report No 224 (see note 15 above) proposes a system under which the court awarding a lump sum would make the discount by reference to the rate of return on government index-linked bonds at the time. The overall effect would be that damages would rise.

17 The Judicial Studies Board publishes a useful booklet of guidelines distilled from the case law (2nd ed 1994). The range for facial scarring is £750 to £38,000 and for sterility £2,000 to £60,000.

18 The awards made in the 1960s for worst case quadriplegia would probably be at least £175,000 in today's money.

private benevolence are not treated as reducing the plaintiff's loss[19] but sick pay in continuing employment is. Social security benefits are deductible in full for the first five years but the defendant must reimburse the state. Thereafter they are not treated as reducing the loss. The plaintiff is entitled to claim the costs of reasonable private (as opposed to state) medical treatment if he chooses to do so. Damages in fatal accident cases are generally lower than in cases of serious injury for two reasons: first, apart from a token sum of £7,500 (fixed by statute) to the spouse or parent of an unmarried minor, there are no damages for non-pecuniary loss; secondly, the fact that the deceased no longer has to maintain himself means that damages in respect of lost earnings (strictly, loss of support from those earnings) are lower, typically by 25 to 33%. However, these factors are to some extent offset by the fact that no benefit from any collateral source is treated as reducing the loss. Costs follow the event (i.e. loser pays all) as is the normal rule in English litigation but legal aid is now much more restricted than it used to be. The 'access to justice' problem may be an important factor in keeping down the overall cost of tort law in this area. We are about to introduce a conditional fee system for these cases but this will not protect the losing plaintiff from having to pay his opponent's costs.

Comparisons of awards in different jurisdictions are difficult because of the differing methods of compensating loss of earnings (for example, some systems have periodical payments). In the case of non-pecuniary loss awards in England are probably at the higher end of the European scale but they are significantly lower than in the United States.[20] England has so far escaped the 'tort reform' controversy which periodically reappears in the United States, perhaps because the courts have held down awards.[21] Nor has there been a great deal of public discussion of the rationale of damages for non-pecuniary loss, the courts contenting themselves generally with the observation that there is no a priori reason for any particular figure for an injury but that the figure should be broadly defensible on a scale of severity in comparison with those for other injuries.

Lack of space precludes even an outline of the assessment of damages in non-personal injury cases. Suffice it to say that (a) in principle 'full' compensation is again the guiding idea (b) that in cases of damage or destruction of property the possibility of obtaining a repair or a reasonable replacement limits the range of

19 Similarly, the proceeds of insurance are treated as *res inter alios acta* in the case of property loss, a proposition which is consistent with the loss insurer's right of subrogation. However, in a mildly revolutionary (and perhaps not fully considered) decision, the Court of Appeal in *Norwich CC v Harvey* [1989] 1 WLR 1180, wielding the sword of what was fair and reasonable and denying a duty of care, held that a sub-contractor was not liable for fire damage to a building when the main contract (to which he was not a party) provided that the building owner was to take the risk of such damage and insure against it.

20 But there is quite a close similarity with Canada.

21 But there is serious concern over damages payable by hospital trusts and health authorities in respect of negligent treatment. In, for example, cases of negligence in childbirth leading to brain damage there may be very large claims for medical and other expenses. Such defendants act as self-insurers and individually face a comparatively small number of claims. It is therefore much more difficult than it would be for a general liability insurer to absorb the occasional very large claim.

recoverable consequential losses more than in personal injury cases and (c) this area may produce litigation of Homeric proportions. In the Lloyd's litigation some 17,000 "names" are seeking to recover £3 billion of losses. An interim judgment has already been given in one of the actions for £210 million.[22] Though up to date figures are hard to come by, it may be that the total annual payment in England for personal injuries from tort sources does not exceed £700 million.[23]

Controlling the scope liability

In the final analysis very many tort doctrines may be traced back to a function of keeping liability within manageable bounds but the whole of tort law is too wide a canvas. Furthermore, it is a rather variegated canvas — there is not very much in common between negligence and defamation, still less perhaps between negligence and conversion or malicious prosecution. What I propose to do, therefore, is to concentrate on those elements in negligence which have produced most judicial activity in the recent past.[24]

The elements of the tort of negligence are: (1) a 'duty of care' (2) owed by D to P (3) broken by D thereby (4) causing damage to P which is not 'too remote.'

The duty of care

Easily the most important and prominent control device in the modern law is the duty of care. Essentially this may be regarded as operating on two rather different types of issue. With regard to the first, there may be no doubt that the event which has occurred and the type of consequent damage are subject to legal sanction, but there may be an issue whether on the particular facts any damage to the plaintiff was foreseeable. In this sense the concept is really redundant since the problems can be dealt with by, for example, asking whether the defendant had fulfilled the standard of care required by the law or whether the damage is too remote a consequence of the negligence. Much more important is the role of the duty of care in determining the situations in which the law of negligence will operate and the type of damage it will compensate. For example, there is a wide-ranging duty of care with regard to acts, a narrower one with regard to omissions or statements; equally, there is a wide-ranging duty in respect of physical damage and a much

22 The Times February 15, 1995.

23 This is a projection of the estimates of the Pearson Commission in the 1970s: Cmnd 7054 (1978).

24 However, it may be of interest to note one recent decision which "mitigates" the level of damages in defamation. English libel damages are very high by European standards. But in *Rantzen v Mirror Group Newspapers* [1993] 3 WLR 953 the Court of Appeal has declared a willingness to interfere more readily with excessive jury awards. This is because the level of awards has threatened to stultify the guarantee of free speech in the European Convention on Human Rights. The Convention is not incorporated into English law but it is regarded as capable of (a) influencing the interpretation of a statute and (b) shaping the common law.

more restricted one in respect of economic loss. Other systems may reach much the same results by means of concepts which look very different but which on closer examination turn out to be very similar to the duty of care: the *Schutzzweck der Norm* is a good example.[25] Even those legal systems with very broad concepts of recoverable damage are likely to think twice about, for example, economic loss suffered by P as a result of physical damage caused by D to X. As Professor Viney has said with reference to claims in French law for *dommage par ricochet*, 'dans l'ensemble pourtant les tribunaux sont restés jusqu'à présent très réservés à l'égard de ces prétentions, notamment de celles qui émanent d'un créancier, d'un employeur ou d'un associé.'[26] Most of the battles have in fact been fought out in England over the question of economic loss.

The original position in the modern common law was that there were clusters of established duties of care rather than a generalized tort of negligence. The great case of *Donoghue v Stevenson*[27] did more than establish a new duty, that of manufacturer to his ultimate consumers, but the famous formula that one must take reasonable care to avoid injury to one's 'neighbour' was not immediately embraced by the courts as even a guiding principle in novel types of case. Then, in *Anns v Merton London Borough*[28] the House of Lords appeared to commit itself to the so-called two stage test, that is to say, one should ask if there was a sufficient relationship of 'neighbourhood or proximity' between plaintiff and defendant and, if there was, a duty would exist unless there were considerations of policy which ought to negative the duty or restrict its scope, for example as to the class of plaintiffs to whom it applied or the nature of the damage recoverable. Though the *Anns* case was controversial on its own particular facts[29] it is not clear that the court regarded itself as laying down any particularly revolutionary doctrine and the general two stage approach was arguably reconcilable with the law on particular duties as it then stood. However, the case was followed by a period of judicial activism which challenged a number of former restrictions on the scope of tort law. For example, in the period immediately after *Anns* it became possible to argue that a manufacturer could be liable to a remote consumer not merely in respect of damage caused by a product but in respect of (hitherto) essentially contractual matters of quality; that a person who had contracted for the use of property or who had agreed to buy property but had neither ownership nor possession, could sue in respect of damage to the property by a third party while it was in the hands of the owner; and that a plaintiff might recover damages for mental trauma suffered as a result of injury to another even though he had not witnessed the event. A reaction

25 The point is particularly clear where the English "norm" is a statute giving rise to civil liability but which is interpreted to cover only certain types of loss: *Gorris v Scott* (1874) LR 9 Ex 125.

26 "Les Obligations; La responsabilité: Conditions" in Ghestin, *Traité de droit civil*, No. 288.

27 [1932] AC 562, a Scots case in fact but the Scots law of delict and the English law of torts are the same in this area.

28 [1978] AC 728.

29 The case imposed on a local authority exercising powers of inspection of new houses a duty to purchasers in respect of defects. This aspect of the case has since been overruled by the House of Lords: *Murphy v Brentwood District Council* [1991] 1 AC 398.

swiftly followed, prompted perhaps in part by conservatism but probably mainly fuelled by two factors. The first was a concern that the law of negligence would become a sort of cuckoo, colonizing and eventually overwhelming other areas of law. An extreme illustration is provided by *CBS Songs v Amstrad Consumer Electronics*.[30] The copyright legislation makes it wrongful not only to commit a breach of copyright but to 'procure' a breach. Amstrad manufactured twin-head domestic tape recorders which made it very easy to copy commercially recorded tapes on to blanks, though they could also of course be used for perfectly lawful purposes. The word 'procure' in its ordinary meaning has a narrower significance than 'facilitate' and this, combined with the fact that the machines carried a warning about copyright, meant that the statute was not infringed. Nothing daunted, the recording company contended in the alternative that Amstrad was liable in negligence for loss of tape sales. To traditional common law thinking there could hardly be a less apt application of the tort and the argument was dismissed in short order by the House of Lords:[31] infringements of copyright were exclusively a matter for the copyright law, not for the law of negligence. The second factor has been a growing consciousness of the burden of liability insurance, particularly for the professions, and of the inability of the insurance market to cover the risks brought within an expanded tort law. The troubles of Lloyd's would appear to have little or nothing to do with English tort law[32] and there are of course features of the American tort system which mean that the 'liability crisis' there cannot necessarily be translated to England.[33] However, in 1992 Britain's ninth largest insurer, which had dominated the public liability sector of the market and hence had borne the greater part of the burden of claims against local authorities following *Anns v Merton*, had temporarily to suspend payment of claims. I do not say that this exposure was the main or even a major cause of the problem, but there is a climate of unease which would have been unthinkable thirty years ago. Employers' liability insurers recently announced that they were no longer willing to offer the unlimited cover which has hitherto been the norm.[34]

It is not too difficult to catalogue the retreats which have taken place in particular areas. What is more difficult is to give a coherent account of the current general approach to the determination of duty. A tenable view collected from the nineteen

30 [1988] AC 1013.

31 Lord Templeman said: "The pleading assumes that we are all neighbours now, Pharisees and good Samaritans alike, that foreseeability is a reflection of hindsight and that for every mischance in an accident-prone world someone solvent must be liable in damages."

32 Though the huge current suits arising out of these troubles of course involve claims for negligence against those who managed the various syndicates. For the dimensions of the litigation see text to note 22 above.

33 In any event, there seems to be a good deal of controversy over how far that crisis has been caused by changes in tort law or litigation and how far by factors in the insurance market (not to mention reckless coverage of risks and assessment of premiums).

34 Standard cover will now be £10 million per occurrence. Premium income between 1989 and 1993 was only 67% of claims.

or so cases in which the House of Lords[35] has considered the duty of care since 1978 would assert that there are no less than four separate elements in the matter: (a) foreseeability (b) proximity (c) fairness (d) policy. At the opposite extreme there is a view that the only formal issue is one of 'proximity' but in effect this is not a test but a coded statement of the conclusion that there should be no duty.[36] Since the common law is not made by treating the words of an individual judge (or even a unanimous judgment) as if they had the force of a statute it would be pointless to search for a single judgment which encapsulates the 'rule.' In any event a rule extracted from these cases would be liable to give a misleading impression of the law as it is in practice by making it look a great deal more complicated than it actually is. The great majority of negligence claims involve physical damage to person or property directly caused by the negligent act[37] of the defendant and with comparatively isolated exceptions[38] no more is in fact required to establish a duty than reasonable foreseeability of harm to the plaintiff.[39] This simple proposition has tended to be obscured in the fog of modern discussions about duty. The problems arise in respect of omissions and other types of damage, particularly economic loss. For this purpose 'proximity' should be understood as a highly relative concept, requiring a much closer relationship between plaintiff and defendant for the recovery of economic loss than is necessary in cases of physical damage. For example, it is obviously highly foreseeable that company accounts will be relied on by investors in and creditors of the company, but no duty of care is owed by the auditors to them as individuals when publishing the accounts because, in the view of the courts, the burden of liability upon the auditors would be too great for a

35 Some of the cases are decisions of the Privy Council on appeal from other jurisdictions. But in terms of personnel it is the same court as the House of Lords.

36 An example of this approach is the judgment of the majority of the High Court of Australia in *Gala v Preston* (1990) 100 ALR 29 denying "proximity" and hence any duty between participants in a criminal use of a motor vehicle.

37 Including, of course, those cases of what superficially appear to be omissions but which are in fact negative elements in a course of conduct -- failing to apply the brakes, failing to keep up with the risk literature, failing to do maintenance and so on.

38 Of which the situation in *Gala v Preston*, note 36 above, is of course one. It would be curious if one safeblower owed a duty of care to his fellow in handling the gelignite while carrying out the "job." In practice the most likely reason for refusing to find a duty of care in respect of physical damage is that it would disturb the allocation of contractual risks in a complex commercial arrangement. See, e.g. *Norwich CC v Harvey* [1989] 1 WLR 828 (building contract, sub-contractor, fire insurance) and *Marc Rich & Co AG v Bishop Rock Marine Co Ltd* [1994] 1 WLR 1071 (advice by marine classification society, loss of cargo, effect of carriage of goods by sea regime).

39 Psychiatric trauma caused by fear for one's own safety is generally regarded in all respects like any other physical damage (though see note 66 below). But psychiatric trauma caused by fear for the safety of others raises more complicated issues. The law has recently been recast in *Alcock v Chief Constable of S Yorks* [1992] 1 AC 310. Very broadly, the courts require (1) a sufficiently close relationship between the plaintiff and the direct victim, foreseeability of psychiatric injury to the plaintiff being presumed in the case of close relations such as parent and child but requiring positive evidence in the case of more remote relationships; (2) sufficient proximity in time and place to the event or its "immediate aftermath"; and (3) the suffering of the mental trauma as a result of witnessing the event or its aftermath and not by being told of it by third parties.

practical system of law,[40] though the Fifth Company Law Directive will no doubt force us to think again about this. We therefore say that proximity exists between a canning company which produces one poisoned can of salmon and any person (even perhaps on another continent) who suffers harm by consuming it[41]; but it will not exist between auditors and half a dozen banks known to the auditors to be lending money to the audited company. Similarly, there is proximity between the manufacturer of a heating boiler and the ultimate user in so far as defects in the boiler cause a fire which burns down the user's property but not in respect of defects in the boiler which cause it not to work efficiently. It is not, however, possible to lay down any absolute rule. If auditors were to respond to a specific enquiry from an investor that would certainly create a sufficiently proximate relationship and the law may go slightly further[42]; a valuer employed by a mortgage lender would normally owe a duty to the borrower/buyer (but not to his successors in title) when he is aware that his report on the condition of the property may be shown to the latter[43]; and in a building project there may be circumstances in which proximity may exist between the building owner and sub-contractors as regards matters of quality.[44] Such cases are commonly said to rest upon 'undertaking and reliance,' an expression with a strong contractual flavour and thereby barely concealing the fact that what is being done is to modify at least the effects, if not the form, of strict contractual requirements of consideration and privity.[45] One group of cases cannot even be explained on the basis of undertaking and reliance. A testator instructs a solicitor to make a will benefiting P. The solicitor makes some error which invalidates the gift to P but the testator dies before it is discovered.

40 *Caparo Industries p.l.c. v. Dickman* [1990] 2 A.C. 605. A duty is of course owed (by contract) to the audited company but if it has been overvalued (the common case) it has not generally suffered loss. The potential liability of auditors on a simple foreseeability basis is very great and the comparatively small number of transactions involved makes it difficult to absorb risks by generally raising prices. The English press in November 1990 reported that US accountancy firms faced claims totalling $3 billion compensatory damages from banking authorities as a result of the savings and loans collapse. It does not, of course follow that all or any of these did or will succeed. But "above cover" damages awards were said to have made a contribution to the Chapter XI bankruptcy of Laventhol & Howarth.

41 This situation might of course now be caught by the strict liability under the Product Liability Directive but the common law liability in negligence continues to exist in parallel.

42 A duty of care could exist if a financial statement were prepared for an identifiable person or perhaps if the audited accounts were confirmed to such a person if it could be said that the auditor must have intended him to act on them: *Morgan Crucible Co plc v Hill Samuel Bank Ltd* [1991] Ch 295; *Galoo Ltd v Bright Grahame Murray* [1995] 1 All ER 16.

43 *Smith v Eric S Bush* [1990] 1 AC 831.

44 This is the controversial case of *Junior Books v Veitchi* [1983] 1 AC 520, which looked as if it would revolutionize the law of economic loss but has been largely explained away. It may even depend upon the sub-contractor's having been a nominated sub-contractor, i.e. one chosen by the building owner, not the main contractor.

45 In some cases rather artificial "collateral contracts" have been found : *Shanklin Pier v Detel Products* [1951] 2 KB 854. Though there are many exceptions (mainly statutory) to the doctrine of privity of contract, the English common law has not, unlike its transatlantic cousin, adopted a general theory of enforceability by an intended third party beneficiary. Nor has it taken the notion of "promissory estoppel" as a substitute for consideration so far as to allow it to be used as a cause of action (cf. Restatement of Contracts 2d s.90).

Alternatively, instructions for a will are given but the solicitor proceeds in such a dilatory fashion that the intending testator dies before it can be executed. The solicitor is in breach of contract to the testator but it is assumed that the estate has suffered only nominal damage. The cases, recently affirmed by a bare majority of the House of Lords,[46] allow P to sue in tort even though P might have been unaware of the proposed gift, partly, it seems, because an 'assumption of responsibility' can in some circumstances give rise to a liability in tort without the element of reliance by the plaintiff but also because otherwise a professional man in this context could breach his duty to his client with comparative impunity. It remains to be seen how far this will be confined to the situation of solicitor/client/beneficiary — the dissenting minority thought it could not. Of course, there is no risk of wide-ranging liability. As was said in one of the cases, the solicitor's contemplation of the beneficiary is 'nominate and direct.'

There are, however, situations in which certainty is regarded as so important a requirement that the courts are unwilling to adopt a flexible approach. That is the case in England with the situation where P suffers economic loss as a result of damage to X's property. One type of case is that where D causes damage to a public utility supply belonging to X and P then suffers loss of production because this facility is not available. No doubt this type of case needs to be handled with great care because of the danger of wide-ranging and crushing liability, but in some situations this risk is absent and a well-defined loss is simply 'transferred' from X to P. This is the case, for example, where P agrees to buy goods from X and they are despatched to P on terms that they become P's property only on arrival and payment but P is to bear the risk in them during transit.[47] The House of Lords in *Leigh & Sillavan v Aliakmon Shipping*[48] categorically rejected a tort claim by P against D, the carrier, since P had neither ownership nor possession when the damage was done. Of course, this is a rather unusual situation because in an international sale transaction of this nature, notwithstanding the normal rule of privity, the rights and duties of the seller (X) are transferred to the buyer (P)[49] and it was only because of the rather unusual facts of the *Aliakmon* case that this did not happen.[50] A powerful motive for excluding the law of tort in this case was clearly to prevent tort subverting the well-understood and established regime of carriage by sea[51]but the same answer would be given by an English court even

46 *White v Jones*, [1995]/ A11 ER 691 (the facts are practically identical to the German *Testamentfall* case (NJW 1965, 1955)).

47 The case of the solicitor and the disappointed beneficiary (above) probably cannot be regarded as a case of transferred loss.

48 [1986] AC 785.

49 Formerly under the Bills of Lading Act 1855, now under the carriage of Goods by Sea Act 1992.

50 On the facts, X could have sued and P might have taken an assignment of X's rights. But a rule depending on X's cooperation is not very satisfactory from P's point of view. It is always possible in theory to outflank rules on economic loss by contractual allocation of risks but (a) this may cut across other interests of the parties and (b) the real parties in a case of this type are likely to be the buyer's loss insurers and the carrier's liability insurers.

51 See also the *Marc Rich* case, note 38 above.

where there was no such factor — for example on facts such as those in the Canadian Supreme Court decision in *CNR v Norsk Pacific*[52] where the P railway suffered loss of business as a result of the damage to X's bridge by D's negligence. A majority (three) of the majority (four) of the court rejected the English rule in favour of allowing a claim to a narrow class of 'proximate' persons with 'relational' interests. The minority (three) would have adhered to the English rule, partly on the grounds of certainty, partly because of the ability of a person in CNR's position to assess his own risks and seek alternative protection.

To return to the general question of determining whether a duty should exist, there are cases in which there is a close relationship between the parties but there are still factors which cast doubt upon the good sense of imposing tort liability (indeed, the *Aliakmon* case discussed above falls under this head). Though it is perhaps heretical to say so, I suggest that separate elements of what is fair and reasonable and 'policy' are really unnecessary because policy is surely subsumed in what is fair and reasonable. Possibly the heading 'policy' might be slightly more apt to describe the situation where there is some public interest in denying a duty but it seems more a question of emphasis than of substance. The relationship between 'fairness/policy' and proximity is illustrated by a group of cases concerning the police. In *Hill v Chief Constable of West Yorkshire*[53] a claim against the police by the estate of a victim of a mass-murderer was dismissed on the ground of lack of proximity, the plaintiff being merely a member of a large undifferentiated class of victims and the defendants being guilty of what was essentially an omission in failing to prevent wilful injury by a third party, liability for which generally requires some special relationship between the defendant and either the victim or the wrongdoer. Similarly, the police are not civilly liable to a person injured by their failure to take effective action against a road hazard which they come across.[54] However, in *Osman v Ferguson*[55] the claim concerned failure to take effective steps against a person whose identity was known and who, after a campaign of harassment against them, finally murdered P's father and seriously injured P. Since P had been the target of the campaign and the father had made repeated complaints to the police it would have been difficult to say there was no proximity, unless that word has severed all connexion with its ordinary, non-legal meaning. However, the Court of Appeal fell back on an argument which had been adverted to in *Hill's* case but had there been considered unnecessary as a basis for the decision: that it would be against the public interest to impose upon the police liability for failures in investigating crimes and apprehending offenders. This view was taken for a number of reasons, that the threat of litigation might encourage a 'looking over the shoulder' attitude within the force, that resources might thereby be diverted from the effective investigation of crime and that claims would be brought (as was to some extent true in the *Hill* case) not to seek compensation but

52 (1992) 91 DLR (4th) 289.
53 [1989] AC 53.
54 *Ancell v McDermott* [1993] 3 All ER 355.
55 [1993] 3 All ER 344.

to obtain a full and expensive investigation of police efficiency for which the civil trial process was not suitable.

A great deal more could be said about the duty of care, especially in the context of claims against public officials and services, where further complications arise because of the interplay with judicial review and the nature of discretions and powers but space precludes pursuing this. The reader who has examined the "duty of care issue" may, however, ask whether all this subtlety, these fine shifts of emphasis and degree are of much practical importance.[56] At one level, the answer is 'no'. Expressions like 'proximity' and 'foreseeability' are so vague that they give the court[57] a good deal of leeway in coming to a decision on the question of duty. Further, it might not have been too difficult to come to exactly the same result in many of the subsequent cases via the two-stage approach as set out in *Anns*. In the police cases, for example, the defendant had failed to protect the plaintiffs against wilful wrongdoing by a third party. Since the law has always shown great reluctance to impose a positive duty to protect strangers, was not that clear and consistent evidence of 'considerations which ought to negative' the duty claimed by the plaintiff? There was no reason to believe, on the basis of *Anns* itself that it was intended to throw over all general, existing, restrictive rules in the area of the duty of care, for these considerations might be present in whole ranges of cases and were not necessarily 'on the line' in every case.[58] However, there is more than a verbal quibble involved in the different approaches, for they reflect different trends in the law of negligence. Whatever *Anns* actually meant it was thought to put great emphasis on the close connection between foreseeability and the prima facie duty and it therefore pointed towards an expanding concept of liability, tolerant of exceptions, but requiring those exceptions to be justified by argument rather than by mere longevity. There appeared to be a mild version of the 'permanent revolution' which Thatcherism has imposed on many of our public institutions. Now that the tide has turned, the prevailing attitude is that expressed by Brennan J in the High Court of Australia and approved by several members of the House of Lords:[59]

> 'It is preferable in my view, that the law should develop novel categories of negligence incrementally and by analogy with established categories, rather than by a massive extension of a prima facie duty of care restrained only by indefinable "considerations which ought to negative, or to reduce or limit the scope of the duty or the class of persons to whom it is owed."'

56 Part of this paragraph is a slightly modified version of Rogers, *The Law of Tort*, 2nd ed (1994).

57 The appellate court is quite ready to interfere on the question of duty, which is regarded as a question of law.

58 Indeed, Lord Wilberforce, who delivered the leading judgment in *Anns*, also delivered much the most cautious judgment (subsequently approved by the House of Lords in *Alcock*) in a psychiatric trauma case, *McLoughlin v O' Brian* [1983] 1 AC 410, emphasizing the need for a gradual and incremental approach to the extension of liability.

59 *Sutherland Shire Council v Heyman* (1985) 60 ALR 1,43.

Other control devices in the substantive law

We would probably not readily think of the standard of care required by the law as a control device but of course it is. What may appear on the surface as a uniform objective standard may conceal practical variations. For example, it is questionable how far the implementation of the Product Liability Directive has actually altered the potential burden of liability in England given the courts' readiness to infer negligence from a defect in a product which appears to be associated with manufacture. Arguably the common law was already a quasi- strict liability system. By contrast, in the context of professional negligence there appears to be a quite wide allowance for differences of opinion and mistaken decisions.[60]

Causation in the 'factual' sense (condition *sine qua non*) is hardly worthy of the title of mitigating or limiting device since some causal connexion between the defendant's act and the plaintiff's loss has so far been regarded as an inescapable element of a law of tort. However, one has to recognize that notions which worked well enough with the comparatively simple physical accident of traditional tort law are under great strain with the aetiology of disease or, even where this is not in doubt, with tracing the damage to the conduct of a defendant where the plaintiff is a victim of, say, a generic drug administered to a parent[61] or of chronic environmental pollution. Recent decisions of the House of Lords on proof of causation[62] have very substantially limited the possibility of success in one type of medical negligence claim. Suppose P is injured in a fall (no-one's fault) and taken to hospital, where the proper treatment is not administered. Had it been administered, the evidence is that there would have been a 25% chance of full recovery (i.e. that 25% of patients in his category recover). P has a continuing disability. Does P recover nothing because he has failed to prove to the civil standard (a balance of probabilities) that but for the defendant's negligence he would have recovered? Or does he recover damages for his disability, discounted by the risk that he would not have recovered anyway (presumably 25% of the valuation of his loss)? According to the House of Lords the answer is the former. It seems, however, that if the plaintiff shows that it is more likely than not that the treatment would have succeeded he recovers full damages and the possibly substantial chance that in his case it would have failed is ignored. In effect, the loss of the chance of recovery is not accepted as legal damage (though loss of a chance is well established as a basis of damages in contract) but once the threshold of probability is passed the causation of

60 Take for example the question of what information should be given to a patient consenting to treatment. While holding to the notion of patient autonomy in saying that an adult of sound mind is entitled to a proper answer to a specific question, the courts have shown great deference to the views of the profession (which may of course contain different schools of thought) on what should be volunteered.

61 For alternative views of the universe in this context see *Sindell v Abbott Laboratories* 607 P 2d 924 (1980) and the Dutch *DES case* RvaW 1992, 219.

62 *Hotson v E Berks AHA* [1987] AC 750; *Wilsher v Essex AHA* [1988] AC 1074.

damage is treated as being fully established[63] even though there may be a significant chance that it would have occurred anyway.[64]

Because causation is established in the mechanical sense it is not necessarily adequate — the damage suffered may be too remote a consequence of the defendant's negligence. While this undoubtedly plays a significant role in containing liability it has not figured very prominently in the case law in recent years, perhaps because solutions which are reached in other systems by reference to the adequacy of causation tend to be handled by reference to the somewhat overloaded concept of duty of care. In most cases the question is whether the injury suffered by the plaintiff would have been reasonably foreseeable to a reasonable person,[65] but the application of this tends to favour the plaintiff for two reasons. First, there is a tendency to describe the risk broadly, so that the precise nature of the injury or its manner of occurrence does not have to be foreseeable. Secondly, provided some injury was foreseeable, the defendant is liable even though a different and more serious injury occurs which was not reasonably foreseeable if it is produced by some physical weakness of the plaintiff[66] — the tortfeasor takes his victim as he finds him.[67] Judging by the reported case law (which may of course not be a wholly reliable guide) it seems that it is rare for a personal injury plaintiff to fail on the basis of remoteness. However, it would be wrong to think that remoteness is governed by an unqualified test of foreseeability. In the case of intervening acts or events there is a tendency to speak in the metaphorical language of a "chain" of causation which may be 'broken.' The case law is certainly not wholly consistent (particularly with regard to the acts of third parties)[68] but it is probably fair to say that the chain of causation will readily be regarded as broken by the wilful acts of

63 But once liability has been established a discounted approach is taken to contingencies (what would have happened to the plaintiff before or after the trial had he not been injured and what will now happen to him in the future) in the assessment of damages. The trial judge in *Hotson* had approached the matter as one of quantification.

64 As Professor Dobbs points out in his paper, it is not possible to say whether this approach or a uniform "damages for loss of the chance" rule favours defendants (in effect insurers) as a group. It is, however, certain that to combine the present rule of non-discounted recovery where causation is more probable than not with discounted damages for loss of the chance where this threshold is not crossed would increase the overall cost of liability.

65 *The Wagon Mound (No 1)* [1961] AC 388.

66 This is true even in the case of psychiatric damage. If P is involved in a minor accident caused by D in which some physical injury was foreseeable but does not occur, P can recover damages for psychiatric trauma (triggering a recurrence of "ME" in the particular case) which he suffers because of his "eggshell personality." *Page v Smith* [1995] 2 All ER 136

67 *Smith v Leech Brain & Co Ltd* [1962] 2 QB 405 (foreseeable burn triggering cancer). In view of *Liesbosch Dredger v SS Edison* [1933] AC 449 it cannot be said that this principle applies so fully to the economic consequences of physical damage.

68 Some confusion is also introduced by the fact that some cases are couched in terms of duty of care. Hence in *Lamb v Camden LBC* [1981] 1 QB 625, where the plaintiff's house had been rendered uninhabitable by the defendant's negligence and further damage was done by the entry of squatters, the discussion was in terms of remoteness; whereas in *Smith v Littlewoods* [1987] AC 241, where the defendant's empty building became a target of vandals, who caused a fire which spread to the plaintiff's property, the House of Lords saw the case in terms of duty of care or of breach of duty.

third parties but not by the act of the plaintiff. The reason no doubt is that in the latter case there is a power to reduce damages on account of the plaintiff's fault under the Law Reform (Contributory Negligence) Act 1945, whereas in the former the defendant's chances of recovering a contribution from the wilful wrongdoer are likely to be slim. It is not easy to find cases which decisively say that a particular consequence was foreseeable and yet there is no adequate chain of causation.[69] A rare example is *Galoo Ltd v Bright Grahame Murray*[70] where a company failed in a claim against its auditors for negligence in failing to discover the company's insolvent situation so that it continued to trade and built up bigger losses than would otherwise have been the case. However, as is so often the case, perhaps the application of the law differs from one type of loss to another. If a doctor were retained to advise a patient on an allergic reaction and negligently failed to discover that it was attributable to his work environment, would it be held that the patient's continuing to work at the job was the sole cause of further illness?

69 No doubt because what is reasonably foreseeable is a somewhat elastic concept.

70 [1995] 1 All ER 16. There was a claim for breach of contract but it was assumed that for this purpose causation was the same in contract and in tort.

How to keep liability within reasonable limits? A brief outline of Dutch law

*J. Spier**

1 Background in formation about Dutch liability law[1]

a. a shift from fault liability to strict liability
Traditionally, Dutch tort law has mainly been based on fault liability (art. 1401 old BW), albeit with some exceptions of marginal importance, such as liability for collapsing premises (art. 1405) and for animals (art. 1404 old BW).

Dutch tort law, however, has also included various strict liabilities, for instance liability levied against parents and employers for acts committed by children and by employees (art. 1403 paras 2 and 3 old BW), respectively. Similar provisions can also be found in the present Code (art. 6:169 and 6:170 BW), along with strict liability for acts committed by non-servants (art. 6:171 BW) and by agents (art. 6:172 BW).

The new Civil Code (which came into force on January 1, 1992) introduces a new strict liability, involving defective movables (art. 6:173 BW). As of February 1, 1995, the new Code also provides for strict liability for dangerous substances (art. 6:175 BW), boreholes (art. 6:177 BW), and dumping sites (art. 6:176 BW).[2]

The EC directive on product liability has, of course, been implemented into Dutch law (art. 6:185 ff BW).[3] The present article, however, is devoted solely to personal injury and damage to property suffered by persons identified as "consumers". In the case of damage incurred by companies, liability must be based on fault. In that event, it is likely that the manufacturer will have to prove:

* Professor of private law, Tilburg University.
1 See also C. von Bar (E.H. Hondius and C.C. van Dam), Deliktsrecht in Europa, Landesberichte Niederlande/Norwegen.
2 See for liability for dangerous substances under the present Code J. Spier and C.H.W.M. Sterk, Rope-Dancing Dutch Tort Law (Geneva 1993), pp 14 ff.
3 See D. and C. Campbell, International Product Liability Law, pp 373 ff.

J. Spier (ed.), The Limits of Liability, 93-126.

- that the defect did not yet exist at the time the product was put into circulation; and
- that the product was not used in a normal way.[4]

b. quasi strict liability

Liability for labour accidents is becoming increasingly important. It is governed by art. 7A:1638x BW.[5] In addition to art. 1638x BW, employees can base a claim on the articles mentioned above.

Art. 7A:1638x requires that employers take all appropriate measures so as to ensure the safety of employees. Yet, the injured employee must, nevertheless, prove the employer to be at fault. The Supreme Court construed this article as being a type of strict liability. The employer must be able to demonstrate that measures have been taken to ensure the safety of its employees and that potential dangers to which its employees may be exposed have been investigated. The mere fact that the employer has taken the safety measures adopted by similar companies does not immunize him from liability. Moreover, the employer must also assume that employees will make mistakes and will not always take the necessary precautions.[6]

Diseases like "asbestosis" and "mesothelioma" have attracted a lot of attention causing this subject area to gain some importance. The amount of the awards at stake can often be considerable.

Major developments have taken place in the law regarding motor vehicle accidents. The Supreme Court has rendered a number of judgements securing solid protection for injured persons who were not passengers in the motor vehicle.[7] Although, on a macro-scale, the amount of the awards in question are high, it does not seem useful to dwell upon this issue. Liability for motor accidents is covered by a mandatory insurance regime. The premiums are clearly on the rise.[8] Yet, one has

4 Whether or not such a rule applies depends on the interpretation of Hoge Raad 24-12-1993, NJ 1994, 214. It remains debatable whether it only pertains to damage suffered by "consumers" or has a more general application. I am inclined to believe that one would be better advised to adhere to the latter view. See for more details Onrechtmatige Daad VIII (Michiels van Kessenich-Hoogendam), nrs 179 ff.

5 This article has not yet been changed. The new version (art. 7:652) -still before Parliament- will not be significantly different from the present one.

6 See for more details J. Spier, A&V 1993/2, pp 33 ff. An advisory committee, chaired by Prof. de Ru, delivered an opinion on this topic (Van Keurslijf naar keurmerk). Briefly, the opinion of the committee is that the new provision provides sufficiently adequate protection from the perspective of civil law.

7 See e.g. HR 1-6-1990, NJ 1991,720 CJHB, HR 31-5-1991, NJ 1991,721 CJHB, HR 28-2-1992, NJ 1993,566 CJHB, HR 24-12-1993, NJ 1995, 236 CJHB.

8 Despite the "loi Badinter", French premiums are still fairly moderate. See A. Tunc, Towards a European Civil Code, p. 332.

to bear in mind that these decisions only apply to the damage suffered by the injured party and not to the damage suffered by the subrogated insurer.[9]

c. liability for improper services

Suing persons or organisations who rendered services is becoming popular. This type of liability targets physicians[10], notaries public[11], attorneys[12], tax consultants[13], auditors[14], banks[15], and the like. Receivers have also been a new target, but this may well be an ephemeron since the Supreme Court appears disinclined to decide in favour of the plaintiffs in these cases.[16]

In cases where physicians, attorneys, and notaries public are implicated, the plaintiff generally is the contractual counterpart. This may also be true for auditors and banks, though it may be less obvious. When the latter are implicated, it will often be third parties who have suffered damages as a result of having relied upon information provided by those auditors and banks. Needless to say, the amounts involved can often be substantial. It is becoming apparent that insurers are increasingly reluctant to provide adequate insurance coverage at a reasonable price.[17]

The standard of care applicable to physicians, attorneys, and the like is that of a reasonable and reasonably capable colleague.[18]

d. liability for damage to the environment

As of January 1, 1995, the provincial executive can demand, in situations where there is "serious contamination", a cleaning order against the person who caused

9 HR 28-2-1992, NJ 1993,566 CJHB. See for a slightly different approach - in relation to the liability of a hospital - HR 13-1-1995, RvdW 1995,31.

10 See e.g. HR 25-9-1992, NJ 1992,751, HR 8-7-1992, NJ 1992,714, HR 18-2-1994, NJ 1994, 368, Rb. Arnhem 10-9-1992, NJ 1993,278 and for more details Onrechtmatige Daad VIII, nrs 32 ff. On April 1, 1995, new provisions came into effect, notably art. 7:446 ff BW. It is apparent that they are in line with existing case law.

11 See for more details T.R. Hidma, WPNR 6120 (1994) pp 29 ff, G.J. Lekkerkerker, WPNR 6176 and -e.g.- HR 20-1-1989, NJ 1989,766 EAAL, HR 19-5-1989, NJ 1990,54 EAAL, HR 28-9-1990, NJ 1991,473 EAAL, HR 7-12-1990, NJ 1991,474 EAAL, HR 25-1-1991, NJ 1992,97 EAAL, HR 27-3-1992, NJ 1993,188 EAAL, HR 18-12-1992, NJ 1994,91 EAAL, HR 31-12-1993, NJ 1994, 275, HR 23-12-1994, RvdW 1995, 10/11 and Hof 's-Hertogenbosch 19-4-1994, NJ 1995, 68. In addition, see for more details Onrechtmatige Daad VIII, nrs 103 ff.

12 See e.g. HR 29-11-1991, NJ 1992,808 CJHB, Rb. Rotterdam 13-8-1993, A&V 1994, pp 55 ff JS and for more details Onrechtmatige Daad VIII, nrs 9 ff.

13 See e.g. HR 3-4-1992, NJ 1992,396 and for more details Onrechtmatige Daad VIII, nrs 31g ff.

14 Hof 's-Gravenhage 19-5-1992, NJ 1993,436 and for more details Onrechtmatige Daad VIII, nrs 5 ff

15 See e.g. HR 10-12-1993, NJ 1994, 667 PS, HR 2-12-1994, RvdW 1994, 263 and W.J. Slagter, A&V 1995 pp 30 ff, Hof Amsterdam 27-5-1993, NJ 1993,682, Rb. Leeuwarden 20-8-1987, NJ 1992,803 and for more details Onrechtmatige Daad VIII, nrs 200 ff.

16 HR 24-2-1995, RvdW 1995, 43 and thereabout J. Spier, A&V 1995/3, pp 64 ff.

17 See F.H.A. Arisz, preadvies NJV 1987 pp 23 ff and J.G.C. Kamphuisen, idem, pp 76 ff and T. Hartlief, A&V 1994, p. 144.

18 See e.g. HR 9-11-1990, NJ 1991,26 and HR 26-4-1991, NJ 1991,455.

the pollution or against the owner or the long-term lessor of the relevant site (art. 43 Wet bodembescherming). The adoption of this executive power met with fierce resistance from legal doctrine.[19] Since this law falls within the realm of administrative law[20], the addressee of such an order can appeal to the administrative court which must, of course, apply the rules of administrative law. These rules are guided by the general principles of good administration (algemene beginselen van behoorlijk bestuur), and more specifically by the requirement of proportionality between the order and the interest of the addressee. The Council of State (which also happens to be the Supreme Administrative Court) has indicated, however, that - under specific cirumstances - it is probable that the government may only be allowed to demand a cleaning order if it provides adequate compensation to the owner.[21] I am inclined to believe that this principle could be a source of inspiration for civil law. See hereunder sub II E.

e. government liability

Government liability is expanding. This observation applies to liability based on tort as well as to liability based on lawful acts. While I do not propose to discuss this issue here, I should like to point out that the government (or more precisely the legislator) could enact specific legislation to keep its own liability within reasonable limits. As long as it refrains from doing so, one must assume that government liability is apparently not (yet) considered to be undesirable. Unlike other defendants, one can hardly argue that the government is *unable* to pay damages.

f. joint and several liability

The issue of joint and several liability is also attaining some prominence. Under the present Code, joint and several liability is triggered by three different situations:

* if two or more persons are obliged to compensate the same damage (art. 6:102 BW);
* if a member of a group of persons unlawfully causes damage and if the risk of causing this damage should have prevented these persons from engaging in their collective conduct (art. 6:166 BW);
* when damage has resulted from two or more events for each of which a different person is liable, and it has been determined that the damage has arisen from at least one of these events. In such a case, the defendant may prove that the damage is not the result of the event for which he himself is liable (art. 6:99 BW).

It is this third scenario that might become particularly significant in joint and several liability (see appendix under 2).

19 See e.g. P. Kuipers, WPNR 6063, p. 690 and J. Spier, A&V 1993, p. 40 and 1994, p. 44.

20 See for details H.E. Uniken Venema, TVVS 1995, pp 6 ff and E.C.M. Schippers, Handboek Milieuaansprakelijkheid D-1200.

21 See for more details J. Spier, A&V 1994, p. 44.

2 The changing scene of liability law

As already highlighted above, litigation in liability cases is on the increase, and the amounts of the awards are continually rising. The issue is significant with regard to ceilings.

The need to maintain liability law as such and liability awards in particular within reasonable limits is linked to the question of whether liability should be fault-based or not. A severe liability law is unlikely to cause serious difficulties if plaintiffs are reluctant to sue tortfeasors. This is especially the case if the amounts claimed remain within reasonable limits. It is feasible that plaintiffs' reluctance is the reason why the limits of liability law have not yet been explored in many countries, unlike in the US where the limits are well known.[22] Yet, one should be careful in interpreting statistics, even more so if they are not abundantly available.[23]

What is the reason behind the increase in litigation and in the awards claimed? It is difficult to give a convincing answer to this question because information about this topic is essentially rather sparse.[24] Nonetheless, it appears to me that the answer is not particularly obscure.

Victims are no longer prepared to absorb their loss. This seems to reflect a change in attitude. Injured parties appear to be less reluctant to sue. The relationship between parties and the feeling that it is "not done" to sue others seem no longer to be serious (moral) obstacles. It is not unlikely that this development is influenced by television and newspapers which devote more and more attention to lawsuits and legal fiction. Information about the "American crisis" and/or American case-law generates, in the Netherlands and elsewhere, the impression that considerable awards can easily be recovered. That this information is often misunderstood is not recognized, since the American situation cannot be compared to that existing in the Netherlands, in that, for example, the Dutch system does not have juries, punitive damages, contingency fees, nor exaggerated awards for pain and suffering.[25]

22 See for details about US: Report of the tort policy working group on the causes, extent and policy implications of the current crisis in insurance availability and affordability (1986) and the update of 1987. The commission suggests various causes for the crisis such as the movement towards no-fault liability, the undermining of causation, the explosive growth in damage awards and excessive transaction costs (pp 30 ff).

23 See for more details B.S. Markesinis, Litigation-Mania in England, Germany and the USA: Are We So Different?, Cambridge Law Journal 49(2), July 1990, pp 233-276. Dutch statistics are not (yet) available. O.A. Haazen and I hope to be able to provide them in our prelimary report for the Nederlandse Juristen Vereniging 1996.

24 See, to a large extent along the same lines, Arisz, op. cit., pp 12 ff.

25 However, the awards are going up. Until mid-1992, the more general view was that an amount of Dfl 150.000 was about the maximum one could recover. If my understanding of HR 8-7-1992, NJ 1992, 714 is correct, we have to reckon with at least a doubling of the claims, if not more. Attorneys specialized in personal injury claims confirm this trend for most (serious) cases of personal injury. The awards for pain and suffering are significantly different in the various EC

For companies, the economic situation is an important factor. The emphasis tends to be on the short term with the costs being relayed to others (counterparts or third "parties") to the greatest extent possible.

Needless to say, such developments will be reinforced by a trend towards no-fault liability or the undermining of the proof of causation.[26]

3 A Dutch tort crisis?

It is apparent from the arguments above that Dutch tort law is in a development phase. A number of new types of liability have been created - each one of them a type of strict liability. Recently, a new - and far-reaching - administrative approach determined upon tackling pollution has been established. It breaks with certain fundamental concepts of civil law such as negligence and causation. The reduction of claims in case of contributory negligence has been abolished or at least restricted to the benefit of victims suffering personal injury. This occurs mostly in cases involving traffic and labour accidents, but it does not seem unlikely that the same may apply more generally. In addition, Dutch case law is lenient with regard to compensation of pure economic loss.

With the exception of the administrative provisions concerning pollution, new liabilities created by the legislator never have retroactive effect. This is rightly so - for a number of reasons.[27] The imposition of new liabilities for acts or omissions which took place in the past means that damages will have to be compensated, despite the fact that:

* at the time of the act or omission, the defendant was not aware - indeed, could not have been aware - of the financial consequences;
* the defendant had no reason to undertake insurance coverage nor to increase the price of products or services to accumulate reserves.

To some extent the same applies to insurers. It is likely that they have insured against various risks, simply because they were unable previously to contemplate the possibility of such risks. In other words, they had no reason to exclude those risks. In the meantime, they are - or, at least, should be - aware of serious future

countries. They vary from ECU 244.000 (Germany), ECU 232.500 (Spain), ECU 73.000 (France), ECU 5.500 (Portugal) to ECU 3.000 (Greece). See C.C. van Dam, A survey of the settlements concerning the compensation for immaterial damage in the EC, p. 41.

26 Those factors play a significant role in the US. See Report of the tort policy working group, pp 30 ff. Similar developments are taking place in Canada, despite the differences between American and Canadian law. See Trebilcock, San Diego Law Review, Vol. 24, pp 929 ff, 1987 and for the differences, pp 931/2.

27 See, more generally, O.A. Haazen, in H.G. Schermers et al., De rol van de rechter in de moderne westerse samenleving, pp 151 ff. His excellent article provides a lot of information, not only about Dutch doctrine and case-law, but also about foreign law.

exposures. Yet, it seems open to debate whether they are sufficiently capable of foreseeing potential eventualities.[28]

As far as case-law is concerned, the situation is worse. In a number of judicial decisions, the Supreme Court undoubtedly changed the law in such a way as not only to have effect on future cases, but also to have a retroactive impact.[29] For example, affected cases include those claiming large awards for pain and suffering, cases protecting victims of car and labour accidents, and cases involving DES. Other supportive examples exist as well, in which the amounts claimed are quite substantial for defendants and for their insurers. This has serious repercussions as mentioned above.

While the Supreme Court is inclined to apply its new rules retroactively - a rather radical initiative, though its negative impact may be difficult to demonstrate - one should not underestimate the undesirability of the administrative solution for pollution. Yet, I do not think that these developments plunge our tort law, at this point, into a crisis.

I stress that thus far tort law is coping, but we might well face serious problems in the future. I have already indicated some potential pitfalls. See under 2. This, however, is apparently not just a Dutch "problem". As my German colleague von Bar put it: "Schiksal und Leiden nimmt man nicht länger widerspruchlos hin". Whether this is also due to the fact that one is "increasingly turning to the courts for relief from a range of personal distress and anxieties"[30], as the former US Chief Justice Warren Burger maintained, may be open to debate. Be this as it may, people have become claim-conscious. Consequently, the propensity to sue has increased considerably. Inflation is also reflected in the amount of the awards claimed.

Often the awards claimed are clearly unjustified and are sometimes quite outrageous. Yet, they must be dealt with. Even if they are dismissed, they are undoubtedly a nuisance, both in terms of time and money. To the best of my knowledge, relevant statistics are unavailable on this point. Nonetheless, they can be disruptive to the system. I strongly believe that the issue should be tackled and a solution for the "nuisance value" problem found.[31]

28 My colleague O.A. Haazen and I will probably touch upon that issue in the very near future.

29 E.g. the DES-case (see appendix, 2), traffic accidents, briefly mentioned under 1b above, labour accidents (idem) and the amounts for pain and suffering (see note 25).

30 Quoted by B.S. Markesinis, CLJ 49(2), July 1990, p. 255.

31 See for more details J. Spier, De grenzen der buitengerechtelijke kosten, A&V 1995/3, pp 55 ff.

4 Piercing the corporate veil

As mentioned, the list of strict liabilities is expanding, and the amounts claimed are increasing. Consequently, the question as to whether or not the defendant is able to pay the compensation awarded for the damage caused arises as a matter of some practical importance.

In the majority of cases, it will be beyond doubt who should be sued. The question needs special attention if the tortfeasor belongs to a group of companies and is itself alone unable to pay. Legally speaking, piercing the corporate veil will be the exception,[32] unless, in short, the other related companies intended to harm the victim's interest. This intention will often be absent. This is because it is standard practice to create a number of group companies (each of them a separate legal entity) for various legitimate reasons such as, for example, tax purposes.

Unless the related group companies are prepared to contribute to the damage caused by one of the group companies (assuming the tortfeasing company is unable to meet its obligations), the question as to whether or not the plaintiff will be compensated depends essentially on coincidental circumstances. I will not elaborate on this point, limiting myself to footnoting relevant case-law and legal doctrine.[33]

II How to keep liability within reasonable limits? A brief outline of Dutch law.

Below is a brief description of the tools that could be used to keep liability within reasonable limits. Many of these appear not to play a significant role, and in fact, application of some of these tools sometimes produces the opposite effect. While some of the statements may be slightly oversimplified, the reader will appreciate that the scope of this paper does not permit attention to detail or subtle distinctions.

A Causation

Art. 6:98 BW deals with causation. Whether the damage can be imputed to the tortfeasor depends on various factors among which the nature of the damage and of the liability are significant. Yet, they are not the only contributing factors.

Much can be gleaned from the case-law. For instance, it appears that:

32 Exceptions are possibile. E.g. art. 2:403 BW; it only applies to debts from legal acts.

33 See e.g. M.J.G.C. Raaijmakers and H.L.J. Roelvink, prelimary report Nederlandse Juristen-Vereniging 1977, R.C. van Dongen, Identificatie in het Rechtspersonenrecht, thesis VU 1995, L.G.H.J. Houwen, A.P. Schoonbrood-Wessels and J.A.W. Scheurs, Aansprakelijkheid in concern-verhoudingen, pp 880 ff, and the case-law to which they refer.

1. in the case of personal injury, the scope of causation is very broad. For example:

* damage aggravated by personal predisposition can be entirely recovered.[34] The case-law provides some rather extreme scenarios.[35]
* generally speaking, the causal relationship will not be interfered with by later events which cause additional damage (e.g. maltreatment in hospital).[36] A different rule applies if an intervening event attributable to the victim results in damage which is unrelated to the tort (e.g. a heart attack, due to which the victim would equally have become unable to work).[37]

2. in the event of an infringement of a "traffic rule" (verkeersnorm) or a "safety standard" (veiligheidsnorm), causation is similarly broadly interpreted. For practical purposes, there is little difference between it and the rule mentioned under 1. The cases are often the same.[38] Until 1995, the Supreme Court targeted infringements of standards which aimed at avoiding traffic and labour accidents.[39] Recent case-law, however, interprets "veiligheidsnorm" as meaning the infringement of a duty of care protecting the safety of the injured party.[40] The consequences of this new approach remain uncertain. For example, could this doctrine be invoked in cases where damage is caused by dangerous substances, even though fault may not be established? I am inclined to answer this question in the negative.

There are other fact patterns which raise the question of foreseeability.[41] Generally speaking, a tortfeasor is not obliged to compensate damage that could not reasonably have been anticipated. Exceptions, however, are possible, such as when

34 See for details Schadevergoeding (Boonekamp), art. 98 aant. 46.

35 E.g. HR 8-2-1985, NJ 1986,137 CJHB; the injured party suffered a "pension neurosis". The BGH understood that the way to deal with it was to restrict the amounts paid (See H. Kötz, Deliktsrecht (5th ed.), nr 155). The Hoge Raad went the other way. Despite the fact that the damage was actually caused by the neurosis, the defendant had to compensate the injured party. See for other examples: HR 21-3-1975, NJ 1975, 372 GJS (a patient dies after a traffic accident from a coronary trombosis brought on by emotional distress caused by the accident) and HR 4-11-1988, NJ 1989, 751 CJHB. (Following a light traffic accident, the plaintiff developed a series of mainly psychologically caused complaints manifesting themselves as difficulties with his wife, his employer, and alcohol were also at stake. The ultimate result was a deterioration in his health. After almost ten years, the plaintiff became unable to work any longer. While the direct effect of the accident only played a minimal role in the outcome of this case, the Supreme Court held that it was significant, since the illness was seen as a consequence of the plaintiff's personality structure.)

36 See e.g. HR 8-2-1985, NJ 1986,136 CJHB.

37 HR 2-2-1990, NJ 1991, 292 CJHB.

38 See Schadevergoeding, art. 98 aant. 29.3.

39 Yet, doctrine already was inclined to apply a similar rule e.g. in product liability. See P. Neleman, BW-krant Jaarboek 1987, p. 49 and Advocate-General Hartkamp though the conclusions were not entirely clear before HR 8-12-1989, NJ 1990, 778 CJHB.

40 HR 13-1-1995, RvdW 1995, 31.

41 Explicitly Memorandum of Reply, Parlementaire geschiedenis book 6, p. 345. See further Schadevergoeding, art. 98 aant. 31, HR 25-5-1990, NJ 1990, 577, and Hof Amsterdam 9-1-1986, NJ 1987, 140 (liability of a bank). It could be argued that one could also take into account whether the defendant ought to have subscribed to some insurance coverage. See J. van Schellen, Toerekening naar redelijkheid, p. 131, in connection with solicitors.

the tortfeasor acted (grossly) negligently.[42] In this connection the nature of the tort also plays a role. Unfortunately, however, the case-law does not give much guidance. The Supreme Court generally focusses on the case to be judged and does not attempt to formulate general rules.[43] See also under C (ad hoc control).

The mere fact that the damage could be foreseen does not necessarily imply an obligation to compensate. One of the relevant factors to be taken into account is the remoteness of the damage. The practical importance of remoteness, however, is rather limited.[44]

3. art. 6:99 BW provides a rule about alternative causation. If the damage could have been caused by different tortfeasors, and it has been determined that the damage has been caused by at least one of them, then each of them is obliged to contribute to making up the entire damage. The Supreme Court applied this rule in the DES case. See for more details Appendix under 2.

4. the mere fact that liability would lead to a cascade of claims is an insufficient reason to refrain from establishing it. This rule was put forward in the following case: a natural gas pipeline was damaged during digging activities. A brick fabrication company suffered damage as a result of stagnation. The far-reaching consequences of holding the digging party liable could not lead to the conclusion that the damage suffered by the company could not be imputed to the tortfeasor.[45]

5. the nature of the liability may have consequences. For instance, the scope of causation may be broader in cases of liability based on fault, whereas it may be more restrictive in cases of strict liability.[46] There is, unfortunately, little case-law to confirm this observation leaving the practical impact of these issues open to debate.

The Explanatory Memorandum on art. 6:175 (strict liability for damage caused by dangerous substances) is not in line with this approach. It describes damage caused by an explosion which resulted in the pollution of a beach. It reads as follows:

> The requirement of a causal relationship (art. 6:98 BW) leads to the conclusion that economic loss (bedrijfsschade) which stems directly from the pollution has to be compensated. In this connection, one must think of the economic loss suffered by the hotels at the beach. Others may well suffer economic loss as well, for example, shopkeepers who would have had the hotel guests as customers, suppliers who deliver food and drinks to the hotels, suppliers who stock the shops, etc. The parliamentary history of economic loss suggests a reluctance in finding connections which are rather remote ("verder weg

42 E.g. HR 13-11-1987, NJ 1988,210 G.

43 See for more details Schadevergoeding, art. 98 aant. 29.4.

44 See Schadevergoeding, art. 98 aant. 32 and HR 2-11-1990, NJ 1991,24.

45 HR 1-7-1977, NJ 1978,84 GJS; see also HR 14-3-1958, NJ 1961,570.

46 HR 13-6-1975, NJ 1975,509 GJS.

liggende schakels"). Ultimately, this issue is open to further development in the case-law.[47]

6. as already set out above (under 1), personal injury will often be imputed to the tortfeasor. The case-law shows a more generous approach towards personal injury than it does in relation to other heads of damage, especially in the case of pure economic loss.[48] Yet, neither doctrine nor case law is explicit on this point; furthermore neither sheds much light on the significance of the distinction among the various heads of "economic loss".[49]

The following damages may be distinguished:

* fixed costs, i.e. that part of the cost associated with the plaintiff and which will accrue irrespective of whether the company operates or not, for example, depreciation;
* overheads, fixed head office charges, for example, insurance premiums;
* the wages of employees who cannot be dismissed (for a while) and who cannot perform any other function which has an equivalent value for the injured party;
* lost profits.[50]

I am inclined to believe that one must be more cautious in imputing loss of profit than in imputing other heads of economic loss. After all, the injured party will *need* compensation for fixed costs, overheads, and wages because these must be paid. If the damage had not occurred, the plaintiff would have received compensation by selling his products. The same does not necessarily apply to loss of profit. In the longer term, a company undoubtedly needs to make profit. We are not, however, referring to the costs that must be incurred.

Another troublesome question is how to calculate fixed costs and overheads. The question seems relevant because companies use various depreciation yardsticks and methods and have different head office charges. In other words, the amount of damage to be compensated will depend on the calculation selected by the plaintiff. The same argument applies to loss of profit which will be greatly affected by certain variables, such as the calculation of depreciation.

It does not seem appropriate to base the amount of damages to be paid on such an arbitrary calculation. I would tend to advocate that one should use an objective

47 Bill number 21202, nr 3, pp. 18/9. See further J. Spier, Kwartaalbericht Nieuw BW 1990, p. 13.

48 See for details Schadevergoeding, art. 98 aant. 30. See about pure economic loss HR 13-11-1987, NJ 1988, 210 G, HR 25-10-1990, NJ 1990, 577, and HR 2-11-1990, NJ 1991, 24. As far as loss of profit is concerned, the Supreme Court held that the plaintiff can only recover the profit he *would* have made, not the profit he *could* have made: HR 13-6-1890, W 5889 and HR 18-4-1986, NJ 1986, 567 G.

49 See for general observations R.A. Salomons, Nieuw BW mon. B38, nr 23 ff and A.R. Bloembergen, Nieuw BW mon. B34, nrs 27 ff.

50 See for details Schadevergoeding art. 96 (Bloembergen) aant., 131 ff and J. Spier, Nieuw BW mon. B36, nr 39.

"yardstick", such as, for instance, the "reasonable company" (or, to be more precise, common accounting principles).[51]

One should bear in mind that the factors mentioned under 2, 5, and 6 are interrelated. But, their interaction will not necessarily produce the same conclusion in different situations. One could well imagine a scenario triggering a restrictive interpretation (such as strict liability) and another scenario urging a generous interpretation (for instance, personal injury). Surprisingly, neither legal doctrine nor case-law is sensitive to disparate situations. However, I believe that personal injury will often be regarded as the prevailing factor.

7. as a general rule the proof of causation rests with the plaintiff. Exceptions are, however, possible, for instance, in cases of infringement of safety standards and labour and traffic accidents. In labour accident claims, the employer will have to prove that the accident was *not* caused as a result of the use of improper procedures or methods.[52] This rule does not apply to defamation cases.[53]

B Non-recoverable damages

A plaintiff may suffer damages defined under different heads of damage:
- material damage;
- damage for pain and suffering;
- loss of profit (pure economic loss).

Naturally, material damage must be compensated. I will not treat the calculation of this type of damage here.[54]

Dutch law is conservative in awarding damages for pain and suffering. This type of compensation is limited to those persons referred to in art. 6:106.[55]

It is interesting to note that the European Court of Human Rights is reluctant to allow such claims. For reasons which remain unclear and explanations which are often less than convincing, the court maintains that its judgements against viol-

51 See also J. Spier, Nieuw BW mon. B36, nr 39 and -albeit in a slightly different context- T.E. Deurvorst, Schadevergoeding, voldoening van een redelijke gebruiksvergoeding en winstafdracht bij inbreuk op intellectuele eigendomsrechten, pp 90 ff.

52 E.g. HR 17-11-1989, NJ 1990, 572 (labour accident) and HR 16-11-1990, NJ 1991, 55 (traffic accident).

53 HR 29-10-1993, NJ 1994,108.

54 See for details Schadevergoeding (Bloembergen), art. 97 and with regard to material damage caused by personal injury, see idem (Bolt), art. 105.

55 See for details Schadevergoeding (Deurvorst), art. 106.

ations of human rights often constitute sufficient just satisfaction for the purposes of art. 50.[56]

Pure economic loss can also be recovered, in principle, without any restriction.[57] Yet, in a specific case such a claim could well be rejected on the basis of lack of (legal) causation[58] or could undergo judicial modification, although the latter course of action is exceptional.

The injured party often has to spend money to convince the tortfeasor that his damage should be compensated. In this regard, a distinction must be drawn between expenditures undertaken before the lawsuit and sums paid pursuant to the legal proceedings, such as attorney fees. As far as the former are concerned, the tortfeasor must compensate the injured party for the reasonable cost of legal services rendered to the plaintiff.[59] Generally speaking though, the greater part of the cost is associated with the lawsuit. The Dutch legal system provides a peculiar method of calculating the costs of the party whose claim is dismissed in court. It takes into account the amount claimed by the plaintiff as well as the *number* of different procedures required of the other party's lawyer, irrespective of quality and time. In real terms, the amount granted to the plaintiff is almost always considerably lower than the amount paid to the attorneys.[60]

C Ad hoc control/modification

For the Netherlands, ad hoc control (hereinafter referred to as "modification") of damages had its origins at the beginning of this century. In 1911, a bill was introduced in Parliament which stated (the translation is mine):

> The court will fix the amount of damages in accordance with equity, taking the circumstances into account.[61] According to the Explanatory Memorandum, one has to consider of the "damnum emergens", "lucrum cessans", and the financial capacity of tortfeasor and victim.[62] The reaction in the Lower House was divided. One point of criticism was that the article was somewhat vague

56 E.g. 23-4-1992, Series A, Vol. 236, NJ 1994, 102 EJD (Castells/Spain) and 28-8-1992, Series A, Vol 242B, NJ 1994, 103 EJD (Schwabe/Austria). See also J. Spier, A&V 1994, p. 155.

57 See for details Schadevergoeding (Deurvorst), art. 96 aant., pp 131 ff.

58 In these cases, there will often be a *conditio sine qua non* link, but this is considered to be insufficient. See under A above.

59 See art. 6:96 para. 2 under c and for details Schadevergoeding, art. 96 aant., 186 ff, F.Th. Kremer, A&V 1994, pp 59 ff and J. Spier, A&V 1995/3, pp 55 ff.

60 In exceptional circumstances (such as frivolous claims), however, one is entitled to the entire amount. See Parlementaire geschiedenis Invoering 3, 5 and 6, Wijziging van het Wetboek van Burgerlijke Rechtsvordering, p. 36 and J. Spier, A&V 1995/3, p. 60.

61 See W. 9099 (1911), p. 1.

62 W. 9099, p. 2.

and did not provide any guidance.[63] For other reasons, this law never came into effect.[64]

The new Code (which came into force January 1, 1992) introduced a vehicle by which the amount to be paid by the tortfeasor is modulated: art. 6:109 BW. According to this article, the courts are allowed to mitigate a legal obligation to repair damage if awarding full compensation would lead to clearly unacceptable results in the circumstances, including the nature of the liability, the legal relationship between the parties, and their financial capacity. The modification may not exceed the amount for which thc tortfeasor is insured or for which he is obligated to be insured.

The article was understandably vigorously debated in Parliament. A similar general provision has hitherto been unknown in Dutch law and could potentially have a major impact. Its efficacy is, however, ultimately dependent upon its reception by the courts which may be somewhat reluctant to give it a liberal interpretation given the drafting of the provision and the uncertainty created as a result of the debates among Ministers and Parliament. The mere fact that the amount of the compensation claimed is substantial or that the defendant may have difficulties in paying is not necessarily sufficient to attract application of the modification principle.[65]

It might be useful to turn our attention to the Parliamentary debates since they discuss the fundamentals of modification and treat the difficult questions of when and how to apply it.

Prior to the commencement of the drafting of the present Civil Code, a number of "vraagpunten" or points of contention were raised for discussion by the Minister of Justice. Modification was one such point. One of the main questions regarding modification was whether the court should obtain a general competence to demand the modification of obligations to pay damages.

The official explanation stated that modification may be desirable in cases where there is:

i - a limited degree of negligence;
ii - inequality between the degree of negligence and the (high) amount of damages caused;
iii - a necessity to make a quick decision;
iv - an employee who assumes a risk for the benefit of his employer that he would not otherwise have assumed;

63 W. 9312 (1912), p. 4.

64 It primarily intended to "overrule" the Supreme Court's most restrictive case-law about the meaning of art. 1401 BW (the predecessor of art. 6:162 BW). In one of its most important judgements (HR 31-1-1919, NJ 1919,161, W 10365 Molengraaff), the Supreme Court adopted the wording of the draft legislation.

65 Parlementaire geschiedenis, book 6, pp 404 ff.

v - strict liability;[66]

vi - the threat of financial ruin; while financial inability to pay compensation was deemed to be insufficient[67] to trigger modification, financial ruin, that is, the situation where a company can no longer continue to operate, may be sufficient to warrant modification.[68]

Generally speaking, the Lower Chamber supported these contentions. Some members, however, stressed that it should not routinely be applied in cases of negligence[69], thoug it should be borne in mind that modification means that the victim cannot recover for the entire damage.[70] Consequently, the Court should be obliged to give reasons why modification was appropriate in the particular circumstances.[71]

The governmental debate led to the drafting of art. 6.1.9.12a. Modification would be possible when full compensation would create an "emergency situation" for the debtor. It could not be invoked in the event of gross negligence or an intentional act.[72]

Professor Meijers suggested that a finding of negligence should be insufficient to attract modification.[73] He further determined that criterion iii was inappropriate, though he found that criterion vi was valid.[74]

The Lower Chamber considered art. 6.1.9.12a to be too narrow and took the view that all relevant circumstances should be taken into account, in particular, that the interest of debtor and victim should be balanced.[75] The Lower Chamber was uncertain as to how cases where several victims suffered damage due to the act of one tortfeasor should be handled. It was inclined to believe that the court should consider the total amount of the different claims.[76] The Minister of Justice supports this approach. He rightly points out that the defendant should do his utmost to ascertain all the claims at the same time.[77]

66 Parlementaire geschiedenis, book 6, pp 404 and 406.

67 Idem, p. 406.

68 Prof. Meijers (Government Commissioner), idem, pp 423, 426, and 440.

69 E.g. Mr van Rijckevorsel, idem, p. 408, Mrs Wttewaall van Stoetwegen, p. 413 and Mr Van der Feltz, p. 416.

70 E.g. Mrs Wttewaall van Stoetwegen, idem, p. 410 and Van der Feltz, p. 418. See also Van Rijckevorsel, p. 431.

71 Idem, p. 411.

72 In addition, art. 6.3.17 was introduced. Its importance was minimal, though subsequently combined with art. 6.1.9.12a to yield the present art. 6:109 BW. The reference to gross negligence and intention to cause damage was deleted at a later stage. Even in those cases, modification *can* be appropriate, e.g. if the event was provoked by the victim (p. 451).

73 Idem, p. 424.

74 Idem, p. 440.

75 Idem, p. 441.

76 Idem, p. 443.

77 Idem, p. 452.

The Minister of Justice argued that the wording of art. 6:109 BW rendered it such that the court ought to be reluctant to apply modification. This argument is in line with the "highly unreasonable" test outlined by the Association of Dutch Lawyers.[78] The Minister of Justice even suggested some circumstances where art. 109 BW could play a role. Relevant situations could include those where:

* there could be rendering of unselfish services;
* the circumstances are as described in iv above;
* the tortfeasor himself also suffers (serious) personal injury;
* either the debtor or the victim could claim compensation through insurance;
* the nature of the liability, whether strict or fault liability, is implicated.[79]

Case-law concerning art. 6:109 BW is sparse. (This is understandable since art. 6:109 only came into force on January 1, 1992.) Furthermore, it was drafted in connection with a similar provision dealing with governmental action to recover the cost of cleaning polluted land from the party who negligently caused the contamination (art. 21 Interimwet bodemsanering[80]). Against the background of the "polluter pays" principle, the lower courts have demonstrated considerable reluctance in moderating.[81]

Modification was denied because:

* the polluter took advantage of the fact that he had not taken the necessary measures to avoid pollution;[82]
* the damage (Dfl 75 million, as it was assessed) was not sufficiently substantial in relation to the assets of the defendant;[83]
* the defendant denied liability (sic!) and hence denied its responsibility for the pollution.[84]

Modification was applied in view of:

the responsibility of the government which flowed from the fact that while it was aware of the activities causing the pollution and of the serious consequences thereof, it failed to take proper preventive action.[85]

Similar provisions had existed previously in the old Civil Code (as from 1838), namely, arts. 1406 and 1407. They dealt with cases of torts causing death or personal injury. The amount to be paid by the defendant depended on "de stand en de fortuin der personen" (the class and fortune of the respective persons) and the circumstances. The case-law illustrates the meaning of these old provisions.

78 Idem, p. 449.

79 Idem, p. 450. Government Commissioner, Mr Snijders, subsequently emphasized the importance of this argument, p. 454.

80 This article has been replaced by art. 75 Wet bodembescherming. The new article remains unchanged in this respect.

81 Handboek Milieu-aansprakelijkheid (Spier) Jurisprudentie, nrs 6, 13, 17, 22, 24, 44, 55, 60, 61, 67, 69, 70, and 72.

82 Rb. 's-Hertogenbosch 20-5-1988, BR 1989, pp 280 ff.

83 Rb. Almelo 12-12-1990, TMA 1991, pp 129 ff.

84 Rb. Alkmaar 25-2-1993, TMA 1993, pp 143 ff.

85 Rb. 's-Hertogenbosch 16-2-1990, TMA 1991, pp 139 ff.

The financial capacity of the defendant can justify modification, though future developments in the defendant's financial situation must be taken into account. In fact, the courts have shown a certain optimism about the positive future developments of the defendant's fiscal affairs.[86]
Curiously enough, however, - and of course without success - the municipality of Amsterdam pleaded that it was unable to pay Dfl 20.000 (in 1963).[87]

The "class" hardly played a role.[88]

Moreover, other factors were invoked, sometimes with success, such as:
- the degree of negligence[89], though a different view was expressed by the same Court 24 years later;[90]
- the offering of unselfish services. However, the Supreme Court held in 1971 that this factor could only be taken into account if the financial situation of the defendant is considered to be bad.[91]

Following an event causing damage to several victims, the amount available for compensation must be apportioned among them.[92] Until the amount to be paid to other victims is known, their portion cannot be taken into account.[93]

The courts have held that defendants are required to provide sufficient facts justifying modification.[94]

Regarding the new legislation concerning governmental action in the area of pollution, the Council of State made a very interesting observation. In the (recent) past, polluters could not have foreseen the possibility that the soil would have to be cleaned[95], nor that the government would deem it appropriate to demand the restoration of the land for different subsequent uses (industrial and other). In other words, even if an obligation to pay damages was deemed to have been operating - an unlikely assumption until ten or fifteen years ago - there was no way of anticipating that the amounts implicated could be so substantial. Thus, the Council seems to be in favour of modulating the compensation awards under such circumstances. The Ministers of Justice and of the Environment are not persuaded and do not see

86 See for details Onrechtmatige Daad II (de Groot), nr 333.
87 Hof Amsterdam 16-5-1963, NJ 1964, 116.
88 The only exception is Hof 's-Hertogenbosch 14-1-1930, NJ 1930, 1596. The defendant, the son of a physician, studied at university. The Court does not make clear the specific importance of this fact.
89 Hof Amsterdam 27-4-1939, NJ 1939, 709.
90 Hof Amsterdam 16-5-1963, NJ 1964, 116.
91 HR 3-12-1971, NJ 1972, 144 GJS.
92 See Onrechtmatige Daad II, nr 339.
93 Rb. Amsterdam 27-1-1961, VR 1964, 60.
94 HR 2-1-1931, NJ 1931, 348 EMM; see for more details Onrechtmatige Daad II, nr 340.
95 See also HR 30-9-1994, RvdW 1994, 185.

any reason for such an approach. It is, however, the lack of financial capacity to pay the damages that leads to modification in a specific case.[96]

D Caps and ceilings

Caps and ceilings (hereinafter referred to as ceilings) are well known in transport law. Generally speaking, the maximum amount of awards is based on treaties. In this context, ceilings have their origin in the Middle Ages.[97] It was considered reasonable at that time that the value of a ship should be the upper limit of liability.[98] The desire to stimulate investment in transport by sea, the "fortune de mer" principle, and the importance of keeping transport by ship relatively cheap (in relation to other countries) played a significant role in determinations with respect to ceilings.[99] In 1854 and 1862, the (English) Merchant Shipping Act, for example, based ceilings on a certain amount per registered ton.[100] I will set aside this topic at this point, though it is interesting especially from a general perspective.

Apart from transport law, ceilings do not play liability an important role in Dutch law. They operate in relation to the liability for nuclear energy as set out in the Treaty of Paris and the subsequent implementing Dutch legislation (Wet aansprakelijkheid kernongevallen). Yet, art. 6:110 BW provides for the keeping of liability within reasonable limits. It reads:

Maximum liability amounts can be set by regulation, so that the liability which may arise from damage does not exceed that which can reasonably be covered by insurance. Separate amounts can be fixed according to, amongst other factors, the nature of the event, of the damage, and of the liability.

Art. 6:110 BW[101] is founded on the idea that liability which is not based on negligence should be capped, a principle that has descended from time immemorial.[102] And, since the new Civil Code introduces new strict liabilities, it has now been deemed equitable to establish a link between the maximum award to be

96 Bill number 23 589 A, pp 6/7.

97 See F.J. de Vries, Wettelijke limitering van aansprakelijkheid, thesis Leiden 1990, p. 5.

98 Op. cit., p. 6.

99 One should bear in mind that the way of limiting liability was then rather different. In the beginning of the 19 th century, Dutch law focussed on the value of the vessel *after* the disaster, whereas English law focussed on the value before the disaster (legislation of 1734): idem, p. 7. The principle was explicitly stated by Devlin, L.J. in *Berry* v. *British Transport Commission*: "Limitation of liability is a principle that is now well recognised. In the case of damage done by a ship .. the basis of it is simply that it is not in the public interest that shipowners should be deterred from seafaring by the prospect that they might be crippled by awards and heavy damages" (quoted in McGregor on Damages, 15 ed., nr 662).

100 Idem, p. 8. This system has been followed in a series of treaties: idem, pp 16 ff.

101 Originally art. 6.3.17 and thereafter art. 6.3.2.12.

102 Toelichting (Explanatory Memorandum) Meijers, Parlementaire geschiedenis, book 6, pp 769 ff.

paid by the "tortfeasor" and the amount which could be covered by insurance.[103] In addition, the Memorandum of Reply has indicated that it should be possible to fix different amounts for personal injury, damage to property, and pure economic loss.[104]

The Senate has raised the issue as to whether liability based on fault should also be limited by a ceiling. It (rightly) pointed out that the difference between strict liability and liability based on negligence could well be minimal in specific cases.[105] The Minister of Justice initially concluded that a ceiling should not apply to fault liability. The rationale for creating a ceiling was based on the realization that the new strict liabilities could not be covered by insurance[106] (obviously a sophism, because insurers will attempt to limit their coverage, leaving the insured to pay the damage not covered by insurance). The Minister of Justice subsequently changed his mind. Since art. 6:110 BW is not restricted to strict liability,[107] he further suggested that the degree of negligence should play a role in the setting of ceilings in the event that a distinction might be made according to the nature of the liability in question.[108]

The Lower House inquired into which criteria ought to be used in determining whether or not - and up to what amount - an obligation to pay damages could be capped. The Minister of Justice's reply to this query was rather nebulous, that is, he merely ventured to say that various circumstances should be taken into account to determine whether limitation is justified.[109] Unfortunately, he does not elaborate on the criteria to which the court should resort in order to decide if limitation is required. He maintains that "indeed" the maximum coverage provided by insurers will be "an important fact".[110] In the Senate, the Minister of Justice argued that a ceiling would be an exception, particularly since it remains barely known in other countries. It will only be used in the event of "bottlenecks". Art. 6:110 BW will be resorted to if excessive damages are claimed and would require restriction through the imposition of a ceiling. Until then, art. 6:109 BW may help resolve potential difficulties. The Minister specifically indicated that the article was not intended to cap the liability of the liberal professions.[111]

103 Idem, p. 770. Meijers' explanation is not entirely clear. It seems to suggest that a ceiling should not be applied in all cases of strict liability, though it fails to indicate in which cases unlimited liability would be appropriate.
104 Idem, p. 771.
105 Idem, p. 771.
106 Idem, p. 772.
107 Parlementaire geschiedenis, book 6 Invoeringswet, p. 1318.
108 Idem, p. 1318.
109 Idem, p. 1319.
110 Idem, p. 1319.
111 Idem, p. 1320. Understandably, some professionals stress the importance of ceilings. See e.g. F.H.A. Arisz and J.G.C. Kamphuisen, prelimary report Nederlandse Juristenvereniging 1987, pp 54 ff and 96. See also T. Hartlief, A&V 1994, pp 146 ff, who is sceptical.

In the meantime, it has become clear that the Minister of Justice does not intend to make use of art. 6:110 BW. He rejects the possibility of ceilings for specific branches of industry and for specific companies. Such limitations would mean a decrease in the financial burden which is something that he feels cannot be justified[112], apart from caps for relatively high amounts resulting from grave disasters. It is evident that he is clearly determined to avoid the application of ceilings, though as he points out, one must be aware that no great disasters have yet occurred in the Netherlands.[113] In short, the Minister of Justice highlights the potential of art. 6:109 BW to solve possible difficulties in specific cases.
In view of the above arguments, I am inclined to believe that the courts should not be too reluctant to moderate obligations to pay damages. Indeed, a number of newly introduced (strict) liabilities were explicitly based on the assumption that the new Code provided adequate means to keep liability within reasonable limits. In this regard, the importance of ceilings is persuasive. Now, however, it appears that one must rely solely on modification (or, as the case may be, causation). Despite the rather restrictive wording of art. 6:109 BW, the balance should be re-established.[114]
The directive on product liability allows Member States to limit the damage awards to be paid. Greece, Portugal, and Germany have taken advantage of this provision,[115] while the Netherlands has not yet done so.

E "Egalité devant les charges publiques" [Equality before public burdens]

On January 1, 1995, a bill came into force introducing a cleaning order targeting the owner or long-term lessor of polluted land or the party who actually caused the contamination, irrespective of whether or not that party had committed a tort.[116]

In its advice to the Queen, the Council of State referred to case-law stating that the government will have to consider whether such orders must be borne entirely by the addressee. It appears that an affirmative answer to this question may well be in conflict with the principle of "égalité devant les charges publiques".[117]

112 See also F.J. de Vries, o.c., p. 52/3. The application of a ceiling implies that victims would be subsidizing industry and companies.

113 Memorandum of Reply Bill number 21202 (dangerous substances and the like), p. 32. Exceptions will be made in the context of the transportation of dangerous substances (idem).

114 See also J. Spier and C.H.W.M. Sterk, Aansprakelijkheid voor gevaarlijke stoffen, pp 17 ff and Sterk, Verhoogd gevaar in het aansprakelijkheidsrecht, thesis KUB 1994, p. 296.

115 See A. Geddes, Product and Service Liability in the EEC, pp 103/104.

116 Art. 43 Wet bodembescherming. See J. Spier and C.H.W.M. Sterk, Rope-Dancing Dutch Tort Law, pp. 27 ff. The relevant provisions are extremely complicated. They provide specific loopholes which I will not address here. See for details E.C.M. Schippers, Handboek Milieu-aansprakelijkheid D 1200.

117 Bill number 23 589, nr A, pp 4/5.

Needless to say, the Ministers who introduced the bill were annoyed by this qualification. They pointed out that the clear intention of the Cabinet and Parliament was to override that case-law. Apart from the question of whether the Ministers' interpretation of Parliament's intention is valid or not - which I do not believe it is - their reaction is quite remarkable, given that the view they espouse is clearly in conflict with the concept of the *Algemene wet bestuursrecht* (general administrative law) which came into force on January 1, 1994![118]

The approach suggested by the Council of State is of considerable importance since it creates a tool for maintaining specific claims lodged by the government within reasonable limits.

F Duty of care towards whom? (Schutznorm)

Art. 6:162 BW does not provide any relief unless the norm violated by the defendant had as its purpose the protection against such damage as suffered by the victim (art. 6:163 BW). While art. 6:163 BW does not currently play an important role,[119] it could potentially be effective in two particular areas:

a. claims by the government, not being the owner of the land, for the cleaning cost; and
b. torts committed by rendering improper services.

Ad a.
The Supreme Court has held that the State has a claim against the polluter who commits a tort by contaminating land or groundwater as of January 1, 1975.[120] As from that date, there is a likelihood that the State would begin a clean-up at its expense.

The government was dismayed by this line of decision because it meant that the State would not have a claim against incidents of pollution which took place in the more distant past. Consequently, the government introduced a bill in Parliament to "overrule" the case-law in question.[121] This met with fierce resistance, especially by the Senate.[122] It was argued that legal certainty would be compromised by this

118 See J. Spier, WPNR 6074 (1992), pp 986 ff.

119 The Supreme Court seemingly reduced the importance of art. 6:163 BW as an "autonomous" requirement: 30-9-1994, RvdW 1994, 185. If negligence is based on the violation of a rule of unwritten law pertaining to proper social conduct, it apparently has been absorbed by art. 6:162 BW. The outcome of a specific case will remain the same, as the Court seems to stress. Only the doctrinal approach changes. See E. Bauw, A&V 1995, pp 9 ff, Jac. Hijma, AA 1995, p. 278 and J. Spier, WPNR 6168 (1995), pp 109 ff.

120 HR 24-4-1992, NJ 1993, 643 CJHB and 644. One should bear in mind that the Supreme Court "only" dealt with cases of pollution of the polluter's own land. The same, however, applies to cases of pollution of land belonging to third parties. HR 30-9-1994, RvdW 1994, 185-188.

121 Art. 47, para. 5 Wet bodembescherming in connection with art. VI.

122 See for details T. Hartlief, A&V 1994, pp 13/14 and for subsequent discussions in Parliament J. Spier, A&V 1994, pp 43/44, 70 ff and 99 ff.

legislation. The Ministers of the Environment and of Justice pledged to amend the law and introduced a revised law in Parliament which restricts claims against polluters whose acts took place before January 1, 1975.[123] Thus, it appears that the criteria for suing tortfeasors now result in a retroactive effect - at least this seems to be the case. In a number of judgements delivered in September 1994, the Supreme Court held that until 1975 it was *not* a tort to dispose of waste by depositing it in the ground since at that time it was assumed that the land would recover.[124] Consequently, the practical significance of the new bill seems to be minimal.

Ad b.
In general, only contractual counterparts will suffer damage from improper services. Exceptions are, however, possible, and the amounts involved may be substantial. This is especially true for torts committed by auditors, banks, and to some extent, by physicians, attorneys, notaries public, and bailiffs. The case-law (at least the published case-law) on this topic is sparse. It is my opinion that the decisive factor, stated in simplified terms, is whether or not the defendant could have foreseen that the victim could suffer damage from his acts or would rely upon his statements or acts.[125]

This rule implies that auditors will not often escape from liability in cases where they make mistakes (e.g. in approving the annual account of a company).[126] The same is true for banks (e.g. in providing incorrect information about the creditworthiness of a debtor[127] or in issuing an inaccurate prospectus regarding a bond emission).[128/129]

123 Bill number 23589.
124 HR 30-9-1994, RvdW 1994,185/187. See J.M. van Dunné, NJB 1994, pp 1329 ff and 1536 (extremely critical) and TMA 1994, pp 166 ff (with the same complaints). See also P.F.A. Bierbooms and R.A. Taams, NJB 1994, pp 1339 ff, G.E. van Maanen, A&V 1994, pp 139 ff, E. Bauw, A&V 1995, pp 6 ff, Jac Hijma, AA 1995, pp 273 ff and J. Spier, WPNR 6167, pp 87 ff and 6168, pp 109 ff.
125 Possibly in the same sense HR 2-12-1994, RvdW 1994, 263 legal ground 5.3. See also Hof 's-Hertogenbosch 28.9.1983, NJ 1985,120 (auditors) and Rb. Almelo 7-7-1993, A&V 1993, 21 (architects).
126 See for case-law -partly unpublished- K.A.J. Bisschop, NTBR 1994, pp 23 ff and especially Hof 's-Hertogenbosch 28-9-1983, NJ 1985, 120.
127 HR 10-12-1993, RvdW 1993, 248.
128 HR 2-12-1994, RvdW 1994, 263 and see about this judgement W.J. Slagter, A&V 1995, pp 30 ff. See also Hof Amsterdam 27-5-1993, NJ 1993, 682. See for more details D. Campbell and R. Meroni, Bankers Liability: Risks and Remedies, pp 151 ff (about the legal situation in the Netherlands). They touch upon granting, continuing and increasing credit, withdrawal of credit, taking security from debtors, and selling security.
129 See for attorneys Rb. Amsterdam 11-11-1947, NJ 1948, 393, Hof 's-Gravenhage 9-5-1979, NJ 1981, 322 (notary public, selling real estate by auction, committing an error in estimating its size), and for bailiffs Onrechtmatige Daad VIII (Michiels van Kessenich-Hoogendam), nr 77.

G Contributory negligence

Contributory negligence can play a major role in keeping liabilities within reasonable limits. It can be invoked irrespective of whether a claim is based on contract[130] or tort. I will, however, only briefly touch upon this topic since it falls slightly outside the scope of this chapter.

Contributory negligence implies that the victim must bear a part of his damage himself. As a general rule, the distribution of damages will depend on which part of the damage was caused by the tortfeasor and which part by the victim (art. 6:101 BW). This apportionment is often not obvious. The case-law seems to indicate that the outcome is far from predictable.[131]

This balancing of the parties' respective causal contribution, however, does not necessarily lead to just results. In view of this, art. 6:101 provides an alternative apportionment required by equity.

The case-law indicates a trend encouraging application of this alternative equitable apportionment in cases of:

a. personal injury of pedestrians or cyclists caused by motor vehicles;[132] and
b. personal injury of children below the age of 14.[133]

Contributory negligence can also play an important role in other cases, such as, for example, professional liability. The damage will often be partly due to the plaintiff who failed to act with sufficient prudence.[134]

It seems likely that equity will restrict the amount of compensation if the victim was grossly negligent or acted deliberately.[135]

130 E.g. Rb. Amsterdam 7-12-1994, NJ 1995, 265.

131 See for a striking example HR 22-4-1994, A&V 1994, 106 JS (and for a similar observation, p. 107 under 3). See also Hof 's-Gravenhage 15-9-1994, A&V 1995, 51 T. Hartlief rightly criticizes this judgement.

132 E.g. HR 1-6-1990, NJ 1991, 720 CJHB, 31-5-1991, NJ 1991, 721 CJHB, 28-2-1992, NJ 1993, 566 CJHB and 24-12-1993, NJ 1995, 236 CJHB. The Supreme Court's case-law seems to be more generous to those who contributed considerably to the event which caused the damage than to victims whose contribution was relatively small. Brunner rightly criticized this approach (NJ 1995, 236, p. 1059 under 3).

133 HR 8-12-1989, NJ 1990, 778 CJHB. It seems likely that the rule, developed in this case, will apply more generally. See for details Schadevergoeding art. 101 (Boonekamp) aant. 17 and J. Spier, mon. Nieuw BW B 36, nr 7.

134 See e.g.: Rb. 's-Gravenhage 12-12-1990, quoted by Bisschop, op. cit., p. 26 (liability of auditor), HR 31-12-1993, NJ 1994, 275 (liability of notary public) and in connection with liability of public authorities e.g. HR 10-12-1993, NJ 1994, 242, A&V 1994, 73 TH, HR 1-10-1993, RvdW 1993, 188, A&V 1994, 47 TH, HR 22-4-1994, RvdW 1994, 107, A&V 1994, 106 JS, HR 13-1-1995, RvdW 1995, 29, A&V 1995, 43 JS. See for a rather uncommon case (liability of the owner of a two-star Michelin restaurant who hits his guest after assuming that the guest, whose behaviour was rather offensive, had not paid the bill: HR 31-3-1995, RvdW 1995, 83).

135 See J. Spier, Nieuw BW mon. B 36, nr 7.

Contributory negligence will be disregarded in cases involving a recourse action by an employer against his employee for damage caused by the latter to a third party, unless the employee acted with malice or conscious recklessness (art. 6:170 para 3 BW). An action based on art. 7A:1638x BW (labour accidents) will not (partly) founder on the ground of contributory negligence of the injured employee. His claim will only be dismissed should there be a finding of wilful recklessness.[136]

H Exoneration

Exoneration is only[137] implicated in contractual relations and arises when one party stipulates that he will only be liable up to a certain amount.

Clauses to this effect are usual, that is, can be found among the general terms and conditions of the contract. Furthermore, they are common in specific contracts for the sale or manufacturing of goods. To the best of my knowledge, they are not (yet) common in the context of services offered by attorneys, notaries public, or auditors.[138] They are also used by architects.[139]

Inevitably, the sale of defective products or improper services can result in major damage to a counterpart, for example, by compromising that party's reputation or by causing breakdowns.

Whether or not an exoneration clause inserted in the general terms and conditions can be invoked[140] depends on the circumstances[141], such as:
- the degree of negligence as it relates to the nature and seriousness of the interests concerned;
- the overall nature and specific contents of the agreement;[142]
- the position of the respective parties and their interrelationships;

136 HR 9-1-1987, NJ 1987, 948 PAS and HR 27-3-1992, NJ 1992, 496 PAS.

137 Exceptions are possible. See for details Contractenrecht III (Wuisman), nr 172 and P. Kuipers, in Aansprakelijkheden, pp 49 ff.

138 However, the situation may well change in the near future. We already have a small number of attorneys who use exoneration clauses. Yet, it is open to debate whether they will (always) apply. More generally, lawyers and businessmen underestimate the issue of applicability. They often take for granted that the mere existence of exoneration clauses means that they will necessarily apply. See on the topic of exoneration of attorneys T. Hartlief, A&V 1994 pp. 143/4 and F.H.A Arisz, op. cit, p. 25/6.

139 See F.H.A. Arisz, op. cit., pp 50 ff and (about auditors) K.A.J. Bisschop, op. cit., p. 27.

140 The application of an exoneration clause is an "either-or" proposition - either it can be invoked or it cannot. This "all or nothing" approach has -rightly, in my view- been criticized by J.B.M. Vranken, WPNR 6142, pp 453/4.

141 See also Verbintenissenrecht I (Hondius) art. 233 aant. 44.

142 See for details Contractenrecht III (Wuisman), nr 181 ff. E.g. Hof 's-Gravenhage 26-5-1975, NJ 1976,237 took into account that the seller promised to deliver goods of a good quality, and that while the plaintiff had no experience with these goods, he was not obliged to find out whether or not they were defective.

- whether or not the counterpart was aware of the exoneration clause;[143]
- whether one or all of the parties are covered by insurance;[144]
- societal opinion.[145]

The mere fact that exoneration clauses may commonly be included along with the general terms and conditions does not necessarily guarantee that the exoneration clause will be successfully invoked, particularly when the other party is unaware of the existence of the clause in the contract. Furthermore, whether or not the other party is deemed to have accepted the clause depends on the interpretation of the agreement.[146]

Art. 12 of the directive on product liability and art. 7 of the proposal directive on defective services[147] explicitly states that liability of manufacturers and of suppliers of services cannot be limited or excluded (as far as damage covered by the respective directives is concerned).

III How to keep liability law within reasonable limits: observations.

It follows from the above that Dutch law makes it *possible* to keep liabilities within reasonable limits. Different methods can be used, and they are obviously interrelated. For the remainder of this article, I will focus strictly on liability based on tort. In any event, where a contractual relationship exists, it is up to the parties to determine the issue of liability.

Although Dutch law provides sufficient tools to cope with the expansion of liability, it is evident that legislation fails to offer a consistent view on the needs of modern tort law. The result is that the courts are left to resolve the difficulties without much guidance.

The main issue in (the expansion of) tort law is how to justify who should bear the cost of the damage suffered in a specific case. One is inclined to believe that the answer should be: either the tortfeasor or the victim - rightly so in the majority of cases. But, exceptional cases deserve our attention. Hence, the question to be asked is when and why is a case exceptional?

143 HR 19-5-1967, NJ 1967, 261 GJS.

144 See for details Contractenrecht III (Wuisman), nr 191 and HR 11-1-1957, NJ 1959, 37 HB and Hof 's-Hertogenbosch 3-3-1959, NJ 1959, 655: the fact that the damage was covered by the plaintiff's insurance was taken into account to his detriment. If the damage was covered by the defendant, this can prevent him from invoking an exoneration clause: Hof 's-Hertogenbosch 8-12-1959, NJ 1961, 158. See more recently HR 31-12-1993, NJ 1995, 389 CJHB.

145 A.R. Bloembergen, BR 1969, pp 362 ff.

146 HR 1-7-1993, NJ 1993, 688. See also HR 31-12-1993, NJ 1995, 389 CJHB.

147 The draft has been withdrawn.

To some extent, the answers to these questions are quite clear. There is no (valid) reason to relieve the tortfeasor from liability if:

1. he is covered by mandatory insurance; or
2. the damage caused is not very substantial.

These criteria, however, do not solve many of the conundrums, such as determining whether the amount of damages should be restricted; whether to take into account the financial capacity of tortfeasor/or victim; and whether to consider the nature of the liability (strict or contractual liability or liability based on (gross) negligence)? I am inclined to respond in the affirmative to all these queries, though in doing so I realize that one is back to square one.

It may be useful at this point to elaborate on and distinguish between the different heads of damage. I tend to believe that one should be reluctant to cut the amount of damages paid to persons who have suffered personal injury. Yet, I do not see any valid reason why damage limitation should apply to subrogated insurers.[148]

It is unclear whether reluctance in creating an obligation to compensate (pure) economic loss is justifiable. I must admit that I even doubt whether such an approach should be encouraged. It may be that economic loss deserves less support than personal injury.[149] Companies need to make profits without which they risk bankruptcy. The effect is often unemployment and negative consequences for unpaid creditors.

Tort law should avoid creating bankruptcies as far as possible. Bankruptcy is neither a solution for the victim nor for the tortfeasor because failed businesses can often be detrimental to employees, contract partners and shareholders (as in the case of pension funds). This is particularly true in the event of bankruptcy of both victim *and* tortfeasor.

In addition to avoiding the creation of bankruptcies, tort law should also refrain from causing the deterioration of the financial capacity of companies (and professional practices)[150] because of their negative effects. From a general perspective, neither of these solutions serves a useful purpose.

In the light of these arguments, it is apparent that there is no need, nor sufficient justification, to modulate or impose a ceiling on the amount to be paid by the liable person unless full compensation would create major financial difficulties for him.

148 To some extent -and slightly to my surprise- the Supreme Court seems to be of a different opinion. Compare HR 13-1-1995, RvdW 1995, 31. However, its case-law in relation to the consequences of contributory negligence in traffic accidents is based on a similar view. See HR 28-2-1992, NJ 1993, 566 CJHB.

149 See also Asser-Hartkamp I, nr 499.

150 I share Eykman's view that one should not distinguish between e.g. a baker and an attorney (HNJV 1987 II, pp 67 ff).

If, however, modification would inflict significant hardship on both victim *and* tortfeasor, it will often be deemed reasonable to sacrifice the well-being of the latter, though exceptions should be allowed, such as, for instance, if bankruptcy of the victim would only lead to a relatively small number of job losses compared to the number of employees who would lose their jobs if the tortfeasor were to go bankrupt.[151]

Whether modification or a ceiling will be applied can not be determined in advance with certainty. This lack of certainty is not attractive, but must be accepted.

The real difficulty of (modern) tort law is to choose between the devil and the deep blue sea. It is clearly justifiable to create strict liabilities. Society, however, needs industry, attorneys, auditors, banks, and so on, and thus they must not be discouraged from carrying on their businesses and professions. As a New York Court in 1873 stated:

> "We must have factories, machinery, dams, canals and railroads. They are demanded by the manifold wants of mankind, and lie at the basis of all our civilization."[152]

It seems clear that tort law must not make these pursuits impossible by creating unlimited liabilities. However, it is not very attractive to harbour a system where victims would have to bear the damage they have suffered (or a substantial part of it). In short, there is no reason why victims should pay in the interest of society.

Is it possible to accommodate these discrepancies? I am inclined to think so. But, in doing so we will have to eschew traditional tort law.[153] I will not attempt to elaborate on this point here except to make a few rough observations:

- the government might (possibly even should) encourage companies to take insurance coverage for potential damages which they might suffer and for which they would prefer not to assume the loss (first party insurance). If such insurance coverage becomes standard, it should be taken into account.
- it might (should) also stimulate companies -and professions- to take adequate insurance coverage,[154] unless:
  * the likelihood of damage is (too) remote; or
  * their financial capacity is sufficient to pay the damages which could reasonably be caused.

151 The specific circumstances should be taken into account, such as, the degree of negligence.

152 *Losee* v. *Buchanan*, 51 N.Y. 476, quoted by Kötz, op. cit., p. 14. See for more details Prosser and Keeton on Torts, 5th ed., pp 548 ff.

153 The more general view is that modification is appropriate in cases where the defendant's financial capacity is insufficient (Asser-Hartkamp I, nr 497), given that he cannot get adequate insurance coverage (Schoordijk, op. cit., p. 284; Asser-Hartkamp I, nr 502).

154 See also: C.J.M. Klaassen, Risico-aansprakelijkheid, thesis Nijmegen 1991, pp 320/321 (if the premium is reasonable) and P. Abas, mon. Nieuw BW A 16, nr 28.

It may, however, be impossible to obtain adequate insurance coverage, and there is always the possibility that a true disaster may occur. In these cases, it does not necessarily seem justifiable to saddle the victim with the damages - nor hand them all to the tortfeasor.

In some situations, proper insurance coverage could be offered by the State. Needless to say, it may be difficult - sometimes even impossible[155] - to calculate the premiums to be paid simply because there is insufficient knowledge about the chance a specific risk will be realized. If a disaster does occur, and if:

* full compensation would detrimentally affect the financial situation of the tortfeasor; or
* adequate insurance could not be obtained (either from private insurers or from the government),

one could well imagine that the damage would be borne by the government.[156]

This approach is not in line with traditional thinking. But, it seems open to debate whether the right questions are being asked. I agree with Brunner that legal entities do not need feelings of humanity.[157] However, their employees do! He also argued that there would be no need to accommodate professions. They would be able to organize themselves into legal entities.[158] This possibility may exist,[159] though I fail to see why one should "punish" those who refrain from such constructions and favour the others. In any event, I do not see any justification for why it should matter fto victims.

And, what about the criteria set out by the legislator, the case-law, and legal doctrine? I doubt whether the nature of liability should be considered to have much importance. The difference between them is often rather limited.[160] Moreover, it is not extraordinary that one acts negligently from time to time. But, this should not lead to the ruin of a person or a legal entity.

155 R. van den Bergh and M. Faure rightly point out that the most difficult question is how to calculate the "moral risk" and the possible size of damage: preadvies Vereniging voor burgerlijk recht 1990, pp 20 and 22. See also Schmidt-Salzer, Kommentar zum Umwelthaftungsgesetz, p. 869.

156 The "Altlasten" topic is an excellent example of the difficulties one will face. It is highly debated, though the (Dutch) government does not show much interest in solving the problem by using public funds. See for more details under I.d.

157 C.J.H. Brunner, Aansprakelijkheid naar draagkracht, p. 16. In the same sense: G.J. Scholten, De beperkingen van aansprakelijkheid met het gehele vermogen en de matigingsbevoegdheid van de rechter, p. 19.

158 Idem, p. 16.

159 See recently e.g. B. Wessels, NJB 1995, pp 233 ff and T. Hartlief, A&V 1994, p. 147.

160 In the same sense H.C.F. Schoordijk, Het algemeen gedeelte van het verbintenissenrecht naar het nieuw Burgerlijk Wetboek p 281. The more general view is that, in modulating, one should distinguish between strict and fault liability: e.g. C.J.M. Klaassen, op. cit., p. 318 and 321, P. Abas, op. cit., nr 11. See also J.J.M. Maeijer, Matiging van schadevergoeding, thesis Nijmegen 1962, pp 162 ff.

Nevertheless, one should always look carefully at the specific situation at hand. If a company, attorney, auditor, and the like often cause damage or act deliberately, the tortfeasor should bear the damage himself, even if it could result in bankruptcy. Society at large does not benefit (any longer) from such "institutions".

I realize that the suggestions mentioned above need careful consideration. One must also discover whether they meet any obstacles, as seen from a practical perspective. Finally, I hope I have been provocative and have encouraged some discussion.

Appendix[161]

1 Liability for dangerous substances

Art. 6:175 -which came into force on February 1, 1995- reads as follows:

1. He who uses or keeps, while operating his company or exercising his profession, a substance which is known to have such qualities that it constitutes a special danger of a serious nature for persons or property, is liable when the danger materialises. Operating a company also includes every legal entity which uses or keeps a substance in the exercise of its task. A substance that is explosive, flamable, easily flamable, very easily flamable, toxic, or very toxic, according to criteria and methods set out in art. 34 para. 3 of the Dangerous Substances Act, is deemed to create a special danger of a serious nature.
2. (..)
3. (..)
4. (..)
5. In the event that the substance is a part of a chattel personal, as referred to in art. 173 para. 1, or is wrapped in such a chattel or is stocked in a building or "werk", as referred to in art. 174, para. 3, the liable person is he who is liable pursuant to the previous paragraphs of this article.
6. A substance is deemed to be dangerous, according to the first sentence of para. 1, when it is referred to as such in an Order in Council.

Art. 175 is a strict liability provision. It serves two purposes. First, it aims to ensure that liability can be construed in case, for instance, damage is caused by gas that is no longer under human control (and, consequently, is not a chattel personal).[162]

Secondly, and more importantly, all dangerous substances can give rise to strict liability; a defect of the substance is not required. A rather extreme example would be that of an airplane crashing into an oil refinery which, in turn, would lead to

161 Para's 1, 2, and to a large extent 4 are borrowed from Rope-Dancing Dutch Tort Law (J. Spier and C.H.W.M. Sterk).

162 Bill number 21202, Explanatory Memorandum, p. 13.

the explosion of some storage tanks causing serious damage to neighbouring premises. The oil, that is, the dangerous substance in this scenario, was itself not defective. Moreover, the oil company cannot be blamed for the damage as it could not have avoided the explosion. Nevertheless, it is deemed to be liable.[163]

Art. 6:173 BW could not have been invoked because the chattel personal was not defective. Moreover, it is even open to debate whether the oil could be considered to be a chattel personal at the time of the explosion.

However, according to art. 175, liability is not absolute. Art. 6:178 establishes a limited number of exclusions, notably:
Liability under art. 175 (...) can not be invoked in cases where:
a. damage is caused by armed conflict, civil war, insurrection, domestic unrest, or mutiny;
b. damage is caused by natural phenomena of an exceptional, inevitable, and irresistable character (....);
c. damage is exclusively caused through compliance with a specific order or compulsory measure by a public authority;
d. damage is caused by an activity involving substances referred to in art. 175, used lawfully in the interest of the person suffering the damage, whereby it was reasonable towards this person to expose him to the risk of damage;
e. damage is exclusively caused by an act or omission of a third person with the intention to cause damage;
f. hindrance, pollution, or other consequences upon which the liability is based, according to the previous article (= 6:162 BW and 6:163 BW, JS), would not have resulted, had the damage been deliberately caused.[164]

These exceptions are rather usual, although they are restrictive in comparison to traditional tort law concepts. "Force majeure" and "fait d'un tiers" are *not* mentioned.[165] So, for example, the oil company can only successfully invoke an exception if it establishes that the plane crashed as a result of an act committed

163 The example has been given by Dutch company lawyers in their discussion with Government Commissioner, Mr Snijders. He did not deny liability in this case. See also J. Spier, Een kritische verkenning van wetsvoorstel 21202, Kwartaalbericht Nieuw BW 1990, p. 14.

164 The exceptions set out in section 6:178 BW are almost identical to those mentioned in section 8 of the Strasbourg Convention on Civil Liability resulting from activities dangerous to the environment. See J. de Boer, Risico aansprakelijkheid voor gevaarlijke stoffen en milieuverontreiniging, NJB 1993 p. 230 and J. Spier and C.H.W.M. Sterk, the Draft Convention on Civil Liability, Milieu & Recht 1992, pp 593 ff.

165 "Force majeure" is an exception in the new German Umwelthaftungsgesetz: § 4. Moreover, it establishes an exception if "die Anlage bestimmungsgemäß betrieben worden (ist)"; in that case, there is no liability for "Sachschäden (..) wenn die Sache nur unwesentlich oder in einem Maße beeinträchtigt wird, das nach den örtlichen Verhältnissen zumutbar ist." In a recent Flemish draft, "force majeure", as such, is insufficient to avoid liability (see art. 9.1.5). However, art. 9.1.6 provides exceptions which are not included in art. 6:178 BW. See for the Belgian draft, H. Bocken et al., Voorontwerp decreet Milieubeleid and about said articles H. Bocken, D. Ryckborst and S. Deloddere, pp 896 ff.

with the intention to cause damage.[166] However, it is not clear whether the third person is required to have intended to cause damage to the oil company or merely to have caused the damage, that is, the explosion of the airplane. The defendant has to prove this intention which may be very difficult.

2 Joint and several liability

The meaning and significance of art. 6:99 BW (mentioned above) were at stake in the DES case, a case involving product liability (under the pre-directive regime)[167] which led to a much disputed judgement by the Supreme Court.[168] The facts are well known: during the fifties and sixties pregnant women ingested DES tablets which in time proved to be harmful to their daughters. The damage arose after a considerable time delay (in the eighties) following the use of the tablets. At that time, it was impossible (for the daughters) to prove which manufacturer had put into circulation the tablets consumed by the respective mothers. The daughters argued that art. 6:99 BW applied.

The Advocate General, Hartkamp, concluded that art. 6:99 BW did not apply because it was impossible that each defendant *could* have caused the entire damage (of all the daughters). In the event of joint and several liability, each defendant would have had to pay considerably more damage than he *could* have caused. The Supreme Court did not follow this argument. It held that:

> As a result of the construction of the rule, one must consider its wording, purpose, and the parliamentary history.
> The case to be decided falls within the ambit of the wording of the rule. (..) Its application, in this instance, is consistent with its intention. The rule aims to remove the injustice suffered by the injured party who remains uncompensated because it cannot prove who actually caused its damage. Such a difficulty of proof arises in this case. It may be true that Meijers's Explanatory Memorandum and the parliamentary papers do not refer to cases such as the DES case, though it is likely that that type of decision was not contemplated at the time.

166 The same applies to the Austrian draft law on environmental liability (Entwürf Bundesgesetz über die Haftung für Umweltschäden § 5, para. 2); moreover, it establishes a further restriction: "sofern der in Anspruch Genommene beweist, daß alle im Hinblick auf die Gefährlichkeit der Anlage oder Tätigkeit zumutbaren Vorkehrungen getroffen worden sind, um einen solchen Schaden zu vermeiden": Schmidt-Salzer, Kommentar zum Umwelthaftungsrecht p. 70. Under Polish law "force majeure" and "faute d'un tiers" are exceptions too; the degree of negligence does not play any role: B. Lewaszkiewicz-Petrykowska, La responsabilité délictuelle fondée sur le principe du risque; in Entwicklungen des Deliktsrecht in rechtsvergleichender Sicht, Arbeiten zur Rechtsvergleichung, nr 136 (1987), p. 195 ff.

167 The Supreme Court indicates that its decision is limited to product liability cases based on art. 6:162 BW; it leaves unresolved the question of whether the same decision applies in cases where liability is based on art. 6:185 ff BW (the article implementing of the European directive on product liability).

168 HR 9-10-1992, NJ 1994, 535 CJHB.

However, the fact that the issue was not considered is no reason for not applying the rule.
Furthermore, it is essential to highlight that the system that was previously applied by the Court of Appeal can no longer be regarded as acceptable.
Although it is assumed[169] that each of the pharmaceutical companies acted negligently by putting DES into circulation and that the DES daughters suffered serious personal injury in consequence of their mothers' use of DES tablets, according to the Court of Appeal, the DES daughters should remain uncompensated due to the fact that they cannot establish which company actually manufactured the DES tablets used by the mothers in each case.[170]

3 Uncertainty about causation

Often, there is uncertainty as to when the damage has been caused. The question may be of considerable importance for different reasons:

- can the victim still sue the tortfeasor? (a question of prescription); and
- was a tort committed at the time the damage was caused?

The Supreme Court delivered a far-reaching judgement on the latter issue.[171] Cijsouw was employed by De Schelde between 1949 and 1967. In 1988, lung cancer was diagnosed, caused by mesothelioma (an asbestos-related disease). In this disease, it is possible for one crystal to cause the entire damage.[172] The incubation period is between 20 and 40 years.
Between 1949 and October 1961, Cijsouw had been employed in the actual operational part of the business; consequently, he had been physically exposed to asbestos. From that time onwards, however, he worked in the offices of De Schelde.
For the sake of argument, the Supreme Court held that De Schelde had acted negligently as of 1960. However, it remained unproven whether the fatal crystal was swallowed before or after 1960.
The Supreme Court held that the employer was responsible for bearing the risk that the cause of the disease will never be proven, and hence that it will be unable

169 The question of whether or not the defendants acted negligently was left open by the Court of Appeal. For procedural reasons, however, it was assumed that they had acted negligently.

170 One should bear in mind that this doctrine goes far beyond the approach of the majority of US Courts in DES cases. Generally speaking, (a kind of) market share liability is accepted. See for details the Conclusion of the Advocate General Hartkamp NJ 1994, pp 2491 ff), L. Dommering-van Rongen, Produktenaansprakelijkheid (thesis Utrecht 1991, pp 298 ff) and K. Otte, Marktanteilhaftung, Rechtsvergleich und Alternativen im US-amerikanischen und deutschen Recht.

171 HR 25.06.1993, NJ 1993,686 PAS.

172 This at least was the Court's assumption. It is questionable whether it is, indeed, correct. See for (technical) details e.g. H.T. Planteydt, Asbestos Exposure and Health, in Asbest en aansprakelijkheid, pp 121 ff.

to exculpate itself.[173] One should bear in mind, however, that the chance that the damage was caused before 1960 is higher (considerably above 70%).

4 Insurability

As already highlighted above, the amounts implicated are often substantial. Claims for many millions of Dutch guilders are no longer exceptional. This is true for a wide range of cases, spanning environmental liability, product liability, employers' liability (e.g. in asbestos cases), and liability for all kinds of services.

Environmental liability and the question of its insurability attract most of the attention. Until some years ago, Dutch - and foreign - insurers[174] did not specifically confront these issues. In fact, these problems barely existed. Damage was covered under liability policies, albeit often for rather small amounts. As a result, subsequent problems for insurers were likely to arise in the event that they had insured certain unforeseen claims under those policies. For example, insurers did not take environmental liabilities into account when calculating premiums. Furthermore, they did not anticipate claims arising from a distant past.

As far as future claims are concerned, it seems likely that strict liability, as such, can be insured,[175] though only for relatively small amounts.[176] One of the reasons for this is that insurers are not able to predict and calculate their potential risk.

It seems likely that product liability and liability for services, for example, can be covered by insurance. Nonetheless, the increase in the number of claims and in the amounts of the claims will undoubtedly have consequences for the availability of insurance coverage or for the premiums to be paid.[177]

173 I have to stress that the judgement is not crystal clear. It is not inconceivable - albeit unlikely in my view - that the decision can be read differently. See J. Hijma, AA 1994, pp 113/114 and J. Spier, in Asbest en aansprakelijkheid, pp 36 ff.

174 J.H. Wansink, Environmental Liability Insurance in Europe and the United States, TMA 1989, pp 69 ff.

175 A. Keller, Kritische Würdigung des Schweizerischen Systems aus Sicht der Versicherung; in Colloque sur les développements récents du droit de la responsabilité (ed. O. Guillod), p. 391.

176 See for many details, Bill number 21202, Explanatory Memorandum, p. 27 ff., J.H. Wansink, Verzekering voor aansprakelijkheid voor gevaarlijke stoffen in het NBW, TMA 1990, pp 65 ff, and A&V 1993/1, pp 10 ff. See for other countries: W. Pfenningstorf (Germany), id., pp 733 ff, J. Deprimoz (France), id., pp 76 ff, J.C. Morrow (US), id., pp 77 ff, C. Oldertz (Sweden), id., pp 80 ff amd J. Rogge (Belgium), id. pp. 82-89. See also Green paper, pp 12/13.

177 F.J. de Vries argued (in 1990) that insuring attorneys does not (as yet) create major difficulties (unlike in the UK), Wettelijke limitering van aansprakelijkheid, pp 74 ff. Difficulties arising for auditors: idem, p. 116. My colleague O.A. Haazen and I will probably provide more specific information about this topic in a report to the Dutch Lawyers' Association 1996.

Insurers dislike joint and several liability and are alarmed by cases like DES. Further, an increase in the basic premium in such a case must be acknowledged; and more significantly, insurers are likely to refrain from offering insurance in view of the DES judgement, something which may begin to affect other areas of liability, such as environmental liability.[178]

178 See for details J.H. Wansink in International Insurance Law Review, (1993), 6, pp 180/181.

Modération et limitation des responsabilités et des indemnisations

Rapport sur le droit français, par Geneviève VINEY
Professeur à l'Université de Paris I (Panthéon-Sorbonne)

Le problème de la limitation des responsabilités et des indemnisations n'a pas été jusqu'à présent l'une des préoccupations essentielles de la doctrine, de la jurisprudence ni du législateur en France. En effet l'attachement au principe de la réparation intégrale a toujours été et demeure très fort, ce qui explique la très grande méfiance qu'inspire toute tentative de limitation.

En revanche, cette question n'a cessé d'occuper une place centrale dans le domaine de l'assurance. Les assureurs plafonnent en effet leur garantie dans la plupart des contrats d'assurance de responsabilité, sauf pour les dommages corporels qui sont aujourd'hui de plus en plus souvent assurés sans limitation.

En outre, toutes les raisons qui ont été évoquées dans les autres pays pour justifier un effort de limitation existent également en France: Extension de la notion de faute, multiplication des cas de responsabilité sans faute, généralisation de l'obligation au tout des co-auteurs du même dommage, générosité croissante des tribunaux pour l'indemnisation de certains dommages, en particulier les dommages corporels, se conjuguent pour accroître l'étendue et le poids des responsabilités et cette aggravation est d'autant plus sensible que certains "risques majeurs" ou "risques de catastrophe" - risques écologiques, nucléaires, industriels, technologiques... - se sont manifestés en France ces dernières années de façon particulièrement éclatante (mareés noires, pollution par les déchets, contaminations par transfusion sanguine...).

Or, dans le même temps, la crise économique a fait prendre conscience des limites des possibilités de financement permettant de couvrir ces risques (assurances ou autres ressources d'origine fiscale ou para-fiscale) et des conséquences très graves, tant sur le plan économique que sur le plan social, qu'entraînent des condamnations très lourdes, lorsqu'elles ne sont pas assurées: faillites, fermetures d'entreprises, chômage...

C'est pourquoi il paraît utile d'amorcer une réflexion sur cette question de la modération des dommages et intérêts et des limitations de responsabilité, dans la perspective précisément d'un ajustement aux possibilités de l'assurance et des autres mécanismes de garantie.

J. Spier (ed.), The Limits of Liability, 127-136.

Il convient donc d'abord de faire le bilan des instruments que le droit positif offre, dès à présent, pour limiter les responsabilités et modérer les indemnisations (I) avant de s'interroger sur les orientations qui pourraient être envisagées afin d'améliorer les choses dans l'avenir (II).

I Les tendances du droit français quant au problème de la limitation des responsabilités et des indemnisations

L'attachement au principe de la réparation intégrale, qui a été étendu à tous les cas de responsabilité civile, y compris à ceux qui ne sont pas fondés sur la faute, explique la méfiance persistante du droit français à l'égard des méthodes officielles de limitation des responsabilités (A). Toutefois, en y regardant de plus près, on s'aperçoit sans peine que ce droit n'est pas resté insensible aux objurgations de ceux qui souhaitaient restreindre l'impact des responsabilités. Mais, pour y parvenir, il a privilégié l'emploi de méthodes indirectes et quasi-occultes (B).

A.- *La méfiance à l'égard des méthodes officielles de limitation des responsabilités* s'est manifestée tant à l'égard des plafonnements légaux ou réglementaires que du pouvoir de modération judiciaire. Quant aux limitations conventionnelles, si leur validité est en principe admise, elles se heurtent aujourd'hui à des obstacles si nombreux que ce principe paraît fortement écorné.

1°) Le droit français connaît, certes, quelques *dispositions légales ou réglementaires plafonnant* l'indemnisation que les victimes peuvent obtenir à l'occasion de certains types de dommages, mais la plupart de ces dispositions ont été imposées par les conventions internationales auxquelles la France a adhéré. C'est le cas des limitations de responsabilité profitant aux transporteurs maritimes[1] et aériens[2] ainsi qu'à certains transporteurs terrestres[3].

1 Articles 40, 43 et 44 L. 18 juin 1966 et D. 23 mars 1967 modifié par le décret du 24 septembre 1986 qui prévoient les limitations en matière de transport interne de passagers.
Pour les transports internationaux de passagers, la Convention de Bruxelles ayant été dénoncée par la France, on doit appliquer désormais, lorsque les règles de conflits désignent la loi française, la loi de 1966.
Pour les transports internes de marchandises, v. art. 28 L. 18 juin 1966 modifié à plusieurs reprises.
Pour les transports internationaux de marchandises, v. la Convention de Bruxelles de 1924 modifiée en 1968.

2 Ici le texte essentiel est la Convention de Varsovie de 1929 modifiée à plusieurs reprises et qui s'applique au transport de personnes, de bagages et de marchandises, qu'il s'agisse d'un transport interne ou international.

3 Les transports ferroviaires internationaux: art. 6 § 2 C.I.V. de Berne; les transports internationaux de marchandises par route (CMR de Genève). - Des plafonnements existent également dans le cadre des transports ferroviaires et routiers internes de marchandises.

On peut en dire autant de celles qui sont prônées par les textes réglementant la responsabilité civile de l'exploitant d'un réacteur nucléaire[4] et celle de l'exploitant d'un navire nucléaire[5].

Ce sont encore des textes internationaux qui ont inspiré la règle permettant au propriétaire d'un navire de limiter sa responsabilité envers ses co contractants ou les tiers pour les dommages qui se sont produits à bord d'un navire à ceux qui sont en relation directe avec la navigation ou l'utilisation du navire[6] ou encore la limitation de responsabilité dont bénéficie celui qui procède à une opération d'assistance ou de sauvetage en mer[7]. Enfin, on relèvera la convention de Bruxelles du 26 novembre 1969 qui est entrée en vigueur en France en 1975 et qui prévoit un plafond de responsabilité pour les dommages dus à la pollution des mers par les hydrocarbures.

Quant aux dispositions de pur droit interne, elles sont rares.

Certes, il en est une au moins qui est très importante, c'est celle qui prévoit une indemnisation seulement partielle des accidents du travail, mais elle s'explique alors par le caractère automatique de la réparation qui ne relève plus du droit de la responsabilité civile.

Pour le reste, on ne peut guère citer que les limitations de responsabilité instaurées au profit de l'hôtelier[8] ou de l'établissement de santé[9] dont la responsabilité est recherchée à la suite du vol ou de la détérioration des objets déposés entre ses mains par ces clients.

D'ailleurs, ces plafonnements peuvent généralement être écartés ou relevés par convention[10]. En outre, ils sont toujours écartés en présence d'une faute intentionnelle, à laquelle, dans la plupart des cas, les tribunaux assimilent la faute lourde qu'ils définissent de façon extensive[11]. Il arrive même qu'une faute simple suffise à faire obstacle au plafonnement qui, dans ce cas, ne s'applique que lorsque la

4 Il s'agit de la Convention de Paris du 29 juillet 1960 modifiée et complétée par un protocole du 28 janvier 1984 et une convention additionnelle du 31 janvier 1963 modifiée en 1964. Ces textes ont été complétés par une loi du 30 octobre 1968 qui a fixé les mesures que la Convention de Paris avait laissées à l'initiative des parties contractantes.

5 Loi du 12 novembre 1965 modifiée par la loi du 29 novembre 1968.

6 L. 3 janvier 1967 portant statut des navires et autres bâtiments de mer, art. 68 et s. modifiés par la loi N° 84-1151 du 21 décembre 1984; Convention de Londres du 19 novembre 1976 sur la limitation de la responsabilité en matière de créances maritimes.

7 L. 84-1173 du 22 septembre 1984 complétant la loi 67-545 du 7 juillet 1967 relative aux événements de mer.

8 Art. 1953 et 1954 du code civil.

9 Article 2 L. 92.614 du 6 juillet 1992 relative à la responsabilité du fait des vols, pertes et détériorations des objets déposés dans les établissements de santé.

10 Voir, par exemple, Civ.l 15 avril 1986 Bull.Civ. I N° 91, Civ.l 13 octobre 1992 Bull.Civ. I N° 254 p. 167. V.G. VINEY: La responsabilité: effets No 315.

11 V.G. VINEY, op.cit. N° 316.

responsabilité est fondée sur un faut non fautif[12]. C'est seulement par application des textes internationaux que le droit français renforce parfois la portée du plafonnement en ne permettant de l'écarter qu'en présence d'une faute inexcusable[13].

Dans ce contexte de méfiance à l'égard de ce type de limitation de responsabilité, on ne s'étonnera donc pas que le projet de loi destiné à introduire en droit français la directive européenne du 25 juillet 1985 sur la responsabilité du fait des produits défectueux n'ait pas mis en oeuvre la faculté de plafonnement que la directive a donnée aux Etats-membres.

2°) Le droit français, qui se montre ainsi assez restrictif à l'égard des plafonnements légaux ou réglementaires de l'indemnisation, est, en apparence au moins, encore plus hostile à toute forme de *modération judiciaire des dommages et intérêts.*

Sans doute, la loi du 9 février 1975 a-t-elle prévu de donner au juge le pouvoir de modérer la clause pénale, mais seulement en cas d'excès manifeste et le juge ne peut jamais, dans le cadre de cette loi, ramener l'indemnisation à une somme inférieure au montant du préjudice.

D'ailleurs, en dehors de ce domaine particulier, ni le code civil, ni le code de procédure civile ne confère au juge un pouvoir général de modération fondé sur l'équité comme celui qui est reconnu par d'autres systèmes juridiques[14] Bien plus, lorsqu'il a été proposé d'introduire un tel pouvoir dans un domaine particulier, le Parlement s'y est formellement opposé[15].

Pas davantage le droit français n'impose-t-il à la victime une obligation quelconque de "mitigation", lui enjoignant de minimiser son dommage sous peine de voir l'indemnisation amputée de la partie correspondant à ce qui aurait pu être évité si elle avait pris toutes les précautions nécessaires.

3°) Quant aux *limitations conventionnelles*, elles ne sont jugées valables que si elles affectent une responsabilité de nature contractuelle. Encore, dans ce domaine,

12 Voir, pour l'hôtelier, art. 1953 al. 3 c.civ.

13 C'est le cas en matière de transport maritime ou aérien: V.G. VINEY: La responsabilité: effets, N° 316.

14 V.H. STOLL, Consequences of Liability: remedies, International encyclopedia of comparative Law, vol. XI, Torts, Ch.8, N° 155 à 157.
M.E. ROUJOU DE BOUBEE: Essai sur la notion de réparation L.G.D.J. 1974, p. 323 et s.

15 Ce refus s'est manifesté lors de la discussion du texte qui est devenu la loi du 3 janvier 1968 sur la protection des incapables majeurs. Dans l'avant-projet gouvernemental, il était en effet prévu, à propos des dommages causés sous l'empire d'un trouble mental, de donner au tribunal un pouvoir modérateur pour l'ivaluation de l'indemnité. Mais cette disposition a été écartée par l'assemblée nationale qui l'a jugée incompatible avec l'ensemble des solutions du droit français en matière de responsabilité civile.

se heurtent-elles à des obstacles de plus en plus nombreux et importants qui s'opposent soit à leur efficacité, soit même à leur validité[16].

Apparemment, le droit français se montre donc très réticent à l'égard de tous les procédés qui, au moins dans le domaine extra-contractuel, réduisent officiellement la responsabilité et font obstacle au principe de la réparation intégrale.

B.- Toutefois, en regardant de plus près la pratique judiciaire, on constate que *les tribunaux parviennent, de façon indirecte, à limiter très efficacement les indemnisations.*

Les procédés employés à cette fin sont assez diversifiés.

1°) Le plus important est probablement celui qui résulte des *pouvoirs laissés aux juges du fond dans l'appréciation des dommages et intérêts*. Le contrôle exercé par la Cour de cassation reste en effet actuellement très limité, même s'il est en progression[17]. Certes, il s'exerce en principe pour censurer la méconnaissance par les juges du fond du principe de la réparation intégrale, mais en cas de motivation très sommaire, le tribunal se contentant, par exemple, d'affirmer que la somme allouée répare effectivement et complètement les préjudices constatés, la décision sera le plus souvent à l'abri de la cassation. La cour régulatrice censure en effet plus volontiers les motifs exprimés que l'insuffisance des motifs, de telle sorte qu'elle laisse aux juges une marge très importante d'appréciation, surtout à propos des chefs de préjudice difficilement évaluables, comme les préjudices moraux et même certains dommages économiques diffus, tel celui que cause un acte de concurrence déloyale ou une pratique économique illicite. Or il n'est guère douteux que les tribunaux profitent effectivement de cette liberté pour moduler l'indemnisation en tenant compte notamment de la gravité ou de la légèreté de la faute commise, des facultés contributives du responsable, de l'existence ou de l'absence d'assurance, etc......

2°) Un autre moyen, pour les tribunaux, de limiter indirectement l'indemnisation passe par l'*appréciation de la causalité*. Sur ce point encore, la Cour de cassation use assez discrètement de son pouvoir de contrôle. En effet, elle n'a jamais pris parti explicitement en faveur de l'une ou de l'autre des théories de la causalité qui ont été présentées et soutenues en doctrine. Or cette neutralité laisse aux juges du fond une grande liberté et il est bien évident que celle-ci est très souvent utilisée afin d'écarter certaines conséquences lointaines et inattendues du fait dommageable initial, lorsque précisément ces conséquences alourdissent de façon excessive la dette du responsable.

Les exemples jurisprudentiels illustrant cette démarche sont légion et, dans certains cas, la convergence entre les résultats auxquels elle conduit et ceux que

16 Voir G. VINEY: La responsabilité: effets, N° 180 à 228.
17 Voir G. VINEY, op.cit. N° 61 à 66.

produirait une obligation de mitigation imposée à la victime est tout à fait frappante.

On citera un exemple, parmi bien d'autres, emprunté à un arrêt de la 2e Chambre civile de la Cour de cassation rendu le 8 février 1989[18]. Dans cette affaire, il s'agissait d'un très grave accident qui avait provoqué une invalidité totale et l'indemnité allouée après l'accident incluait le salaire d'une tierce personne afin d'assister le blessé à plein temps. Or, plusieurs années après, un incendie se déclara dans la chambre du blessé et celui-ci, qui apparemment était seul, mourut brûlé dans son lit qu'il n'avait pu quitter du fait de sa paralysie. La veuve de la victime assigna alors l'auteur de l'accident initial pour obtenir réparation de ses préjudices par ricochet. La Cour d'appel accueillit cette demande, mais la Cour de cassation censura cette décision: "Doit être cassé", affirma-t-elle, "l'arrêt qui, pour condamner le responsable de l'accident de la circulation à indemniser la veuve de l'invalide en raison du décès de celui-ci, survenu plusieurs années après, dans l'incendie de son lit, énonce que le handicap de la victime, consécutif à l'accident initial, est la seule cause qui l'a empêchée de quitter le lieu du sinistre, alors que le décès avait pour cause immédiate l'incendie du lit et que l'auteur de l'accident avait versé une indemnité pour assistance d'une tierce personne, de nature à inclure la prévention des risques inhérents à l'invalidité de la personne".

Dans cette affaire, il est clair que l'utilisation de la notion de causalité pour limiter l'indemnisation n'est qu'une façade. D'ailleurs, dans d'autres hypothèses où la situation était, du point de vue de la causalité, analogue à celle-là, la Cour de cassation a affirmé la solution inverse[19]. Ce qui a été déterminant, c'est, très vraisemblablement, la constatation de l'existence d'une indemnisation pour assistance d'une tierce personne qui aurait dû permettre, si elle avait été effectivement utilisée pour l'objet auquel elle était destinée, d'éviter le drame qui s'est produit. Autrement dit, si la veuve de la victime s'est vu refuser l'indemnisation de son préjudice par ricochet, c'est tout simplement parce qu'elle n'avait pas pris les précautions qui auraient pu empêcher le décès de son conjoint et qu'elle était en mesure de prendre du fait de l'indemnisation du dommage initial.

Il y a donc là une démarche qui s'apparente à la reconnaissance d'une obligation de mitigation incombant à la victime ou, en cas d'incapacité de celle-ci, à ses proches.

3°) D'ailleurs, *la prise en considération de la faute de la victime, en tant que cause d'exonération partielle* joue souvent le même rôle. Certes, tel n'est pas le cas de la faute antérieure à l'apparition du dommage, mais dans beaucoup d'hypothèses la faute de la victime est invoquée pour refuser de prendre en compte, dans l'indemnisation, certaines aggravations du dommage initial. Il s'agit alors très

18 Bull.civ. II N° 39 p. 20.

19 Voir, par exemple, pour la contamination par transfusion à la suite d'un accident de la circulation Civ.I 17 février 1993 Bull.civ. I N° 80 p. 52.

fréquemment de l'omission d'une précaution qui aurait pu empêcher l'extension du préjudice[20]

Ici encore, l'analogie avec l'affirmation officielle d'une obligation de mitigation incombant à la victime est évidente.

4°) Enfin, on peut se demander si *le principe de non-réparation du dommage imprévisible* que formule l'article 1150 du c.c. n'est pas également susceptible de fournir aux juges un moyen de modérer certaines indemnisations.

A vrai dire, cette disposition n'est pas, pour l'instant, d'un usage très courant et la jurisprudence considère qu'elle ne concerne que la responsabilité contractuelle[21]. Mais, dans ce domaine, il semble bien qu'elle soit utilisée parfois dans cette perspective d'une modération judiciaire des dommages et intérêts[22] et la souplesse de la notion d'imprévisibilité se prête d'ailleurs bien à cet usage. Il n'est donc pas exclu que, si le besoin de renforcer le pouvoir d'équité du juge sur l'ampleur des condamnations se fait sentir de manière plus pressante, elle soit, dans l'avenir, davantage utilisée et même transposée à la responsabilité délictuelle.

Ainsi, l'approche du droit français apparaît-elle assez ambiguë et irrationnelle à propos de cette question de la limitation des responsabilités et des indemnisations. D'un côté, on observe une grande réserve à l'égard des procédés officiels de limitation qui sont maniés avec beaucoup de précautions, tandis que, de l'autre, les tribunaux n'hésitent pas à se servir de moyens indirects afin de modérer les condamnations.

Cette situation paraît donc assez paradoxale et appelle une mise au point.

II Les orientations à envisager

Pour sortir de l'ambiguïté actuelle, il conviendrait de regarder le problème en face et d'adopter des positions claires aussi bien quant au domaine des limitations à envisager (A) que quant aux méthodes à employer pour les mettre en oeuvre.

A.- *Dans quel domaine peut-on envisager d'instaurer des limitations de responsabilité ou de réparation?*

Pour définir ce domaine, il semble a priori assez naturel de tenir compte non seulement des causes de la responsabilité, mais aussi des possibilités de l'assurance et surtout de la nature des dommages.

20 V.C. LAPOYADE-DESCHAMPS: La responsabilité de la victime thèse Bordeaux 1977, préface A. TUNC.

21 V.G. VINEY, La responsabilité: effets, N° 319 à 333.

22 Voir, par exemple, Civ.[3] 13 mai 1992 Bull.civ. III N° 151 p. 92.

1°) Il semblerait d'abord assez logique de *distinguer selon les causes et la responsabilité*. En effet il paraît plus naturel de limiter la responsabilité sans faute ou objective que les responsabilités fondées sur la faute et on peut d'ailleurs observer que certains systèmes juridiques considèrent que toute responsabilité objective doit en principe être plafonnée.

Cependant, en France, la notion de faute est aujourd'hui définie très largement: elle englobe des maladresses ou erreurs parfois insignifiantes et c'est sans doute la raison pour laquelle la jurisprudence ne s'est pas fixée à cette distinction entre responsabilité pour faute et responsabilité sans faute mais lui en a préféré une autre en admettant que les limitations légales ou conventionnelles de la réparation sont en principe écartées en présence d'une faute intentionnelle ou d'une faute lourde. Les tribunaux ont ainsi opposé les responsabilités fondées sur le risque ou sur la faute simple, d'une part, qui sont susceptibles d'être limitées ou modérées à celles qui découlent d'une faute intentionnelle ou lourde, d'autre part, qui doivent subsister intégralement.

Cette réparation paraît judicieuse car elle permet d'éviter que les limitations de responsabilité n'encouragent la mauvaise foi ou de graves négligences.

2°) Une autre distinction, à laquelle on pourrait songer, *prendrait en compte les possibilités de l'assurance*. Par exemple, il serait concevable de lier les plafonnements légaux de responsabilité à une obligation d'assurance ou d'admettre la validité de certaines clauses limitatives de responsabilité à condition qu'une assurance garantisse cette responsabilité plafonnée[23]. Ces combinaisons permettraient en effet de garantir une indemnité minimale sur laquelle pourraient compter les victimes tout en donnant aux assureurs la possibilité d'évaluer les risques et, par conséquent, de les assurer à un coût raisonnable.

3°) Enfin et surtout, ce qui paraît le plus important, c'est de *déterminer quels sont les dommages dont l'indemnisation peut être écartée ou plafonnée.*

Or, sur ce point, il est évident que certaines distinctions sont nécessaires car l'utilité sociale de l'indemnisation apparaît très inégale selon les types de préjudices: Alors que, par exemple, pour les conséquences économiques d'un dommage corporel, le principe de la réparation intégrale répond à une exigence d'équité qui paraît trop essentielle aujourd'hui pour que l'on puisse y déroger, au moins par convention, il semble, en revanche, beaucoup moins indispensable en ce qui concerne les atteintes aux biens ainsi que les pertes de profits économiques. Pour ces dommages, un aménagement de la réparation dans un sens restrictif est en effet plus facilement concevable.

23 Voir par exemple, en ce sens, Civ.1 13 octobre 1992 Bull.civ. I N° 257 p. 162.

Quant aux préjudices moraux, ils sont, par définition même, sans équivalent pécuniaire. Il ne saurait donc être question de les réparer intégralement par l'allocation de dommages et intérêts. C'est pourquoi, dans ce domaine, il serait envisageable non seulement de plafonner les indemnités, mais même de prévoir des forfaits plus ou moins symboliques.

Ainsi les limitations de responsabilité qui apparaissent normales dans certains cas, se révèlent beaucoup plus contestables ailleurs. Il est donc important de chercher à définir rationnellement leur domaine d'application.

B.- Mais il convient également de choisir *les méthodes adaptées à leur mise en oeuvre.*

Or, sur ce point l'expérience peut apporter certains éléments de réponse.

1°) Elle révèle d'abord le *caractère souvent insatisfaisant des plafonnements légaux*. En effet, même si ces limitations sont justifiées au moment où les textes qui les édictent sont promulgués, elles deviennent très vite obsolètes et inadaptées à la situation visée.

Le cas des transports aériens est, à ce point de vue, exemplaire. En effet tout le monde s'accorde aujourd'hui - et depuis longtemps - à constater que les plafonnements institués en 1929 par la Convention de Varsovie sont devenus, même après les diverses révisions dont cette convention a fait l'objet, d'une faiblesse ridicule eu égard à la gravité des dommages qui peuvent résulter d'un accident aérien. Or les progrès de la sécurité aérienne rendent aujourd'hui ce risque facilement assurable, ce qui justifierait des indemnisations beaucoup plus généreuses.

A l'inverse d'ailleurs, lorsqu'elles fixées à un niveau très élève, ces limitations deviennent inutiles. C'est la raison pour laquelle, par exemple, la faculté reconnue aux Etats membres par la directive européenne du 25 juillet 1985 sur la responsabilité du fait des produits défectueux d'introduire un plafonnement n'a guère été utilisée par les législateurs nationaux, le chiffre minimal prévu par le texte étant apparu aux intéressés comme trop important[24] et susceptible de "tirer vers le haut" les évaluations.

2°) Doit-on alors préférer *l'octroi au juge d'un pouvoir de modération fondé sur l'équité?* A priori, la solution est séduisante par sa souplesse, mais elle peut aussi effrayer car elle introduit officiellement dans le droit de la responsabilité civile un élément d'arbitraire. Cependant il ne serait pas impossible, semble-t-il, d'aménager et de discipliner ce pouvoir modérateur en le soumettant à certaines conditions et en définissant ses critères d'application. Il pourrait ainsi acquérir une certaine efficacité.

24 70 millions d'écus.

3°) Reste enfin *la méthode conventionnelle*, qui est probablement la meilleure à condition qu'elle soit soumise à un contrôle strict des clause abusives, mais elle n'est, en toute hypothèse, utilisable qu'à propos des responsabilités dont la survenance est prévisible à l'avance.

L'aménagement d'un régime cohérent et efficace de limitation des responsabilités et des indemnisations exigerait donc un effort important de coordination et de rationnalisation. Certes, le droit actuel n'est pas inexistant dans ce domaine. Bien au contraire, les techniques de limitation sont, nous l'avons constaté, nombreuses et diversifiées, mais elles sont employées de manière assez anarchique, sans vue d'ensemble. Or il s'agit là d'une question dont l'importance est capitale aussi bien pour les victimes que pour les responsables et leurs assureurs. Elle mériterait donc de retenir davantage l'attention aussi bien de la doctrine - pour proposer des solutions - que de la jurisprudence et du législateur - pour les mettre en oeuvre -.

Détermination et réduction de la réparation en droit suisse

Pierre Widmer / Lausanne

I Le soi-disant principe de la réparation intégrale

1 Dans l'enseignement du droit de la responsabilité civile en Suisse, lorsqu'il est question de la réparation du préjudice, on entendra souvent poser comme principe que, si la responsabilité de l'auteur de l'atteinte est établie, *la personne lésée a droit à être indemnisée pour l'ensemble du dommage souffert*[1]. Il est vrai que la clause générale de l'article 41 al.1 du Code suisse des obligations (COS)[2] prévoit de façon apparemment très catégorique que

> *"Celui qui cause, d'une manière illicite, un dommage à autrui ... est tenu de le réparer."*

Des énoncés semblables, bien que rédigés en termes encore plus généraux, et sans référence précise à la réparation comme telle, se retrouvent par ailleurs tant dans les dispositions du Code civil suisse (CCS)[3] et du COS qui consacrent des hypothèses spécifiques de responsabilité, dites *"responsabilités objectives simples [einfache Kausalhaftungen]"*[4], que dans la plupart des lois spéciales instituant une responsabilité à raison du risque (ou *"responsabilité objective aggravée [Gefährdungs-*

1 OFTINGER, *Schweiz.Haftpflichtrecht I: Allgemeiner Teil*, 4e éd., Zurich 1975, § 7, p.261: *"Vorweg gilt die Regel, dass der Schaden grundsätzlich ganz zu ersetzen ist"*; plus nuancé maintenant: OFTINGER/STARK, *Schweiz. Haftpflichtrecht I: Allgemeiner Teil*, 5e éd. Zurich 1995 (cité ci après: OFTINGER/STARK, *AT 5*) § 7, N.1 ss., pp.377 ss.. Cf. aussi: GUHL/MERZ/KOLLER, *Das schweizerische Obligationenrecht*, 8e éd., Zurich 1991, § 10 IV/2, p.77: *"Grundsätzlich ist der Schaden ganz zu ersetzen. Ausnahmsweise kann sich aber in verschiedener Richtung eine Begrenzung des zu leistenden Schadenersatzes ergeben."*; dans le même sens: HONSELL, *Schweiz. Haftpflichtrecht*, Zurich 1995, § 9, p.72:*"Grundsätzlich hat der Schädiger den vollen Ersatz zu leisten, sofern nicht einer der in OR 44 genannten Reduktionsgründe vorliegt"*.

2 Recueil systématique du droit fédéral [ci-après: RS] 220.

3 RS 210.

4 Il s'agit des dispositions suivantes: art.333 (chef de famille) et 679 CS (propriétaire d'immeuble) ainsi que 55 (employeur), 56 (détenteur d'animal) et 58 COS (propriétaire d'ouvrage). On peut y ajouter la nouvelle responsabilité du fait des produits (cité infra n.17/8) ainsi que la responsabilité prévue à l'art.39, al.1, de la nouvelle loi sur la radioprotecion/LRaP (RS 814.50) entrée en vigueur le 1.10.1994.

J. Spier (ed.), The Limits of Liability, 137-162.

haftung]"[6]. C'est ainsi que, pour ne citer qu'un exemple, l'art.58, al.1 de la Loi fédérale sur la circulation routière (LCR)[6] prévoit que

> "Si, par suite de l'emploi d'un véhicule automobile, une personne est tuée ou blessée ou qu'un dommage matériel est causé, le détenteur est civilement responsable."

Et la Loi fédérale sur la responsabilité civile en matière nucléaire (LRCN)[7] de renchérir sur ce ton en proclamant même, à l'article 3, alinéa1, que

> *"L'exploitant d'une installation nucléaire répond* ***de manière illimitée*** *des dommages d'origine nucléaire causés par des substances nucléaires se trouvant dans son installation."*

2 Or, l'affirmation selon laquelle la réparation intégrale constituerait l'idée directrice du droit de l'indemnisation - une opinion que l'on peut à la rigueur soutenir en se plaçant à un niveau d'abstraction très élevé - doit immédiatement être relativisée. Car en réalité (et c'est de la réalité du droit positif que nous parlons), *le principe en question n'a en fait qu'une portée négative.* Nous entendons par là qu'il n'implique nullement une garantie pour la victime d'être entièrement dédommagée, mais que - si l'on veut à tout prix maintenir l'image d'une règle fondamentale - il signifie uniquement que la réparation ne pourra en aucun cas excéder le dommage effectif. "*Le montant du dommage ... constitue l'indemnité maximum que le défendeur peut devoir payer ... La réparation doit placer le lésé dans la situation qui était la sienne avant l'atteinte; elle ne doit pas l'enrichir*"[8].

3 On pourrait même soutenir que, à proprement parler, ce soi-disant principe représente *l'exception qui confirme la règle.* Et la règle, ce serait alors celle qui est énoncée à l'art.43 al.1 COS, selon lequel:

> *"Le juge détermine le mode* ***ainsi que l'étendue*** *de la réparation* ***d'après les circonstances et la gravité de la faute.****"*

3.1 Dans le même ordre d'idées, mais formulé cette fois de manière facultative, l'article suivant (art.44 al.1 COS) confère au juge la compétence de

> *" ...* ***réduire les dommages-intérêts ou même n'en point allouer,*** *lorsque la partie lésée a consenti à la lésion ou lorsque des faits dont elle est responsable*

5 Sur les deux catégories de *responsabilités "causales"*, cf. DESCHENAUX/TERCIER, *La responsabilité civile,* 2e éd., Berne 1982, § 2, NN.30 ss, pp.42 s; A.KELLER, *Haftpflicht im Privatrecht I,* 5e éd., Berne 1993, p.37 ss.

6 RS 741.01.

7 RS 732.44.

8 DESCHENAUX/TERCIER, *La responsabilité civile* (cité supra n.5) § 28 N.2, p.242.

ont contribué à créer le dommage, à l'augmenter, ou qu'ils ont aggravé la situation du débiteur."

L'alinéa 2 de cette disposition prévoit en outre que

> *"Lorsque le préjudice n'a été causé ni intentionnellement, ni par l'effet d'une grave négligence ou imprudence, et que sa réparation exposerait le débiteur à la gêne, le juge peut équitablement réduire les dommages-intérêts."*

Notons enfin que cette dernière idée est également exprimée, mais mais sous l'optique inverse de la victime, à l'art.62 al.2 de la LCR[9], une loi qui, en matière de responsabilité civile, est généralement considérée comme une loi-modèle et (malgré ses trente-six ans d'existence) comme une loi moderne[10]. En vertu de cette disposition

> *"Lorsque la personne tuée ou blessée jouissait d'un revenu exceptionnellement élevé, le juge peut, en tenant compte de toutes les circonstances, réduire équitablement l'indemnité."*[11]

3.2 Il est vrai que les trois exemples mentionnés en dernier n'infirmeraient pas fondamentalement le principe de la réparation intégrale, à supposer qu'il existe. Ils ne font en effet qu'attribuer au juge une faculté et une *marge d'appréciation*; et l'hypothèse de la réduction d'une indemnité en fonction de la situation économique difficile du débiteur ou, au contraire, d'une aisance particulière du créancier, revêt clairement un caractère exceptionnel; l'article cité de la LCR le dit d'ailleurs clairement, même si, du point de vue strictement grammatical, l'adverbe "*exceptionnellement*" se rapporte au niveau de fortune de la victime et non pas au pouvoir du juge.

3.3 En revanche, et bien qu'il soit possible, sur un plan théorique, de les distinguer selon leur champ d'application[12], les normes énoncées aux articles 43 al.1, et 44 al.1 COS reposent sur une *idée unique et générale* que le législateur a nuancée en la modulant de façon plus ou moins impérative. Ainsi, même si à l'art.44 al.1 COS, la possibilité pour le juge de réduire l'indemnité en cas de responsabilité concomitante du lésé n'est présentée que sous une forme facultative, elle n'est pas une

9 Cité supra n. 6.

10 WIDMER, *La réforme du droit de la responsabilité civile et son impact sur les règles régissant la circulation routière*, in: Pratique Juridique Actuelle [PJA] 9/92, p.1086 ss (1094, N.21).

11 Ce motif de réduction était déjà prévu dans une des plus anciennes lois de responsabilité objective: la loi sur la responsabilité des entreprises de chemins de fer du 28 mars 1905 [LRC], art.4; il avait aussi été repris dans la loi sur l'utilisation pacifique de l'énergie atomique de 1959 (LEA; RS 732.0) et il se retrouve à l'art.7 al.2 de la LRCN (cité supra n.7) dont l'al.1 exclut pourtant expressément l'application de l'art.44 al.2 COS.

12 BREHM, *Commentaire bernois* VI/1, t.3/1, Berne 1986-90, N.31 ad art.43 COS; IDEM, *L'étendue des dommages-intérêts (dans le cadre des art.43 al.1 et 44 al.2 COS)*, in: *Die Verantwortlichkeit im Recht*, vol.2, Zurich 1981, p.499 ss (500).

simple recommandation à l'adresse du juge dont celui-ci pourrait tenir compte ou non, selon son humeur et son bon plaisir. La contribution causale du lésé à la survenance du dommage est en même temps l'une des "*circonstances*" qui doivent obligatoirement être prises en considération dans le cadre de l'art.43 al.1 COS. Cette conclusion s'impose en tout cas lorsqu'on admet que *déterminer l'étendue de la réparation ne signifie au fond rien d'autre que l'ajuster en fonction du principe de responsabilité* sur laquelle elle se fonde, c'est-à-dire: la rendre *"adéquate"*.[13]

4 Les règles qui viennent d'être évoquées ont une *portée générale*, à l'exception de celles qui figurent uniquement dans certaines lois spéciales[14], mais qui pourraient également être généralisées dans le cadre de la revision totale du droit suisse de la responsabilité civile qui est actuellement en voie de préparation[15].

4.1 Ainsi, la plupart des lois spéciales renvoient aux dispositions des articles 43 et 44 COS dans des termes plus ou moins identiques à ceux de l'article 62, alinéa1, de la LCR[16]:

> *"Le mode et l'étendue de la réparation ... sont régis par les principes du code des obligations concernant les actes illicites."*[17]

13 Cf. infra ch.8 et 9.3 i.f.; OFTINGER/STARK, *AT 5* (cité supra n.1), adoptent à cet égard une attitude un peu équivoque, puisque, après avoir en principe admis que les règles sur la réduction de la réparation s'imposent d'office au juge (§7 N.7, p.381), ils déclarent un peu plus loin (§ 7 N.12, p.383) que: *"Die Berücksichtigung der Proportionalität zwischen Verschulden und Haftpflicht ist daher nicht als gesetzlich vorgeschrieben zu betrachten; OR 43 I gibt dem Richter diese Möglichkeit, schreibt sie aber nicht vor"*. Dans un sens plus proche de la position défendue ici: HONSELL, *Schweiz.Haftpflichtrecht* (cité supra n.1), § 9, p.72.

14 Supra ch.3.1 i.f., n.11.

15 OFFICE FEDERAL DE LA JUSTICE (éd.), *Rapport de la Commission d'étude pour la revision totale du droit de la responsabilité civile*, Berne 1991; les 102 thèses de la Commission sont aussi publiées dans PJA 9/92 (cité supra n.10), p.1099 ss.
Sur la vocation générale de l'ar.62 al.2 LCR: WIDMER, *La réforme du droit de la responsabilité* (cité supra n.10), p.1096 N.28.

16 Citée supra n.6.

17 Une formule semblable se retrouve notamment dans les lois suivantes: **1)** LF concernant les installations électriques/LIE (RS 743.0) art.36 al.1; **2)** LF sur la navigation aérienne/LNA (RS 748.0), art.79; **3)** LF sur les installations de transport par conduites/LITC (RS 746.1) art.34; **4)** LF sur la chasse/LChP (RS 922.0), art.15 al.2; **5)** LF sur la protection des eaux/LEaux (RS 814.20) art.69 al.3; **6)** LF sur les substances explosibles/LExpl (RS 941.41) art.27 al.1 i.f.; **7)** LF sur la responsabilité civile en matière nucléaire (LRCN; cité supra n.7) art.7; **8)** LF sur la responsabilité du fait des produits/LRFP (RS 221.112.944), art.11 al.1 (une version antérieure excluait l'application de l'art.44 al.2 COS comme incompatible avec la Directive CE 85/374; la non-adhésion de la Suisse à l'EEE a permis de renoncer à cette exclusion); **9)** Projet de revision de la LF sur la protection de l'environnement (LPE) du 7 juin 1993, in: Feuille fédérale [FF] 1993 II p.1337 ss (1447 et 1468 s), art.59a al.3.
La LRC de 1905 (citée supra n.11) était jusqu'à présent la seule loi spéciale de responsabilité civile à ne pas prévoir ce genre de renvoi au COS qui, dans sa version actuelle, est entré en vigueur en 1912, donc sept ans plus tard; elle ne se réfère à l'ancien COS de 1881 qu'en ce qui concerne la prescription (art.14 al.2) et règle elle-même les questions relatives à l'exonération ainsi qu'à la fixation et à la réduction de la réparation (art.4 ss).

Ces lois instituent régulièrement une responsabilité objective à raison du risque. Logiquement, la gravité ou la légèreté de la faute (du responsable ou de ses auxiliaires) ne devrait donc en principe pas pouvoir influencer l'étendue de la réparation, puisque que la responsabilité comme telle repose sur un autre fondement et qu'elle est précisément indépendante de toute faute subjective.[18]

4.2 Il y a cependant lieu de nuancer quelque peu cette conclusion - car, même en cas de *responsabilité dite "causale"*, la faute du côté du responsable peut encore jouer un rôle pour la fixation de la réparation. Elle ne peut, certes, pas justifier une réduction des dommages-intérêts, puisque le simple fait que le risque en question se soit réalisé suffit à fonder l'obligation de réparer. Il est par contre généralement admis qu'elle peut agir dans le sens inverse au titre de "*faute additionnelle*" qui s'ajoute au chef objectif de responsabilité; ceci signifie que lorsqu'il y aurait en principe lieu de réduire l'indemnité en raison d'une autre circonstance, notamment une faute concomitante du lésé, cette dernière pourra être entièrement ou partiellement neutralisée par la faute additionnelle (personnelle ou à la charge d'un auxiliaire) imputable au "responsable causal"[19]. Il s'agit là d'une hypothèse qui, à notre avis, est également couverte par la formule très générale de l'art.43, al.1 COS. Il paraît néanmoins opportun de profiter de la revision totale du droit suisse de la responsabilité civile pour consacrer explicitement le rôle de la faute additionnelle dans la loi[20].

Une faute additionnelle entre également en ligne de compte dans le cadre des responsabilités "semi-objectives", dites *"responsabilités causales simples"*[21]. C'est ainsi que l'on désigne les hypothèses particulières de responsabilité prévues par le CCS et le COS et qui, selon la doctrine dominante, se fondent sur la *"violation présumée d'un devoir de diligence" ou sur une "irrégularité"*[22]. Il s'agit en fait de reponsabilités dans lesquelles la faute est radicalement objectivée, de sorte que même la capacité de discernement du sujet responsable devient sans importance[23]. Si on les considère comme de véritables responsabilités objectives, une faute du responsable ou de ses auxiliaires s'ajoute de la même manière au chef principal de

La nouvelle loi sur la radioprotection (citéé supra n.4) reste totalement muette en ce qui concerne l'applicabilité des règles générales du COS; il semble que le parlement, qui a introduit le nouvel art.39 en cours de débat, ait considéré leur application comme allant de soi.

18 BREHM, *Commentaire* (cité supra n.12), N.41 ad art.43 COS; IDEM, *L'étendue des dommages-intérêts* (cité supra n.12) p.509s.

19 DESCHENAUX/TERCIER, *La responsabilité civile* (cité supra n.5), § 7, N.5, p.79; § 28, NN.28/29, pp.246 s et § 29, N.11, p.251; OFTINGER, *Haftpflichtrecht I* (cité supra n.1) p.139 et p.264 s; A.KELLER, *Haftpflicht im Privatrecht I* (cité supra n.5), pp.97 et 352 ss; plutôt critique: STARK, *Ausservertragliches Haftpflichtrecht/Skriptum*, 2e éd., Zurich 1988, N.330, p.73.

20 Cf. *Rapport de la Commission d'étude* ... (cité supra n.15) ch.V/3.3.7, p.67 s, et thèse 53-4, al.4.

21 Supra ch.1, n.4.

22 OFTINGER/STARK, *Schweizerisches Haftpflichtrecht II/1*, 4e éd., Zurich 1987, § 17, N.6 ss, p.127 ss; A.KELLER, *Haftpflicht im Privatrecht I* (cité supra n.5), pp.38 ss.

23 Pour une approche critique, cf. WIDMER, *Le visage actuel de la responsabilité civile en droit suisse*, in: O.GUILLOD (éd.), *Colloque: Développement récents du droit de la responsabilité civile*, Zurich 1991, p.7 ss (12 ss).

la responsabilité. Si, en revanche, on les rapproche de la responsabilité aquilienne, il ne semblerait pas illogique d'appliquer directement l'art.43, al.1 COS: *Pourquoi, en effet, la faute "objective" ou "objectivée" ne serait-elle pas également susceptible de gradation?* Ce d'autant plusque, précisément, ces responsabilités sont censées appréhender ce que les pandectistes auraient appelé une "*culpa levissima*"[24].

Par contre, il n'est guère contesté (bien que certains anciens arrêts se soient montrés plutôt réticents) que le juge peut réduire le montant de la réparation par rapport au dommage effectif en tenant compte d'autres "circonstances", et notamment d'un cas fortuit, *aussi dans le cadre d'une responsabilité objective*[25].

4.3 Le champ d'application des dispositions générales sur la fixation et la réduction de la réparation s'étend également à la *responsabilité contractuelle*, pour laquelle l'art.99 al.3 COS dispose que:

> *"Les règles relatives à la responsabilité dérivant d'actes illicites s'appliquent par analogie aux effets de la faute contractuelle".*[26]

Doctrine et jurisprudence ont cependant tendance à se montrer plus réservées dans l'application des art.43 et 44 COS au domaine contractuel. Cette retenue s'imposerait, selon les auteurs qui la défendent, essentiellement pour deux motifs: d'une part, parce que le lésé est normalement tenu, en tant que cocontractant, à une contre-prestation ou rémunération, et, deuxièmement, parce qu'il serait inéquitable de faire supporter au créancier le risque professionnel du débiteur[27].

Ces arguments ne paraissent pas entièrement convaincants. Le fait que l'auteur du dommage et la victime soient liés par un contrat ne justifie pas en soi et automatiquement une attitude plus sévère dans la fixation de la réparation. Le législateur a déjà tenu compte de la particularité du lien contractuel en opérant un renversement du fardeau de la preuve en ce qui concerne la faute du débiteur (art.97 al.1 COS); la responsabilité de celui-ci prend ainsi un caractère d'obligation de garantie - correspondant précisément à son risque professionnel - et se rapproche d'une

24 La doctrine, pour autant qu'elle ait vu le problème, rejette cette idée ou la refuse implicitement: cf. BREHM (dans les passages cités supra n.18) qui mentionne cependant plusieurs arrêts du Tribunal fédéral qu'il qualifie de *"inconséquents"* et où une réduction a été accordée en fonction de la légèreté de la faute; cf. également A.KELLER, *Haftpflicht im Privatrecht I* (cité supra n.5), p.352 ss, ainsi que OFTINGER/STARK, *AT 5* (cité supra n.1), § 7 N.12a, n.23, p.384.

25 BREHM, *Commentaire* (cité supra n.12), N.43 ad art.43 COS (avec mention des arrêts contraires: ATF [= Arrêts du Tribunal fédéral suisse] 60 II 156 et 62 II 191); IDEM, *L'étendue des dommages-intérêts* (cité supra n.12), p.510; cf. également: OFTINGER/STARK, *AT 5* (cité supra n.1), § 7 N.36, p.401.

26 Pour une analyse circonstanciée de cette norme, cf. BRUNNER, *Die Anwendung deliktsrechtlicher Regeln auf die Vertragshaftung,* Fribourg 1991.

27 Dans ce sens notamment: BREHM, *Commentaire* (cité supra n.12), N.38 ss ad art.43 COS; IDEM, *L'étendue des dommages-intérêts* (cité supra n.12) p.502.

responsabilité (semi-)objective[28]. Il n'y a pas de raison de l'aggraver encore plus en modifiant les principes sur la fixation de la réparation. D'ailleurs, l'ar.99 COS, après avoir énoncé, dans son premier alinéa, que *"en général, le débiteur répond de toute faute"*, prévoit expressément à l'al.2 que:

> *"Cette responsabilité est plus ou moins étendue selon la nature particulière de l'affaire; elle s'apprécie notamment avec moins de rigueur lorsque l'affaire n'est pas destinée à procurer un avantage au débiteur".*

L'élément de la gratuité ou de la complaisance est ainsi expressément pris en compte pour les cas oû il y a lieu d'apprécier la responsabilité sous cet aspect spécifique. Il ne serait pas correcte d'en déduire que l'application des règles normales, prévue par l'al.3, serait d'emblée exclue lorsqu'il s'agit d'une transaction à titre onéreux.

II Facteurs d'exonération et de réduction de lege lata et de lege ferenda

5 La présentation des normes qui régissent la détermination de la réparation a montré que *le droit suisse de la responsabilité ne repose par sur le principe du "tout ou rien (Alles-oder-Nichts-Prinzip)"*, mais qu'il consacre au contraire un système permettant de doser l'obligation de réparation en fonction de diverses circonstances. Il ne nous semble pas exagéré, dans ces conditions, de parler d'une conception de *"responsabilité proportionnée"*[29] qui peut être comparée - mutatis mutandis, bien entendu - à celle de la responsabilité pénale.

Cela est particulièrement évident pour la *responsabilité fondée sur la faute*; même en admettant que la "faute civile" puisse ou doive être conçue différemment de celle dont se sert le droit pénal, elle reste une notion foncièrement relative et saisissable uniquement par rapport aux données objectives et subjectives d'un événement concret. De ce fait, elle est susceptible d'une infinité de nuances et de gradations qui peuvent et doivent influencer l'étendue de la réparation.

Il ne devrait en principe pas en aller autrement dans les *responsabilités objectives*. Au lieu de parler de *"gravité"* comme on le fait pour la faute, on préférera utiliser le terme d' *"intensité"* en l'appliquant au rapport de causalité[30] existant (ou supposé) entre le dommage et le risque typique qui caractérise le fait de rattachement de la responsabilité en question (détention d'un animal ou d'un véhicule,

28 Cf. à cet égard l'opinion très catégorique de A.KELLER, *Haftpflicht im Privatrecht I* (cité supra n. 5), p.371 s.

29 Cette façon de voir les choses est contestée par DESCHENAUX/TERCIER, *La responsabilité civile* (cité supra n.5), § 28, N.15, p.244. STARK, *Skriptum* (cité supra n.19), N.521, p.113, se montre également réservé en parlant du "pragmatisme" de l'ordre juridique suisse. Cf. également les passages de OFTINGER/STARK, *AT 5* (cité supra. n.1), cités supra n.13.

30 Le "rapport de causalité" doit être compris dans un sens normatif comme *"lien d'imputation"*; cf. infra ch.8.

exploitation d'une entreprise de chemins de fer ou d'une centrale nucléaire etc.). L'intensité de ce lien peut également varier en fonction des circonstances qui concourent à la réalisation du risque, et elle peut et doit trouver une correspondance dans l'évaluation adéquate et équitable de la responsabilité (ou des responsabilités) en jeu.

6 Cette *gradation selon la "gravité" ou l' "intensité"* du critère d'imputation peut donc en effet aller du "tout" au "rien". C'est ce qui ressort expressément de l'art.44 al.1 COS selon lequel le juge peut, suivant l'importance des facteurs retenus à la charge du lésé, réduire l'indemnité jusqu'à zéro; il peut

> "*réduire les dommages-intérêts, ou même n'en point allouer* ...".

Et il ne faut pas se méprendre sur le fait que ce principe n'est énoncé explicitement que pour le cas d'une faute ou d'un fait concomitant imputables à la victime. *Le cas de la réduction à zéro équivaut en fait à une exonération totale du responsable*, et celle-ci correspond à un principe général. Un événement dommageable qui semblait à première vue - c'est-à-dire sur la base d'une appréciation sommaire de la causalité naturelle - engager la responsabilité d'une personne déterminée, peut, lors d'un examen plus approfondi, s'avérer être dû à des causes extérieures dont le rôle apparaît comme prépondérant, compte tenu du fondement de la responsabilité initialement admise et de sa portée normative.

On admet en général *trois motifs classiques d'exonération*, à savoir - en plus de *la faute ou du fait prédominant du lésé - la force majeure et la faute ou le fait prédominant d'un tiers.*

6.1 Jusqu'ici, le droit suisse a adopté, sur ce point, un attitude plutôt éclectique, pour ne pas dire: incohérente. Comme on vient de le voir, le COS - dans son chapitre consacré aux actes illicites - ne mentionne que les faits imputables au lésé. Certaines lois spéciales énumèrent les trois causes d'exonérations, tel que la LCR[31] à son art.59 al.1:

> *"Le détenteur est libéré de la responsabilité civile s'il prouve que l'accident a été causé par la force majeure ou par une faute grave du lésé ou d'un tiers sans que lui-même ou les personnes dont il est responsable aient commis de faute et sans qu'une défectuosité du véhicule ait contribué à l'accident".*

Dans d'autres lois on ne trouve de référence qu'à une ou deux causes d'exonération, et il n'est pas toujours facile de déterminer si l'omission correspond à une volonté positive - un *"silence qualifié"* - du législateur ou si elle est tout simplement due à un inadvertance[32]. Nous pensons que, sur le plan des principes, il faut

31 Cité supra n.6.

32 Pour un aperçu général de ces divergences: STARK, *Probleme der Vereinheitlichung des Haftpflichtrechts*, in: Revue de Droit Suisse [RDS] 86 (1967) II, p.1 ss (20 et 23 ss).

admettre que les *causes dites "d'interruption du lien de causalité"* sont valables dans tous les domaines; cela est en tout cas incontesté en ce qui concerne les faits imputables au lésé lui-même[33] .

Il se peut cependant que, dans certaines hypothèses de responsabilité pour risque, la force majeure ou le fait d'un tiers ne présente *pratiquement jamais une intensité suffisante à écarter complètement la cause primaire* inhérente à l'activité dangereuse en question. Il en va ainsi, par exemple, de la responsabilité de l'exploitant d'un aéronef (pour les dommages causés sur la surface de la terre): on peut difficilement imaginer une force naturelle qui puisse être qualifiée comme *"majeure"* par rapport au risque particulièrement élevé de ce moyen de locomotion, ou le fait d'un tiers qui ne soit pas d'emblée compris dans ce risque[34]. Des considérations analogues s'imposent à plus forte raison en matière de responsabilité nucléaire; ici, le fait de ne citer que la faute grave de la victime comme possible motif exonératoire procède d'une intention précise du législateur qui, d'une part, n'a pas voulu reconnaître un effet libératoire à la force majeure (ni même aux conséquences comparables d'un conflit armé) et qui, d'autre part, a tenu à "canaliser" la responsabilité exclusivement sur l'exploitant de l'installation nucléaire[35].

6.2 Il n'en reste pas moins que l'exonération totale doit pouvoir être admise dans tous les cas où une responsabilité qui n'était qu'apparente s'avère être entièrement inadéquate; les causes d'exonération ne sont en définitive que les *"conditions négatives" de la responsabilité*. C'est afin d'établir clairement ce principe et de lui donner tout son poids et sa portée globale, qu'il est proposé, en vue d'une revision totale du droit de la responsabilité civile en Suisse, d'introduire dans ce que nous appellerons la *"Partie générale du droit de la responsabilité civile"* une norme générale qui pourrait être libellée comme suit:

> *"Une personne est exonérée de toute responsabilité si un fait qui ne lui est pas imputable a contribué de manière manifestement prépondérante à la survenance du dommage ou à son aggravation, notamment une force majeure ou des faits ou des risques caractérisés imputables à un tiers où à la personne lésée".*[36]

Pour la Commision d'étude qui a soutenu cette proposition, il ne s'agissait pas de révolutionner le système, mais uniquement de transformer en droit positif une pratique en principe bien établie ou en train d'évoluer dans un sens clairement déterminable. Le seul élément qui pourrait apporter une certaine innovation, est la

33 Cf. infra ch. 10.

34 La LNA (citée supra n.17/2) ne mentionne aucune cause d'exonération; il semble raisonnable d'admettre - avec A.KELLER, *Haftpflicht im Privatrecht I* (cité supra n.5), p.241 - que: *"Wer sich in die Gewalt der Höhe begibt, kann sich nicht wohl .. auf höhere Gewalt berufen"*, et d'exclure en même temps le fait d'un tiers comme motif d'exonération.

35 Sur la *"canalisation" de la responsabilité nucléaire*, cf. A.KELLER, *Haftpflicht im Privatrecht I* (cité supra n.5) p.310, et OFTINGER/STARK, *Schweiz.Haftpflichtrecht II/3: Übrige Gefährdungshaftungen*, 4e éd., Zurich 1991, § 29, NN.113 ss, p.200 ss.

36 *Rapport de la Commission d'étude* (cité supra n.15), ch.V/2.2.2.2, p.48 ss, et thèse 59-2.

mention expresse du *"risque caractérisé"* (imputable à la victime ou à un tiers) *comme possible cause d'exonération.* Le besoin de souligner ce point doit être vu en relation avec la décision de proposer une *clause générale de la responsabilité pour risque*[37]; il est en outre motivé par les flottements et les controverses qu'avait suscitées à cette égard la disposition de l'art.51 al.2 COS qui règle la répartition définitive du dommage entre coresponsables solidaires et qui ne tient pas compte du "facteur risque" en cas de collision de responsabilités objectives avec des responsabilités contractuelles ou délictuelles fondées sur la faute[38]. L'idée maîtresse de cette conception générale est donc simplement de faire admettre que *"ce qui constitue un fait générateur de responsabilité ... à la charge du lésé si c'était lui qui avait causé un dommage à autrui, devient un élément réducteur* (ou exonératoire [ajouté par l'auteur]) *des dommages-intérêts pour le dommage que lui-même a subi"*[39].

6.3 Signalons en passant que la norme générale sur l'exonération totale laisse subsister une autre controverse qui est celle de savoir, *si le fait non fautif du lésé ou d'un tiers, notamment en cas d'incapacité de discernement, peut également avoir un effet libératoire.* La jurisprudence et la doctrine répondent plutôt par la négative, en considérant que seule une faute subjectivement reprochable (et d'une gravité majeure) est susceptible d'interrompre le lien de causalité adéquate; elles corrigent cependant les conséquences inéquitables que ce principe peut entraîner en applicant par analogie la disposition de l'art.54 al.1 COS qui permet au juge, à certaines conditions, de condamner une personne incapable de discernement à une réparation entière ou partielle du dommage qu'elle a causé[40].

A notre avis il s'agit d'un détour inutile et qui méconnaît le sens de l'exonération comme *"condition négative de la responsabilité"*: l'exonération doit toujours être admise lorsque le facteur extérieur a agi avec une intensité telle que la responsabilité du sujet recherché en premier devient inadéquate. La question de l'imputabilité subjective de ce facteur extérieur est en principe sans importance, sinon il ne serait

37 *Rapport de la Commission d'étude* (cité supra n.15), ch. V/3.3, p.60 ss et thèse 53-4.

38 A ce sujet: WIDMER, *Ethos und Adäquanz der Regressordnung nach Art.51 Abs.2 OR*, in: Mélanges ASSISTA 1968-1978, Genève 1979, p.269 ss; voir aussi: M.KELLER/GABI, *Haftpflichtrecht,* 2e éd., Bâle/Francfort 1988, p.111 s. - BREHM, *Commentaire* (cité supra n.12), NN.76 s et 133 ss ad art.51 COS, continue à défendre la position traditionnelle. Cf.également A.KELLER; *Haftpflicht im Privatrecht I* (cité supra n.5), p.344 ss (notamment 349 s et 353 s), et IDEM, *Haftpflicht im Privatrecht II,* 1e éd., Berne 1987, p.164 ss.

39 RUSCONI, *Les principes sur la détermination de l'étendue des dommages-intérêts,* in: *Die Verantwortlichkeit im Recht,* vol.2 (cité supra n.12), p.537 ss (552).

40 BREHM, *Commentaire* (cité supra n.12), N.40 ad art.44 COS; RUSCONI, *Les principes* ... (cité supra n.39), p.551; A.KELLER, *Haftpflicht im Privatrecht I* (cité supra n.5) p.137; OFTINGER, *Schweiz. Haftpflichtrecht I* (cité supra n.1), § 5, p.165 ss; OFTINGER/STARK, *AT 5* (cité supra n.1), § 5 N.141 ss, p.230, et N.163 ss, p.237 ss; STARK, *Skriptum* (cité supra n.19), N.334 ss, pp.74 s.
La Commission d'étude propose de maintenir une norme sur la responsabilité des incapables, tout en la déclarant nettement comme une dérogation au principe de la faute et en lui conférant un caractère strictement exceptionnel; cf. *Rapport de la Commission d'étude* (cité supra n.15), ch.V/3.2.3 et thèse 53-3, p.57 ss.

pas concevable de reconnaître un effet libératoire à la force majeure et au cas fortuit. A nos yeux, cette attitude s'impose en tout cas aussi longtemps que le droit de la responsabilité civile continue à partir du principe "*casum sentit dominus*" et que le transfert du dommage d'une personne à l'autre présuppose une justification particulière[41]. Si, dans un cas concret, cette justification - le chef de responsabilité - s'avère comme inexistante ou insuffisante, cela signifie précisément qu'on est en présence d'un "*casus*", d'une fatalité; il faut alors être conséquent et accepter qu'il n'y a ni responsabilité ni responsable[42].

7 Après s'être occupée des problèmes de la causalité adéquate et de l'exonération (totale) qu'elle considérait comme les deux faces d'une seule et même médaille, la Commission d'étude chargée de préparer la revision du droit suisse de la responsabilité civile a examiné la forme à donner à une règle complémentaire: *la compétence du juge de réduire la réparation - selon les mêmes critères* - dans les cas où une cause étrangère (toujours par rapport au fait de rattachement et au critère d'imputation d'une responsabilité admise "*prima vista*") n'aurait pas la gravité ou l'intensité nécessaire à interrompre entièrement le lien d'imputation, mais apparaîtrait néanmoins comme un facteur concurrent suffisamment essentiel et décisif pour justifier une *exonération partielle.* Elle a en effet estimé qu'il ne s'agissait au fond que d'une différence graduelle et qu'il était dès lors logique de traiter les deux formes de limitation de la responsabilité entre le "rien" et le "tout" sous une optique commune[43]. Cette conception peut se résumer comme suit:

> *"¹ Une personne peut être partiellement exonérée de sa responsabilité dans la mesure où un fait qui ne lui est pas imputable a contribué de manière décisive à la survenance du dommage ou à son aggravation, notamment un cas fortuit ou des faits ou risques caractéristiques dont répond la personne lésée.*
>
> *² Lorsque les faits ou risques qui ont contribué à la survenance ou à l'aggravation du dommage sont imputables à un tiers, les règles sur le concours de responsabilité s'appliquent."*

Sans entrer dans une exégèse approfondie de ce texte, nous relèverons un point: c'est le fait qu'ici - *pour tenir compte du principe de la solidarité - la faute ou le fait d'un tiers* est envisagé sous un angle différent qu'en cas d'exonération totale et qu'il est par conséquent réglé dans un alinéa séparé.

41 WIDMER, *Fonction et évolution de la responsabilité pour risque*, in RDS (cité supra n.32) 96 [1977] I p.417 ss (417s) où est également citée la phrase de OLIVER WENDELL HOLMES: *"Sound policy lets losses lie where they fall, except where a special reason can be shown for interference"*; dans le même sens: *Rapport de la Commission d'étude* (cité supra n.15), ch.V/2.1, p.38 s.

42 WIDMER, *Standortbestimmung im Haftpflichtrecht*, Revue de la Société des Juristes Bernois [RJB] 110 [1974] p.289 ss (328 ss).

43 *Rapport de la commision d'étude* (cité supra n.15), ch.V/2.2.2.3, p.50 ss et thèse 52-10.

En effet, lorsque plusieurs personnes répondent d'un même dommage, elles ne peuvent normalement pas prétendre à bénéficier d'une exonération partielle; *dans les rapports externes envers le lésé*, chacune est tenue, dans un premier temps, à dédommager la victime, et la répartition définitive - qui tiendra compte de toutes les circonstances et nuances de gravité ou d'intensité propres à chacun des intéressés - se fera sur le plan interne par le jeu des recours. En réservant expressément cette situation, la Commission d'étude a manifesté son intention de trancher une question qui s'était posée dans le contexte de l'art.43 al.1 COS, et que la doctrine avait examinée sous l'aspect de la *"connexité des fautes (Verschuldenskonnexität)"*[44]. La jurisprudence avait en effet admis dans certains cas isolés que la faute concurrente d'un tiers pouvait faire apparaître celle du premier responsable comme plus légère et qu'à ce titre elle pouvait donner lieu à une réduction de l'indemnité due par ce dernier. La plupart des auteurs s'étaient montrés réticents à accepter cette idée[45], et, dans une décision récente, le Tribunal fédéral avait lui-même reconnu que cette possibilité était largement théorique et qu'elle ne pouvait *"viser qu'une situation tout à fait exceptionnelle"*. Il poursuivait son raisonnement en déclarant que la seule hypothèse envisageable serait celle "*où la faute de l'auteur recherché apparaîtrait si peu grave et dans une telle disproportion avec celle du tiers qu'il serait manifestement injuste et choquant de faire supporter au défendeur l'entier du dommage en appliquant à la lettre les rigueurs propres à la solidarité*"[46].

En réalité, *le problème est doublement mal posé*: D'abord parce que, pour l'évaluation de la faute d'une personne, on doit toujours tenir compte de l'ensemble des circonstances dans lesquelles celle-ci a agi ou omis d'agir. Lorsqu'un tiers intervient dans un telle situation, il représente certes une de ces "circonstances" qui conditionnent la faute de l'autre, mais la gravité de la faute du tiers, qui lui est entièrement personnelle, ne peut ni amoindrir ni aggraver celle - tout aussi individuelle - du coresponsable. Deuxièmement, c'est précisément au *"rigueurs de la solidarité"* qu'il faut s'en prendre, car elles ne sont que les émanations d'une conception beaucoup trop grossière de ce principe: *"Solidarité" ne signifie pas nécessairement l'obligation de chacun des coresponsables de réparer l'ensemble du dommage*; comprise dans un sens différencié et approprié, elle a uniquement pour effet d'imposer à chacun des responsables une fonction de garant pour les autres, mais qui ne peut jamais aller au-delà de sa responsabilité personnellement adéquate. La personne recherchée ne doit pas pouvoir profiter de l'existence de plusieurs responsables, mais leur présence ne doit pas non plus jouer en sa défaveur. Une fois la solidarité ainsi "redimensionnée"[47], le problème de la "connexité des fautes" devient pratiquement sans objet.

44 *Rapport de la commission d'étude* (cité supra n.15), ch.V/2.2.2.3, p.51.

45 BREHM, *Commentaire* (cité supra n.12), N.81 ss ad art.43 COS; A.KELLER, *Haftpflicht im Privatrecht I* (cité supra n.5), p.130 s, et *Haftpflicht im Privatrecht II* (cité supra n.38 i.f.), p.158 s.

46 ATF 112 II 138 ss (c.4a, p.143 s).

47 *Rapport de la Commission d'étude* (cité supra n.15), ch.V/9, p.102 ss et thèse 59-2; cf. également A.KELLER, *Haftpflicht im Privatrecht II* (cité supra n.38), p.156 s.

8 Bien que la Commission ait en principe admis qu'exonération totale et exonération partielle ne sont que des *degrés d' "adéquation" de la responsabilité* et donc des échelons d'un seul et même problème, elle a hésité sur la *collocation systématique* de ces dispositions. Elle a envisagé toutes les solutions possibles et a finalement laissé la question ouverte en proposant des règles identiques aussi bien sous l'aspect des conditions de la responsabilité que dans le chapitre consacré à la fixation des dommages-intérêts[48].

Cette indécision est symptomatique: Elle montre que - malgré l'acceptation quasi unanime des théories normatives[49] - on continue à s'inspirer d'une conception scientifico-mécanique de la causalité et on persiste à considérer que *"celle-ci existe ou n'existe pas"*[50]; en conséquence, la responsabilité elle-même est aussi - "en principe" - soit acquise où ne l'est pas du tout. Ce ne serait qu'ensuite, pour ainsi dire: dans une deuxième phase - la responsabilité étant "en principe" établie -, que le juge pourrait se demander s'il y a lieu de réduire la réparation en fonction de divers éléments plus ou moins déterminés et déterminants.

Cette scission de l'analyse juridique en deux approches complètement indépendantes satisfait peut-être à un besoin didactique ou systématique, mais elle obnubile la vue d'ensemble sur la question fondamentale de la responsabilité proportionnée et adéquate qui est en soi indivisible. Ainsi, si le juge, en procédant à la fixation de l'indemnité, arrive à la conclusion que celle-ci doit être réduite à zéro, il admet en effet qu'il n'y a aucune responsabilité. De même, s'il la réduit en tenant compte de différentes circonstances, il constate simultanément que la responsabilité n'existe que jusqu'à ce degré. Dans la plupart des cas, les résultats varieront probablement assez peu, que l'on adopte l'une ou l'autre optique. Mais en procédant par étapes successives, le juge aura l'impression d'avoir simplement un peu corrigé - selon un sentiment de justice diffus et approximatif - un résultat qui autrement aurait été inéquitable. Et c'est la raison pour laquelle, *"le juriste confronté à l'art.43 CO éprouve fréquemment un embarras, nous dirons même: des sentiments mélangés"*[51]. Ces sentiments sont mélangés parce que le juriste croit effectuer des manipulations problématiques et difficilement vérifiables. Il se cramponne à *l'idée erronée que le droit est une science exacte*, et il se sent coupable de porter atteinte à l'objectivité et à la dignité de cette science. En réalité, il exerce tout à fait correctement *son art*

48 *Rapport de la Commission d'étude* (cité supra n.15), ch.V/2.2.2.3, p.51 s, et ch.V/7.2, p.99 ss et thèse 57.

49 DESCHENAUX/TERCIER, *La responsabilité civile* (cité supra n.5), § 4, N.44 ss (46), p.61: *"Se demander si la causalité est adéquate revient à examiner si le dommage qui s'est produit est encore couvert par la norme fondant l'obligation de réparer. C'est la question dite de la 'relation normative' "*; cf. également: HONSELL, *Schweiz. Haftpflichtrecht* (cité supra n.1), § 3 II, p.23 ss.. Plus réverencieux à l'égard de la théorie classique en revanche: OFTINGER/STARK, *AT 5* (cité supra n.1), § 3, N.14 ss, p.109 ss.

50 BREHM, *Commentaire* (cité supra n.12), N.128 ad art.41 COS; OFTINGER/STARK, *AT 5* (cité supra n.1), § 3 N.25, p.116. Avis contraire: HONSELL, *Schweiz. Haftpflichtrecht* (loc. cit. supra n. 49) qui mentionne expressément l'art.43 COS dans ce contexte.

51 BREHM, *L'étendue des dommages-intérêts* (cité supra n.12), p.500.

(*"ars aequi et boni"*) *qui est de rechercher la responsabilité adéquate, dosée et proportionnée selon son fondement ("suum cuique tribuere"*)[52].

9 Ce *"malaise scientifique"* explique le fait qu'*aussi bien la doctrine que la jurisprudence se montrent passablement réservées* dans l'application pratique notamment de l'art.43 al.1 COS. Certains auteurs le déplorent franchement, en constatant que le nombre toujours plus élevé de responsabilités objectives nous a habitué à admettre trop rapidement et trop machinalement que la réparation doit être entière[53]. D'autre part, lorsque la possibilité d'une réduction est néanmoins envisagée, on n'en fait usage qu'avec rentenue, et la tendance est de ne l'admettre que lorsqu'une *faute particulièrement légère* peut justifier le refus de la réparation intégrale.[54]

9.1 Il est d'ailleurs frappant de voir que la majorité des cas, dans lesquels la réduction a été accordée, concerne des *enfants*[55]; on éprouve, semble-t-il, moins de scrupules à procéder à une réduction lorsqu'on a affaire à un responsable dont la capacité de discernement est *ab initio* douteuse. Cette attitude est principalement due à une compréhension schématique et "objectivée" de la capacité de discernement en général; la doctrine majoritaire adopte, là aussi, une optique du "noir ou blanc" - du "tout ou rien"- qu'elle corrige ensuite *ex aequo et bono*, soit en distinguant le côté objectif du côté subjectif de la faute, soit en invoquant l'art.54 CO[56]. Si l'on conçoit au contraire, et comme nous le préconisons, *la faute comme une et indivisible*, mais susceptible de varier entre le gris foncé et le gris clair en fonction de la capacité délictuelle du sujet - elle-même conditionnée par tous les éléments objectifs et subjectifs de l'espèce[57] - on ne recontrera pas la moindre difficulté

52 A.KELLER, *Haftpflicht im Privatrecht I* (cité supra n.5), p.84: *"Man sieht, wie sich die Kreise der Verursachung und ihrer Angemessenheit immer weiter ziehen und sich mit jenen der Schadenersatzbemessung bzw. -minderung und schliesslich der damit zusammenhängenden Haftungskollisionen verschlingen. Betrachtet man die Dinge so, dann kann man allgemein sagen, dass es darum gehe, in jedem Falle den Ursachen, die zu einem Schaden geführt haben (Verschulden, Betriebsgefahr, Zufall usw.) ihren Anteil zuzumessen. Hier das Angemessene, eben das Adäquate, zu finden, das ist die Aufgabe und ist die Kunst."*

53 A.KELLER, *Haftpflicht im Privatrecht I* (cité n.5), p.124; du même avis: FELLMANN, *Der Verschuldensbegriff im Deliktsrecht*, in RDS (cité supra n.32) 106 [1987] I pp.339 ss (343 ss). BREHM, *L'étendue des dommages-intérêts* (cité supra n.12), p.501, est moins catégorique; selon lui: *"... la réduction des dommages-intérêts dans le cadre de l'art.43 CO n'est ni fréquente ni exceptionnelle"*, mais il constate également que: *"Parfois aussi, elle nous semble avoir été oublié tant par l'avocat du défendeur que par le juge"*.

54 OFTINGER/STARK, at 5 (cité spura n.1), § 7 N.11 s, p. 382 s.

55 Cf. A.KELLER, *Haftpflicht im Privatrecht I* (cité supra n.5), p.125, et BREHM, *L'étendue des dommages-intérêts* (cité supra n.12), p.505 s.

56 Cf. WERRO, *La capacité de discernement et la faute dans le droit suisse de la responsabilité*, Fribourg 1986, notamment N.475 ss, p.118 ss; OFTINGER, *Haftpflichtrecht I* (cité supra n.1), p.155. A propos de l'art.54 CO, cf. supra ch.6.3 et n. 40.

57 Dans ce sens également: BUCHER, *Commentaire bernois* (cité supra n.12) I/2, t.1, Berne 1976, N.24 des remarques préliminaires ad art.12-19 CCS, N.3 ss (4a) et 108 ss ad art.16 CCS ainsi que N.374 ad art.19 CCS; FELLMANN, *Der Verschuldensbegriff* (cité supra n.53), p.351 ss. Dans son arrêt ATF 102 II 363, le Tribunal fédéral a expressément admis la notion de capacité restreinte, mais en

d'admettre que l'évaluation de la faute et la pondération correspondante de la réparation doivent se faire *de la même manière chez les adultes que chez les enfants*[58].

9.2 Il est certainement juste d'accorder *la réparation intégrale* lorsque le responsable a provoqué le dommage *intentionnellement ou par une négligence grave*, c'est-à-dire en cas de faute "noire" ou d'un gris très foncé[59]; et nous voyons mal comment, dans telle hypothèse, on pourrait encore envisager une réduction en invoquant d'autres *"circonstances"*, puisque celles-ci auraient précisément dû être prises en considération pour apprécier la faute[60]. Or, si la faute grave constitue le plafond, rien ne s'oppose à ce qu'une réduction de l'indemnité puisse être justifiée en cas de *faute moyenne*[61]. Lorsqu'enfin la faute devient gris clair et se rapproche du blanc, une réduction substantielle s'impose; comme nous venons de le dire, la pratique n'est souvent pas conscient du fait que l'art.43 CO lui en fait une obligation et qu'il ne s'agit pas d'un pouvoir discrétionnaire[62].

9.3 Pour ce qui en est de la possibilité de tenir compte de la *légèreté d'une "irrégularité objective"* dans le cadre des responsabilités objectives simples, nous renvoyons à nos remarques au chiffre 4.2 ci-dessus[63]. Il importe d'ailleurs peu que la réduction se fasse sous le titre de la faute (objectivée) ou sous celui de "circonstances". Or, la *"laxité"* du lien de causalité constitue justement une telle circonstance, soit que le dommage paraisse très éloigné ou *"indirect"* par rapport au fait

limitant son application aux enfants. Cf. la critique de cet arrêt par WESSNER, *Le discernement: Contre la notion de capacité restreinte en droit de la responsabilité civile*, in: Revue Suisse de Jurisprudence [RSJ] 79 [1983] p.333 ss.

58 BREHM, *Commentaire* (cité supra n.12), N.78 ad art.43 COS; IDEM, *L'étendue des dommages-intérêts* (cité supra n.12), p.507.

59 BREHM, *Commentaire* (cité supra n.12) N.73/74 ad art.43 COS; IDEM, *L'étendue des dommages-intérêts* (cité supra n.12), p.505.

60 Dans l'exemple de l'ATF 44 II 77 ss (88 s) cité à cet égard par BREHM - *Commentaire* (cité supra n.12), N.75 ad art.43 COS - le Tribunal fédéral adopte en effet une attitude contradictoire en admettant d'abord à la charge de la défenderesse une négligence grave frisant le dol, et en réduisant ensuite la réparation parce que le comportement insouciant du lésé n'était pas prévisible, de sorte que le lien de causalité adéquate paraîtrait affaibli. S'il en est ainsi, le véritable motif de la réduction ne peut être que la faute concomitante du lésé et, logiquement, la faute du responsable s'en trouve amoindrie. - Il est d'ailleurs symptomatique qu'il s'agissait, en l'espèce, d'un cas typique de *"dommage purement économique"* (renseignements inexacts d'une banque sur une entreprise en difficultés; un cas semblable a été jugé dans l'ATF 101 II 69 ss ou il s'agissait d'un certificat de travail euphémique taisant les activités criminelles de l'employé). Cf. à ce sujet, infra ch.14.

61 BREHM, *Commentaire* (cité supra n.12), N.79 ad art.43 COS; IDEM, *L'étendue des dommages-intérêts* (cité supra n.12), p.508 s.

62 C'est ce que semblent admettre DESCHENAUX/TERCIER, *La responsabilité civile* (cité supra n.5), § 28, N.15 f, p.244, qui refusent ainsi implicitement la possibilité de réduire en cas de faute moyenne; cf. également M.KELLER/GABI, *Haftpflichtrecht* (cité supra n.38), p.102, et OFTINGER, *Haftpflichtrecht I* (cité supra n.1), p.264, qui rejette *"la contrainte à la réduction"* (position maintenue dans OFTINGER/STARK, *AT 5* [loc.cit.supra n.13]).

63 Avant n.24.

imputable à la personne responsable[64] ou démesuré par rapport au manquement ou au risque dont elle répond[65], soit que l'on constate qu'un *cas fortuit*[66] (le petit frère de la force majeure) y a contribué de manière non négligeable.

Ce dernier élément peut théoriquement aussi jouer un rôle dans le domaine des responsabilités pour risque, s'il s'agit d'un facteur extérieur par rapport au danger typique créé par l'activité en question.[67] Il semble d'ailleurs difficile et quelque peu artificiel de distinguer nettement ces différents aspects qui s'enchevêtrent les uns dans les autres[68]; mais ceci n'a rien d'étonnant ni d'inquiétant, dès lors que l'on veut bien reconnaître qu'il s'agit simplement de *différentes facettes d'une seule et même question: celle de la responsabilité adaptée et proportionnée à son fondement, c'est-à-dire: adéquate.*

10 Les causes d'exonération - et par conséquent, aussi de réduction - de loin les plus importantes en pratique, sont les *faits ou circonstances imputables à la personne lésée.* Ce sont aussi ceux et celles que le COS, à l'art.44 al.1[69], mentionne expressément. La prise en compte de ces "*faits dont la partie lésée est responsable*" est souvent présentée comme découlant du *principe de la bonne foi* ou de son pendant négatif que constitue l'interdiction de l'abus de droit.

Cette approche repose sur l'idée que le fait de demander réparation d'un dommage dont on est soi-même responsable serait contraire au devoir général de loyauté[70]. Le principe de la bonne foi est aussi le fondement d'une obligation (ou plutôt: d'une incombance) à la charge du lésé, en vertu de laquelle il est tenu de prendre toutes les mesures que l'on peut raisonnablement exiger de lui afin de réduire le dommage qu'il a subi; il doit se comporter comme s'il ne pouvait pas s'attendre à

64 BREHM, *Commentaire* (cité supra n.12), N.53 s ad art.43 COS. La N.54 montre d'ailleurs nettement l'incohérence de la conception courante en matière de *"causalité adéquate"*: selon le commentateur, l'art.43 COS sert à corriger les effets pervers de cette théorie qui n'admet que "blanc ou noir" (cf. également du même auteur: *L'étendue des dommages-intérêts* [cité supra n.12], pp.515 s) - en réalité, l'art.43 COS est la conséquence logique et organique de la conception normative de la causalité, et il sert à la mettre en oeuvre dans toute sa flexibilité.

65 BREHM, *Commentaire* (cité supra n.12), N.61 ad art.43 COS; IDEM, *L'étendue des dommages-intérêts* (cité supra n.12), p.518; A.KELLER, *Haftpflicht im Privatrecht I* (cité supra n.5), p.130.

66 BREHM, *Commentaire* (cité supra n.12), N.52 ad art.43 COS; IDEM, *L'étendue des dommages-intérêts* (cité supra n.12), p.514 s; A.KELLER, *Haftpflicht im Privatrecht I* (cité supra n.5), p.130.

67 OFTINGER, *Haftpflichtrecht 1* (cité supra n.1), p. 100 et 279; STARK, *Skriptum* (cité supra n. 19), N.355 ss, p. 78 s.

68 BREHM, *L'étendue des dommages-intérêts* (cité supra n.12), p.516: *"Lorsque la faiblesse du lien de causalité est ainsi retenue au titre de 'circonstance', elle fait généralement double emploi avec d'autres circonstances qui recouvrent le même domaine, à savoir le cas fortuit".*

69 Supra, ch.3.1.

70 OFTINGER/STARK, *AT 5* (cité supra n.1), § 5 N.139, p.229; HONSELL, *Schweiz. Haftpflichtrecht* (cité supra n.1), § 9 II/1, p.73; MERZ, *Commentaire bernois* (cité supra n.12), I/1, Berne 1966, N.556 ad.art.2 CCS.

être dédommagé par une autre personne (*"Schadenminderungspflicht"*). Le non-respect de ce devoir équivaut à une faute concomitante.[71]

La faute du lésé est ainsi retenue comme motif d'exonération et de réduction même dans le cadre de responsabilités objectives se rattachant à un risque aussi élevé que celui du nucléaire[72]

Là encore, il s'agit à notre avis d'une conséquence du *principe fondamental de la responsabilité (et non: de la causalité!) adéquate*; dans la mesure où la victime a elle-même contribué à la survenance du dommage (ou à son aggravation), la responsabilité du ou des tiers devient inadéquate[73]. Conçue de cette manière, l'auto-responsabilité de la victime entre en collision avec la responsabilité des co-auteurs du préjudice[74].

11 Il découle également de cette conception que la personne lésée doit se laisser imputer non seulement sa faute individuelle et subjective, mais tous les faits et circonstances qui rentrent dans sa propre sphère de risque.

11.1 Ceci signifie tout d'abord qu'elle doit assumer les conséquences de son comportement personnel, indépendemment du fait que l'on puisse ou non formuler à son égard un reproche subjectif, *indépendemment donc aussi de sa capacité de discernemen*t restreinte ou même inexistante[75].

Pour la même raison, l'obligation du tiers responsable de réparer un dommage doit en principe être réduite lorsque la victime présentait une *prédisposition constitutionnelle*; dans la mesure où - notamment en cas de lésions corporelles - le lésé était déjà affecté d'une maladie ou d'une infirmité, cela constitue une "circonstance" qui ne peut être imputée à aucune autre personne. La jurisprudence se montre pourtant plutôt généreuse en admettant que la causalité adéquate peut s'étendre même à des conséquences anormales et inattendues; elle estime que le hasard d'avoir porté atteinte à une personne de faible constitution ou affectée d'une maladie préexistante doit être supporté par le responsable et que celui-ci ne peut pas prétendre à être traité comme s'il avait eu affaire à une victime valide[76]. Cette attitude est manifestement dictée par des considérations d'ordre social qui sont en soi tout à fait

71 OFTINGER/STARK, *AT 5* (cité supra n.1), § 6 N.37 ss, p.261 ss et § 7 N.16, p.386 s; DESCHENAUX/-TERCIER, *La responsabilité civile* (cité supra n.5), § 28, N.23 ss, p.245 s.

72 Cf. art.5 LRCN (cité supra ch.1, n.7).

73 Avis contraire: BREHM, *Commentaire* (cité supra n.12), N.17 ad art.44 COS.

74 Cf. notamment: A.KELLER, *Haftpflichtrecht I* (cité supra n.5), p.349s.

75 Supra ch.6.3, après n.40.

76 Cf. ATF 113 II 86 ss (90, c.1b). A.KELLER, *Haftpflichtim Privatrecht I* (cité supra n.5), p.75 s et 129; BREHM, *Commentaire* (cité supra n.12), N.54 ss ad art.44; RUSCONI, *Les principes...* (cité supra n.39), p.553 ss.

respectables, mais qui vont à l'encontre du principe "*casum sentit dominus*"[77] et qui nous semblent d'autant plus problématiques que la sécurité sociale est précisément là pour couvrir ce genre de risque existentiel et personnel et pour le rendre plus supportable en le répercutant sur l'ensemble de la société.

11.2 L'art.44 al.1 COS assimile à la faute concomitante du lésé le cas de son *consentement à l'atteinte.*

Dans un système qui, comme le droit suisse, fait de l'illicéité (*"Widerrechtlichkeit/Rechtswidrigkeit"*) une condition autonome de la responsabilité, le consentement de la victime - pour autant qu'il soit valable sous l'aspect de la protection de la personnalité[78] - constitue en principe un *motif justificatif* ("*volenti non fit iniuria*"). L'atteinte perd dès lors d'emblée son caractère illicite dans le mesure où elle est *légitimée* par le consentement de la personne lésée. Si le préjudice en question apparaît comme entièrement couvert par le consentement, celui-ci a le même effet qu'un cause d'exonération, et il n'y a plus lieu de réexaminer la même question sous l'aspect de la causalité, c'est-à-dire de la responsabilité adéquate dans le cadre des articles 43 et 44 COS. Souvent toutefois, le *consentement n'est que partiel ou que partiellement valable ou incertain*, notamment lorsque la victime n'en a pas envisagé toutes les concéquences ou n'était pas entièrement consciente de l'étendue possible du dommage.

C'est ce type de situations que recouvre la notion d' *"acceptation d'un risque"* que l'on rencontre notamment en rapport avec des activités sportives. Ces cas pourraient parfaitement être résolus dans le contexte de l'illicéité, car cette notion est elle aussi susceptible de nuances et de gradations; il s'agirait de déterminer dans quelle mesure la personne lésée a valablement consenti à une atteinte, s'est accomodée d'une telle éventualité ou aurait dû s'en rendre compte si elle avait fait preuve de l'attention nécessaire. Le consentement est alors donné par acte concluant. Etrangement, doctrine et jurisprudence n'envisagent la question que sous l'aspect de la *faute concomitante* dans le cadre de l'art.44 al.1 COS. On parle alors de *consentement "non authentique"*, et on reproche au lésé non pas son acceptation du risque comme telle, mais le fait d'avoir *commis une négligence en s'exposant à un risque prévisible*[79]. Voilà une construction assez bizarre pour qui serait prêt à admettre que - sous réserve des droits inaliénables - on n'est normalement pas tenu d'obser-

77 STARK, *Skriptum* (cité supra n.19), N.364 ss, p.80 s, considère à juste titre que la prédisposition est une forme particulière de "cas fortuit". Il en déduit que ce n'est pas l'art.44 al.1, mais l'art.43 al.1 COS, qui doit s'appliquer, et il émet des réserves générales sur la prise en considération du cas fortuit et de la prédisposition comme facteurs de réduction (loc.cit, N.373 ss, p.82). Cette opinion méconnaît à notre avis le fondement commun des deux dispositions et le fait que l'auto-responsabilité au sens de l'art.44 al.1 COS inclut toutes les circonstances qui rentrent objectivement dans la sphère de risque propre du lésé. Cf. également: OFTINGER/STARK, *AT 5* (cité supra n.1), § 3 N.95 ss, p.141 ss, et § 7 N.37 s., p.401 s.

78 Art.27 al.2 CCS en combinaison avec l'art.20 COS.

79 BREHM, *Commentaire* (cité supra n.12), N.6 ss ad art.44 COS; RUSCONI, *Les principes* ...(cité supra n.39), p.546 ss; OFTINGER/STARK, *AT 5* (cité supra n.1), § 5 N.147 s, p.232..

ver des devoirs de diligence envers soi-même. Mais le résultat doit forcément être le même - que l'on tienne compte de la contribution du lésé sous l'aspect de l'illicéité ou sous celui de la causalité normative: le tiers responsable doit être exonéré dans la mesure où il n'existe pas ou plus de rapport adéquat entre, d'une part, son comportement ou les faits appartenant à sa sphère de risque et, d'autre part, le dommage subi par la personne lésée.

11.3 Un facteur de réduction apparenté à celui du consentement ou de l'acceptation du risque et dont il a déjà été question en rapport avec la responsabilité contractuelle[80], est celui de la *complaisance* ou du fait que l'auteur du dommage a rendu un service à la personne lésée gratuitement ou contre une rémunération modique. Ces facteurs de réduction, et même d'exonération, étaient expressément mentionnés dans la LCR[81] pour les transports par véhicule à moteur; lors d'une revision en 1975, cette disposition (art.59 al.3) a été abrogée[82]. Selon la doctrine dominante, il s'agit cependant d'une règle générale qui reste applicable en vertu de l'art.43 al.1 COS[83]. A notre avis, on pourrait également la fonder sur l'art.44 al.1, car le motif déterminant ne peut être que l'idée que le lésé accepte le risque lié soit à l'activité dont il bénéficie à des conditions avantageuses, soit à la personne dont il accepte ou sollicite un service bénévole. En agissant ainsi, il ne commet certainement pas de faute, mais il "contribue" néanmoins à la survenance du dommage avec une volonté et une intensité qui le distinguent de n'importe quelle autre victime n'ayant eu aucun rapport préalable avec l'auteur du dommage.

11.4 Pour en revenir encore au conséquences qui découlent d'une conception cohérente de l'exonération (totale ou partielle) comme application et mise en oeuvre directe du principe de la responsabilité adéquate, nous rappellerons que parmi les "*faits dont (la partie lésée) est responsable (et qui) ont contribué à créer le dommage*", il faut aussi ranger *le risque caractéristique d'une activité dangereuse* soumise à une responsabilité pour risque[84].

Il en va d'ailleurs *de même pour le risque inhérent au fait de se servir d'auxiliaires*: la personne lésée doit se laisser imputer la part du dommage qui a son origine dans le comportement de personnes dont elle est responsable (tel l'employeur pour ses employés, ou le chef de famille pour les mineurs et interdits qui vivent

80 Supra ch.4.3.

81 Cité supra n.6.

82 Le législateur s'était inspiré d'une considération écologique: on voulait inciter les gens à utiliser une voiture pour plusieurs personnes (notamment pour les transport entre domicile et place de travail) et donc ne pas les exposer au risque de voir - en cas d'accident - leur droit à réparation réduit pour cause de complaisance ou de gratuité.

83 BREHM, *Commentaire* (cité supra n.12), N.55 ss ad art.43 COS; IDEM, *L'étendue des dommages-intérêts* (cité supra n.12), p.516 ss, et notamment: OFTINGER/STARK, *Haftpflichtrecht II/2*, 4e éd., Zurich 1989, § 25, N.579 ss (583), p.262 ss. A.KELLER, *Haftpflicht im Privatrecht I* (cité supra n.5), p.282, estime en revanche que le motif de réduction de la complaisance ne peut plus être invoqué dans le cadre de la LCR revisée.

84 Supra, ch.6.2 et n.37-39.

avec lui en ménage commun)[85]. Dans les hypothèses de responsabilité pour risque, la responsabilité du sujet principal (détenteur, exploitant) pour toutes les personnes qui participent à l'activité en question et contribuent ainsi à la réalisation du risque est automatiquement incluse dans le chef de responsabilité[86]. Etant donné que - depuis qu'il a découvert les vertus caches de l'article 55 COS comme source d'une nouvelle responsabilité du fait des produits[87] - le Tribunal fédéral juge la responsabilité de l'employeur avec un extrême sévérité, on attend avec curiosité de voir s'il fera preuve de la même rigueur lorsqu'il s'agira d'évaluer le rôle des auxiliaires sous l'aspect de l'exonération ou de la réduction pour faute concomitante de l'employeur lésé.

12 Il nous reste à mentionner un dernier critère que le droit suisse envisage comme une des circonstances permettant d'adapter l'étendue de la réparation aux données spécifiques du cas concret: c'est la *prise en compte de la situation économique* respective du responsable et du lésé. Certaines dispositions mentionnées plus haut prévoient en effet la possibilité pour le juge de réduire l'indemnité soit en fonction de la gêne du débiteur (art.44 al.2 COS), soit en "imputant" au créancier sa situation particulièrement aisée (art.62 al.2 LCR et semblables)[88]. Dans le cadre de l'art.43 al.1 COS, on peut aussi imaginer des situations inverses: une situation précaire du créancier qui pourrait inciter le juge à renoncer à une réduction qui se serait justifiée pour d'autres motifs; ou encore le cas d'un débiteur particulièrement fortuné qui pourrait avoir le même effet[89].

12.1 Dans la pratique, ces *dispositions sont rarement appliquées* et on ne peut pas dire que l'existence toujours plus fréquente, de part et d'autre, d'une assurance ait considérablement influencé l'attitude des tribunaux. Tout au plus, le fait, pour le responsable, d'être assuré en responsabilité civile, excluera-t-il normalement l'application de l'art.44 al.2 COS, puisque le risque qu'il tombe dans la gêne à cause de cette dette est automatiquement écarté. Pour la même raison, en matière d'accidents de la circulation - où, de surcroît, le responsable est normalement *couvert par l'assurance obligatoire* - le revenu exceptionnellement élevé de la victime n'a quasiment jamais joué de rôle. En ce qui concerne les prestations d'assurances (privées ou sociales) qui profitent directement au lésé, il n'y a pas lieu non plus d'en tenir compte, étant donné que, soit elles conditionnent déjà le calcul du dommage et alors l'assureur est régulièrement subrogé dans les droits du lésé envers le responsable, soit il y a cumul - lorsqu'il s'agit d'une assurance conclue et

85 BREHM, *Commentaire* (cité supra n.12), N.42 ad art.44 COS; RUSCONI, *Les principes* ... (cité supra n.39), p.548 s; OFTINGER/STARK, *AT 5* (cité supra n.1), § 5 N.154 ss, p.234 ss, et § 7 N.28, p.391.

86 STARK, *Probleme der Vereinheitlichung* (cité supra n.32), p.52 ss. Cf. également: *Rapport de la Commission d'étude* (cité supra n.15), ch.V/3.3.6 et thèse 53-4.

87 ATF 110 II 456 ss; cf. à ce sujet: WIDMER, *La responsabilité du fait des produits en droit suisse*, in: Journées de la Société de législation comparée - année 1989, Paris 1990, p.597 ss (607 s, N.14).

88 Supra, ch.3.1 (n.11) et 3.2.

89 BREHM, *Commentaire* (cité supra n.12), N.62 ss ad art.43 COS; IDEM, *L'étendue des dommages-intérêts* (cité supra n.12) p.520 et 522 ss.

payée par la victime dans un but de prévoyance - et, dans ce cas, il ne se justifie pas d'en faire profiter le responsable (et encore moins son assurance)[90].

12.2 D'une façon générale, il convient de séparer très nettement ces *considérations d'ordre social et économique*[91] de celles dont il a été question auparavant et qui se rapportaient directement au fondement de la responsabilité.

La situation économique des parties est en effet totalement étrangère aux principes qui régissent la compensation des préjudices selon les canons du droit privé. Le droit de la *responsabilité civile n'est pas le mécanisme approprié pour faire de la charité ou pour rédistribuer les fortunes* afin de corriger des inégalités sociales. Sa structure même s'y oppose puisque ces corrections n'interviendraient que de façon purement aléatoire, selon le rythme irrégulier et les coups aveugles de la fatalité; elles ne profiteraient donc qu'aux personnes qui ont la "chance" d'être victime d'un préjudice imputable à une personne aisé ou, au contraire, de tomber sur un Crésus en causant eux-même un dommage. Ni la pauvreté ni l'abondance peuvent dès lors être admises comme critères d'imputation valables[92].

Ces propos peuvent sembler excessivement rigoristes et empreints d'un manque total de sensibilité sociale. Aussi voudrions-nous ne pas être mal compris: il ne s'agit en aucune manière de nier la légitimite - tant pour le législateur que pour le juge - de tenir compte d'aspects sociaux pour déterminer l'étendue de la réparation, d'autant moins que cette opération s'inspire inéluctablement d'une multitude de considérations et qu'elle exige une grande liberté d'appréciation. Dans le cadre de la revision du droit suisse de la responsabilité civile, il est d'ailleurs prévu non seulement de maintenir cette compétence du juge de tenir compte de la situation économique des parties, mais de la consacrer dans une disposition formulée de manière plus générale, en mentionnant expressément une éventuelle couverture d'assurance, mais en souligant en même temps le *caractère exceptionnel* de l'opération. Ce qu'il faut éviter, c'est que ces considérations métajuridiques deviennent d'un usage trop commun et qu'elles commencent à se glisser discrètement dans les fondements de la responsabilité. Il ne faudrait pas que des slogans du genre *"richesse oblige"* ou *"assurance oblige"* se transforment en véritables critères d'imputation et que la personne civilement responsable fasse figure de *"bon samaritain malgré lui"*. L'expérience montre que de telles craintes ne sont pas purement chimériques[93].

90 Sur ces questions: RUSCONI, *Les principes* ... (cité supra n.39), p.556 ss.

91 DESCHENAUX/TERCIER, *La responsabilité civile* (cité supra n.5), § 28, N.42 ss, p.248 s.

92 Dans ce sens également: BREHM, *L'étendue des dommages-intérêts* (cité supra n.12), p.526.

93 WIDMER, *Standortbestimmung* (cité supra n.42), p.314 ss.

III Autres aspects de la limitation de la réparation

13 La détermination et pondération de l'indemnité en fonction du critère d'imputation et de sa portée normative constitue certainement l'instrument le plus efficace et le plus conforme au système de la responsabilité civile pour parvenir à une limitation adéquate de la réparation. Mais il n'est pas le seul. Il existe d'autres moyens permettant d'atteindre ce but.

Nous laisserons ici de côté toute la question relative aux *méthodes de calcul du dommage* qui peuvent avoir des effets considérables sur le résultat final, avant même que l'on songe à des réductions au sens propre. D'ailleurs, les deux démarches sont parfois difficile à distinguer l'une de l'autre[94]. Pour ne citer qu'un exemple: la "prédisposition" dont il a déjà été question, peut aussi être considérée comme un élément permettant de calculer le "dommage net", puisque celui-ci est défini comme représentant la différence entre la fortune du lésé telle qu'elle se présente après l'événement dommageable et celle qui, par hypothèse, aurait été la sienne sans cet événement[95]. La même question peut aussi se poser sous l'aspect de la causalité hypothétique ou "causalité outrepassante"[96].

14 Il s'impose, en revanche, de donner un aperçu de la façon dont la responsabilité et, par conséquent, la charge de la réparation peuvent être limitées en fonction des *différents types de dommage.*

14.1 En droit suisse, cette question est *étroitement liée au concept de l'illicéité*[97]. Selon la doctrine et la jurisprudence largement majoritaires, notre système - bien qu'il repose essentiellement, comme le droit français[98], sur une clause générale de la responsabilité aquilienne (art.41 al.1 COS) - qualifie le dommage réparable selon des critères qui s'inspirent plutôt de la conception allemande[99]. On distingue ainsi les *atteintes à des droits dits "absolus"* - tels que la vie, l'intégrité physique et psychique, la personnalité et les droits réels - de celles qui n'affectent que le patrimoine de la personne lésée. Dans la première hypothèse, l'illicéité est acquise *ipso iure*, et toutes les pertes économiques qui en résultent sont en principe réparables (sous réserve d'une éventuelle exonération totale ou partielle dans le cadre de l'examen de la causalité adéquate). En revanche, le dommage qui affecte uniquement le patrimoine sans passer par une atteinte à la personne ou à des biens matériels, n'est considéré comme réparable que si l'auteur à violé une *norme de*

94 BREHM, *Commentaire* (cité supra n.12), N.29s ad art.43 COS.

95 A.KELLER, *Haftpflicht im Privatrecht II* (cité supra n.38), p.26.

96 BREHM, *L'étendue des dommages-intérêts* (cité supra n.12), p.520; cf. également ATF 115 II 440 ss.

97 Cf. supra N.11.2

98 Art.1382 Code civil français; dans cette disposition, l'illicéité n'apparaît pas comme condition distincte de la responsabilité civile; elle est quasiment intégrée dans la notion de faute.

99 § 823 BGB.

protection particulière ou s'il a agi avec l'intention de nuire ou contrairement aux bonnes moeurs (art.41 al.2 COS)[100].

Il y a donc là une barrière susceptible d'éviter un débordement de la responsabilité et que l'on justifie en général par la nécessité de ne pas entraver la libre concurrence économique[101]. Il s'agit toutefois d'une barrière assez fragile dans la mesure où il existe une tendance à "inventer" des nouvelles normes protectrices (*"Verkehrssicherungspflichten"*) à fur et à mesure que le besoin s'en fait sentir[102].

14.2 Il existe cependant des domaines où la loi définit elle-même clairement le dommage réparable en écartant d'emblée les *dommages dits "purement économiques"*.

C'est par exemple le cas de la LCR, déjà citée à plusieurs reprises[103], dont l'art.58 al.1 ne prévoit la responsabilité objective du détenteur du véhicule à moteur expressément que:

> *"Si ....une personne est tuée ou blessée ou qu'un dommage matériel a été causé ..."*

Des formules semblables se trouvent aussi dans d'autres lois, pour la plupart déjà anciennes, et certaines d'entre elles prévoient des restrictions supplémentaires en ce qui concerne les dommages aux choses[104]. La limitation aux dommages corporels et matériels (avec des conditions restrictives pour ces derniers) se retrouve d'ailleurs dans la Directive communautaire sur la responsabilité du fait des produits, de même que dans le Projet (entretemps abandonné) de directive sur la responsabilité des prestataires de services où elle excluait d'emblée un grand nombre d'activités du champ d'application de cette réglementation.

Dans les lois suisses de date plus récente qui instituent une responsabilité à raison du risque, on parle normalement de dommage sans autre qualificatif, ce qui signifie en principe que tous les dommages sont considérés comme réparables[105]. Dans la

100 Sur la définition et la fonction de l'illicéité et les questions qu'elle soulève, cf. notamment: OFTINGER/STARK, *AT 5* (cité supra n.1), § 4, N.3 ss., p.167 ss.; OFTINGER/STARK, *Haftpflichtrecht II/1* (cité supra n.22), § 16, N.41 ss, p.16 ss; DESCHENAUX/TERCIER, *La Responsabilité civile* (cité supra n.5), § 6, p.67 ss; A.KELLER, *Haftpflicht im Privatrecht I* (cité supra n.5), p.89 ss; BREHM, *Commentaire* (cité supra n.12), N.33 ss et 75 ss ad art.41 COS.

101 M.KELLER/GABI, *Haftpflichtrecht* (cité supra n.38), p.36.

102 A ce sujet: WIDMER, *La responsabilité "du fait des services"*, in: *Liability for services rendered/Responsabilité des prestataires de service* (Colloque A.I.S.J. 1993), Société de législation comparée (éd.), Paris 1994, p.151 ss. (N. 8.3). Dans un arrêt récent, le Tribunal fédéral semble vouloir freiner quelque peu son propre élan dans la découverte de nouvelles normes d'illicéité à l'aide du code pénal (ATF 119 II 127).

103 Supra n.6.

104 Pour un aperçu: STARK, *Probleme der Vereinheitlichung* (cité supra n.32), p.58 ss.

105 Cf. A.KELLER, *Haftpflicht im Privatrecht I* (cité supra n.5), p.53 ss.

LRCN[106], le législateur a même expressément précisé que le *"dommage nucléaire"* comprend aussi les pertes liés à des mesures d'évacuation (sauf le gain manqué) qui sont des exemples classiques de dommage purement économique. Cela n'a cependant pas empêché le Tribunal fédéral, dans le seul cas (heureusement) qu'il a jusqu'ici eu à juger dans ce domaine, de se demander en passant si les dommages purement économiques étaient véritablement couverts par cette loi[107].

14.3 Indépendemment du souci général de contenir la réparation des préjudices dans des limites raisonnables, on peut en effet se poser la question de savoir si, dans le domaine des responsabilités rattachées à un risque technique (tel que celui de la production d'énérgie nucléaire ou celui lié à l'utilisation de véhicules motorisés), la limitation de la responsabilité aux dommages corporels et matériels ne découle pas déjà du fondement même de cette responsabilité. Il ne fait aucun doute que, dans ces cas, le motif principal qui a amené le législateur à prévoir une responsabilité objective, était l'intention de garantir la réparation des dommages physiques (au sens large du terme) causés par des forces physiques. On pourrait dès lors trouver, dans le principe même de ces types de responsabilité, une raison valable pour exclure de la réparation les dommages purement économiques (ce qui est en revanche beaucoup moins évident pour la responsabilité fondée sur la faute). Une telle justification serait aussi en harmonie avec l'échelle générale des valeurs qui est à la base de notre système juridique et qui s'exprime dans une certaine hiérachie des biens protégés[108].

C'est dans cet esprit - et bien que la Commission d'étude n'ait pas réussi à adopter une orientation claire sur ce point[109] - qu'il est envisagé de poser comme principe dans la future Partie générale du droit suisse de la responsabilité civile que:

> *"En matière de responsabilité pour risque et sauf disposition contraire, seuls sont en principe réparables les dommages résultant d'une atteinte à la vie ou à l'intégrité physique ou psychique d'une personne, aux choses ou à l'environnement."*

Cette restriction vaudrait donc automatiquement pour toutes les hypothèses de responsabilité objective instituées par le droit positif et dont la réglementation spécifique ne prévoit pas d'exceptions; et à plus forte raison s'appliquerait-elle à chaque nouvelle forme de responsabilité pour risque que le juge serait amené à sanctionner sur la base de la clause générale[110]. En ce qui concerne d'éventuelles

106 Cité supra n.7: art.2, al.1.

107 ATF 116 II 480 ss (490 s, c.4).

108 TERCIER, *De la distinction entre dommage corporel, dommage matériel et autres dommages*, in: Mélanges ASSISTA 1968-1978 (cité supra n.38), p.247 ss (261).

109 *Rapport de la Commission d'étude* (cité supra n.15), ch.V/2.2.1.2 i.f., p.44, et ch.V/3.3.5, p.66 s.

110 Supra ch.6.2 et n.37. Cette proposition a d'ailleurs déjà suscité un débat doctrinal sur le traitement des *"dommages purement économiques"* dans la revision totale du droit suisse de la responsabilité civile; cf. les prises de positions de SEILER et WIDMER in RJB (cité supra n.41) 131 (1995) p. 398 ss. Cf. également WIDMER, *Die Vereinheitlichung des schweizerischen Haftpflichtrechts - Brenn-*

nouvelles lois spéciales qui pourraient être créées à l'avenir, des dérogations à ce régime général ne seraient tolérées plus que dans la mesure où la spécificité d'un secteur particulier l'exige et le justifie réellement[111].

15 Pour terminer, nous aborderons brièvement la question d'une *limitation générale de la réparation par des sommes plafonnées.*

La position du droit suisse à cet égard est assez nette et catégorique: tant les responsabilités de droit commun que les responsabilités pour risque prévues par des lois spéciales[112] sont en principe illimitées. Les quelques exceptions qui confirment la règle sont pratiquement toutes dues à l'influence du droit international, notamment dans le domaine du droit des transports[113]. Ainsi, lors de la transposition "autonome" de la Directive communautaire sur la responsabilité du fait des produits, le législateur suisse a aussi renoncé à faire usage de l'option qui lui aurait permis de limiter la responsabilité du producteur pour les dommages corporels à un montant égal ou supérieur à 70 millions d'Ecus.

L'exemple qui illustre le mieux cette attitude de principe est celui de la responsabilité nucléaire. L'ancienne loi de 1959 sur l'utilisation pacifique de l'énergie atomique[114] qui s'inspirait largement de la Convention de Paris prévoyait une limitation de la responsabilité de l'exploitant à 40 millions de francs (portée à 200 millions en 1977), correspondant à la somme couverte par l'assurance obligatoire. En 1983, à la suite de diverses interventions parlementaires, cette réglementation a été remplacée par une loi spéciale sur la responsabilité civile en matière nucléaire (LRCN)[115] dont le but principal était précisément d'éliminer cette limitation; et en adoptant ce nouveau système, le législateur était parfaitement conscient du fait qu'il se privait de la possibilité de ratifier les conventions internationales de Paris, Bruxelles et Vienne qui, à l'époque, prévoyaient la limitation d'une façon impérative[116]. Il est vrai que le système mis en place par cette loi est très particulier, puisqu'il se base sur une couverture d'assurance à deux échelons - assurance privée jusqu'à 500 + 50 millions de francs, complétée par une assurance étatique jusqu'a 1 milliard + 100 millions - et que, au-delà de cette somme, pour les "grand sinistres", un régime spécial d'indemnisation *ad hoc* peut être établi par l'Assemblée fédérale (art.29 LRCN). Celui-ci n'entre cependant en ligne de compte que de façon subsidiaire, c'est-à-dire lorsque - après épuisement des couvertures des assurance privées et fédérales - "*les moyens financiers dont dipose la personne responsable ... ne suffisent pas à satisfaire toutes les demandes de réparation*". Dans ce sens et dans l'optique des personnes responsables (l'exploitant et le propriétaire de l'instal-

punkte eines Projekts, in: RJB (cité supra n.42) 130 (1994) p.385 ss., N.VI, p.397 ss.

111 *Rapport de la Commission d'étude* (cité supra n.15), ch.V/1.1, p.35.

112 Supra ch.4.1, n.17.

113 STARK, *Skriptum* (cité supra n.19), N.403, p.88.

114 Citée supra n.11.

115 Cf. supra, N.1 i.f. et n.7.

116 Sur ces questions, cf. OFTINGER/STARK, *Haftpflichtrecht II/3* (cité supra n.35) § 29, N.36 ss, p.180 ss.

lation comme responsables solidaires), il s'agit donc effectivement d'une responsabilité illimitée.

L'idée de base de cette conception peut se résumer ainsi: du point de vue du droit suisse, *une responsabilité est soit bien fondée comme telle* et à partir du premier franc, et alors elle l'est aussi pour le dommage entier, *soit elle n'est pas justifiée du tout*[117]. *Tertium non datur.* Contrairement à une opinion répandue en Allemagne, nous considérons d'ailleurs que cette idée doit également être valable pour les responsabilités objectives, et qu'elle ne dépend pas non plus de l'assurabilité du risque en question. La couverture d'assurance peut être limitée, et elle l'est en général puisque les assureurs ne peuvent pas être contraints à fournir une garantie illimitée; mais cela n'a pas d'influence sur le principe de la responsabilité qui reste entière. On accepte donc en pleine connaissance de cause que l'obligation de réparer le dommage puisse entraîner la ruine et la faillite du responsable. Cette conséquence correspond en fait à la fonction spécifique que la responsabilité pour risque est censée exercer en plus du but primaire de la réparation: en faisant du risque un facteur des coûts d'exploitation de l'entreprise, affectant sa position sur le marché et sa compétitivité, elle incite l'exploitant à prendre toutes les mesures de sécurités disponibles, raisonnables et économiquement supportables pour réduire le risque à un minimum; elle a donc un effet préventif. Or, si toutes ces mesures ne suffisent pas à contenir le risque dans des limites appropriées ou si leur coût ou celui des primes d'assurances dépasse la capacité financière de l'entreprise, le poids de la responsabilité aura pour effet de faire cesser l'activité en question qui se sera avérée socialement et économiquement inadéquate. La disparition d'une entreprise dont l'activité trop hasardeuse constitue un élément de passif dans le bilan socio-économique est dès lors une conséquence logique de la structure et du fondement même de la responsabilité objective qui représente la contrepartie d'un risque toléré dans l'intérêt général[118].

Le présent exposé ne peut évidemment donner qu'un aperçu relativement sommaire et une impression générale de la manière dont le droit suisse tente de contenir la réparation des dommages dans des limites raisonnables. Notre intention principale est de montrer que le système suisse - malgré les apparences et sauf le recours exceptionnel à des considérations d'ordre social - ne repose pas vraiment sur un *concept de "mitigation"*, en ce sens qu'il s'efforcerait de corriger après coup un résultat inéquitable ou indésirable obtenu par une application (trop) stricte des normes de responsabilité, mais qu'il cherche justement à atteindre ce but *en laissant le fondement de la responsabilité déterminer de façon organique non seulement le principe, mais aussi l'étendue de la réparation.*

117 STARK, *Skriptum* (cité supra n.19), N.402, p.88; OFTINGER/STARK, *AT 5* (cité supra n.1), § 7 N.78 s., p.414s..

118 WIDMER, *Fonction et évolution* ... (cité supra n.41), p.428.